CRACKING OLD TESTAMENT CODES

CRACKING OLD TESTAMENT CODES

D. BRENT SANDY &

RONALD L. GIESE, JR.

A Guide to
Interpreting
the Literary
Genres of
the Old
Testament

BROADMAN
& HOLMAN
PUBLISHERS

Nashville, Tennessee

4210–93
0-8054-1093-7

Dewey Decimal Classification: 221
Subject Heading: Bible O.T.—Criticism, Interpretation, Etc.
Library of Congress Card Catalog Number:94-39677

Interior design by Leslie Joslin
Cover design by Steve Diggs & Friends

Library of Congress Cataloging-in-Publication Data

Cracking Old Testament codes: a guide to interpreting Old Testament literary forms / D. Brent Sandy and Ronald L. Giese, Jr., editors
       p. cm.
Includes bibliographical references.
   ISBN 0-8054-1093-7
    1.Bible O.T.—Criticism, Form. 2.Bible. O. T.—Criticism, interpretation, etc. 3. Bible as literature.
I. Sandy, D. Brent, 1947- II. Giese, Ronald L., 1960—
BS1182.C7   1995
221.6'6—dc-20
                         94-39677
                         CIP

7 8   04 03 02

TO
RICHARD D. PATTERSON

CONTENTS

ABBREVIATIONS

ABD	*Anchor Bible Dictionary*
AJBI	Annual of the Japanese Biblical Institute
AnBib	Analecta biblica
ANET	J. B. Pritchard, ed., *Ancient Near Eastern Texts*[3]
ARM	Archives royales de Mari
BJS	Brown Judaic Studies
BO	Bibliotheca orientalis
BSac	*Bibliotheca Sacra*
BZAW	Beihefte zur *ZAW*
CahRB	Cahiers de la Revue biblique
EI	*Eretz Israel*
FOTL	The Forms of the Old Testament Literature
GTJ	*Grace Theological Journal*
HDR	Harvard Dissertations in Religion
HSM	Harvard Semitic Monographs
HTR	*Harvard Theological Review*
IBT	Interpreting Biblical Texts
Int	*Interpretation*
JANES	*Journal of the Ancient Near Eastern Society of Columbia University*

JAOS	*Journal of the American Oriental Society*
JBL	*Journal of Biblical Literature*
JETS	*Journal of the Evangelical Theological Society*
JSOT	*Journal for the Study of the Old Testament*
JSOTSup	Journal for the Study of the Old Testament—Supplement Series
JSS	*Journal of Semitic Studies*
NAC	New American Commentary
NICOT	New International Commentary on the Old Testament
OTL	Old Testament Library
RGG	*Religion in Geschichte und Gegenwart*
SBLDS	SBL Dissertation Series
SBLMS	SBL Monograph Series
TDOT	G. J. Botterweck and H. Ringgren, eds., *Theological Dictionary of the Old Testament*
TJ	*Trinity Journal*
TOTC	Tyndale Old Testament Commentary
TynBul	*Tyndale Bulletin*
UF	*Ugarit-Forschungen*
VT	*Vetus Testamentum*
WHJP	World History of the Jewish People
WTJ	*Westminster Theological Journal*
ZAW	*Zeitschrift für die alttestamentliche Wissenschaft*

CONTRIBUTORS

Martin G. Abegg, Jr.
Trinity Western University

Richard E. Averbeck
Trinity Evangelical Divinity School

Kenneth L. Barker
NIV Translation Center

Trent C. Butler
Broadman & Holman Publishers

John S. Feinberg
Trinity Evangelical Divinity School

Ronald L. Giese, Jr.
Liberty Baptist Theological Seminary

Ted A. Hildebrandt
Grace College and Theological Seminary

Andrew E. Hill
Wheaton College

Walter C. Kaiser, Jr.
Gordon-Conwell Theological Seminary

Tremper Longman III
Westminster Theological Seminary

Eugene H. Merrill
Dallas Theological Seminary

Walter B. Russell III
Talbot Theological Seminary

D. Brent Sandy
Ghent Grace Brethren Church, Roanoke, Virginia

Michael E. Travers
Mississippi College

Willem A. VanGemeren
Trinity Evangelical Divinity School

Branson L. Woodard, Jr.
Liberty University

INTRODUCTION

The morning newspaper contains a diversity of forms of writing, from news reporting to commentary, from classifieds to comic strips. These different forms are almost unnoticed by most readers, who unconsciously adjust their expectations when reading the different content, ways of expression, and purpose of what is written. For example, classified ads have a distinct content, form, and purpose. The meaning of the words "steel sinks" in that context is unmistakable. But in a column reporting on the work of scientists, the content, form, and purpose is very different. There the words "steel sinks" will refer to the density of metal in comparison to water. Will readers two thousand years from now—if someone unearths some "ancient" newspapers—recognize the differences between a classified ad and a column on scientific facts? Will they see that "steel sinks" means two completely different things, depending on the form, content, and function of the context where those words appear in our newspapers? In the same way, do readers of the Bible—a document written more than two thousand years ago—recognize the differences in form, content, and function of the diversity of forms of expression in it? Do they realize that to understand the Bible correctly, they cannot treat every portion of Scripture the same, as if it all were created equal?

This book exists to help Christians understand their Bibles better, in particular the Old Testament. Though the original readers intuitively recognized the diversity of forms in the Bible and the differences of meaning of words and phrases in those forms, readers today are often unprepared for some of the ancient ways of expressing things. Ways of thinking and writing have changed through the millennia.

Fortunately, it is possible to identify the different forms used by the authors of Scripture. Even as a newspaper has certain codes implicit in the variety of sections within it that guide us in reading it correctly, so the Bible has literary codes that reveal how authors were expressing the word of the LORD and what they intended to communicate. Understanding what these codes are and the significance of them will help keep readers from misinterpreting Scripture and will guide them into correct interpretation and application.

Because the literary forms of the Old Testament are so diverse and sometimes complicated, a team of scholars was selected to write the chapters in this book. Each an expert in his individual field of study, the contributors to this volume represent leading evangelical scholarship on the Bible. The intent of this book is not for individual scholars to present positions and ideas that are unique to themselves, but rather to reflect a consensus of how Christians can better read and study their Bibles.

The central chapters of this book, based on ten literary forms in the Old Testament, introduce readers to the unique characteristics of the forms, to literature from the ancient world that is similar to the Bible, to guidelines for interpretation, to a sample text where the guidelines are applied, and to recommended reading for additional insight. In addition to the chapters on the literary forms of the Old Testament, three introductory chapters treat important issues related to the diverse ways in which the Bible was written. A final chapter applies the material in the book to proclamation of the truths of the Bible.

Though this book is written by scholars, it is not written for scholars, though some of them may find it helpful in certain ways.

The goal of these chapters is to make available to students, pastors, and a more general audience the results of the work of scholars on the text of Scripture. This has meant more than usual amounts of editing, rewriting, and supplementing the chapters submitted by the contributors, in order to ensure unity and readability throughout the chapters. Though each contributor was asked to revise his chapter one time, second and third revisions were done by the editors. We express our deep thanks to each of the contributors for their excellent work and cooperation.

This is the first book to be devoted specifically to the literary forms of the Old Testament, with the purpose of providing clear principles of interpretation for Bible readers and for teachers and preachers. The emerging consensus that the codes embedded in the literary forms of the Old Testament are indispensable to correct interpretation makes this book an important contribution to the study of the Bible. The closest book in print to the purpose and content of the present volume is the very helpful *How to Read the Bible for All Its Worth: A Guide to Understanding the Bible* by Gordon D. Fee and Douglas Stuart, 2d ed. (Grand Rapids: Zondervan, 1993). In addition to the literary forms in the New Testament, they discuss five forms for the Old Testament. Though Fee and Stuart's book is still highly recommended, the present volume puts the study of the Old Testament on even surer footing, by treating ten literary forms and by rooting those forms in similar literature from the biblical world.

The specific occasion for this book is the desire of the editors and contributors to honor an esteemed colleague, teacher, friend, and gentleman. This book is dedicated to Richard D. Patterson, on the occasion of his retirement after more than thirty years of outstanding teaching and publishing. A graduate of Wheaton College, Los Angeles Baptist Seminary, Talbot Theological Seminary, and University of California at Los Angeles (M.A. and Ph.D.), Dick has been Professor of Old Testament at four seminaries and a department chair in two of those. He has published important essays spanning such topics as "The Widow, the Orphan, and the Poor in the Old Testament and the Extra-Biblical Literature," "Special Guests at the First Christmas," and "Of Bookends, Hinges, and Hooks: Literary Clues to the Arrangement of Jeremiah's Prophecies." He has contributed numerous articles and notes to Bible encyclopedias, dictionaries, and study Bibles. He has been involved in editing two commentary series. He has written commentaries on Joel, 1 and 2 Kings, Nahum, Habakkuk, and Zephaniah.

Dick Patterson is especially known for his research on the Old Testament as literature and his commitment to rooting the study of Scripture in the ancient world. He has often told his students that the stool on which rests the study of God's Word has four legs, not three. In addition to the legs of historical, grammatical, and theological interpretation, the fourth leg is interpretation according to the literary forms in which the text was written. May this book be a fitting tribute to the legacy that Dr. Patterson leaves in the lives of students, colleagues, and friends.

1

LITERARY FORMS OF THE OLD TESTAMENT

Ronald L. Giese, Jr.

This book is about context. A correct understanding of something spoken or written depends fundamentally on context. Conversely, taking statements out of context almost always deprives them of their true meaning. For Scripture, the most common fallacy of interpretation is failing to recognize the context. Proverbs 9:17 says, "Stolen water is sweet; food eaten in secret is delicious!" So does the Bible mean that water will taste better if we steal it from a neighbor, and food will taste better if we eat it alone rather than with someone? Not if we consider the context. Matthew 7:7–8 says, "Ask and it will be given to you; seek and you will find; knock and the door will be opened to you. For everyone who asks receives; he who seeks finds; and to him who knocks, the door will be opened." So does the Bible mean that we can have absolutely anything we want if we simply ask for it? Not if we consider context.

Anyone who wants to understand Scripture correctly must be sensitive to three levels of written context:

- Every word and phrase of Scripture belongs to the context of the sentence and paragraph where they appear. What the grammatical form of a word is, or what the role of a word or phrase is in relation to the sentence as a whole (syntax), are important considerations in determining meaning. This is *immediate context.*

- Every statement in Scripture is expressed in a certain way, whether it is giving praise to God as in the psalms, proclaiming God's judgment as in the prophets, predicting the expected outcome of certain conduct as in the proverbs, or telling the story of God's chosen people as in the historical books. This middle level of context is that of *literary forms.*

- Every statement in Scripture is part of the total context of the canon of Scripture. Since no single statement can completely reveal all of divine truth on any topic, the whole counsel of the Word of God is important for understanding the individual statements in the Bible. This is *distant context* (sometimes called theological context).[1]

The middle level of context, that of literary forms or categories of literature, has been recognized since people began to study literature. Prose and poetry are the most easily distinguished forms, for instance. Within these two broad categories there are many subdivisions, which encompass all the different ways in which we express ourselves. Literary form is commonly referred to as *genre,* a French term that means "kind." It is extremely important to those who study English literature to identify the genre of a piece of writing and to understand the significance or use of that particular genre during the time when it was written. The same could be said of those who study French literature, German literature, or any written legacy of a modern language.

Unfortunately, many who study the Bible are unaware of genre as a critical step in interpretation. Rather, the first and third levels of context receive the majority of attention, though in the last two decades the context of literary forms has begun to be discussed in the scholarly literature. Even with this beginning, little has been written for a more general audience, and that is especially unfortunate.[2] Ignorance of this level of context leads to some of the worst

---

1. There is another level of context: the context outside of the biblical text, that is, the cultural world of the author and the hearers. The meaning of words and the significance of ideas, for instance, hinges in part on the historical and cultural framework where they appear.

2. An exception to this is the very helpful work by Fee and Stuart, *How to Read the Bible for All Its Worth* (see "Recommended Reading" at the end of this chapter).

mistakes of interpretation. On the other hand, familiarity with this context provides a window through which we can greatly increase our understanding of what the biblical authors were trying to say.

This middle level of context, that of literary forms, should be considered the most important stage in the interpretive process. Let's say I have a friend named Otto who, when I give him a ride, feels compelled to tell me how to drive, park, and navigate short-cuts. One day he asks me, "What would you do if I ever stopped telling you how to drive?" and I reply, "I would give you a thousand dollars." Otto's application of this statement depends entirely upon his understanding of its genre. It is not the immediate context that matters. Looking up words like *give* or *thousand* in a dictionary does not help, and any syntactical analysis (like diagramming the two sentences) is of no value in discovering the way the statement functions (and hence how the receptor should apply it). It is the middle level of context, that of literary forms, that is determinative. The sentence "I would give a thousand dollars" is couched within a larger genre which is the conversation. Whatever label is given to the kind of statement, it is given in jest as part of the give-and-take banter and discussion of superficial topics between friends that sometimes characterizes car rides, short walks, or conversations in hallways or lounges.

If, on the other hand, the same words are used ("I" as the subject, "give" as the verb, and "thousand dollars" as the object) in a different genre, a legal one, the way that the statement functions and the way that the receptor applies it changes completely. If these words are in response to the question, "What will you do with your assets when you die?" it is the genre of "will and testament" that is paramount in interpretation. No amount of syntactical or lexical study (immediate context), and no amount of study on the concept of financial matters in the life of the author (distant context) will crack this code. It is only the deciphering of genre that enables readers to see not only what an author desired to communicate but what an author desired his readers to *do* with his communication—how he wanted them to *respond*.

Almost any passage of Scripture can illustrate the perils of trying to understand the Bible apart from literary context.

- "The waves of death swirled about me; the torrents of destruction overwhelmed me." Without knowing the context we might think of Jonah after his deliverance from near drowning at sea, for these words could describe his plight of floundering in the waves of a terrible storm.

- "Smoke rose from his nostrils; consuming fire came from his mouth, burning coals blazed out of it." Deprived of its context, this statement might raise several questions. Is it describing real smoke and fire? Is it describing a terrible creature, and the smoke, fire, and coals are simply pictorial language to add to the terrifying appearance of the creature? Is it describing a dragon? Or Satan?

- "He reached down from on high and took hold of me; he drew me out of deep waters." These words might call to mind Peter's experience of trying to walk on the water in his own strength when Jesus had to rescue him.

But all three of these verses come from one passage in 2 Samuel 22 (vv. 5, 9, and 17; cf. Ps. 18). It is one of David's psalms of praise for God's deliverance. As a psalm it is poetry, hence David expresses his thanksgiving in very vivid language. He was not threatened with drowning, though his life was in danger like that of drowning. His description of almighty God in terms of smoke, fire, coals, and even nostrils and mouth are not literal descriptions of a dragon-like creature: it is a poetic way of underscoring how awesome God is. What Scripture says needs to be carefully understood in light of the genres in which the authors wrote. Failure to do so results in a mishandling of God's communication to us.

What *Literary Form* Does *Not* Mean

Genre criticism works with the canonical form of the text and not any form *before* that. Searching for an oral stage for forms and ultimately an original "setting in life" (German, *Sitz im Leben*) before the written stage is an unnecessary pursuit, in part because the exercise is all too often a biased one.[3] Furthermore, genre may

---

3. Such a pursuit could be helpful, but not necessary, to understand a literary genre (see Rolf Knierim, "Old Testament Form Criticism Reconsidered," *Interpretation* 27 [1973]: 435–68). C. S. Lewis' criticisms concerning scholarly musings on the pre-written stage of biblical texts, though a bit too harsh, hold true to this day ("Fern-Seed and Elephants," in C. S. Lewis, *Fern-Seed and Elephants and Other Essays on Christianity*, ed. Walter Hooper [Glasgow: Collins, 1975], 113–22).

(and often does) change when a piece of communication passes from an oral, isolated stage to that of a written, contextual one.[4]

Genre criticism also works with the canonical form of the text and not any form *after* that. "Which text do we read?" is a conundrum that plagues other literatures where multiple copies or generational editing is involved. For instance, R. S. Crane's *The Red Badge of Courage* was published in 1895 in a different form than that written by the author (the publisher deleted parts of the original). A restored version that included all of the original text started appearing in the 1979 edition of the *Norton Anthology of American Literature*. In studying this novel, a description of the genre differs depending upon which version is read. The story may be seen as a war novel in which the hero matures into quiet bravery (the publisher's 1895 scaled-down version) or a tale of egotism that the main character never outgrows (the author's original and the 1979 restored version). With the Old Testament, different literary forms are not encountered when we move from one manuscript to another, which is simply to say that any standard English translation will reflect, as much as can be done in translation, the unique characteristics of the genre at hand. Therefore, genre study does not focus on pre- or post-canonical shapings of a text.

There is one other thing that literary form does not mean. Terminology within a statement does not determine the literary form of the statement. Take the question "Will you be playing basketball tomorrow?" to which an answer comes, "I'll be there." As with the question and statement about the gift of a thousand dollars, without information about the genre we have no idea what kinds of conventions, or shared understandings about such statements, are at work between the two individuals. The reponse "I'll be there," by itself, in this limited context, does not help. For instance, the reply to the question could be a *promise*, in which case the speaker of the reply has an obligation—a failure to fulfill the commitment would result in harm to the friendship. On the other hand, the reply could be an *optimistic prediction*, in which case there is

---

4. A point perhaps best made by Muilenburg, the name most commonly associated with rhetorical criticism in biblical studies (see, e.g., Thomas F. Best, ed., *Hearing and Speaking the Word: Selections from the Works of James Muilenburg* [Missoula: Scholars Press, 1984], 18–19).

no serious expectation on the part of the questioner, and a failure to show the next day would not harm the friendship. In this case the genre of the relationship between the two speakers, specifically the genre of the relationship during participatory sporting events, is as important (perhaps more so) than the genre of the conversation. This is evident since there might not be a larger context of conversation between the two within which the above statement can be interpreted.

Two points can be related from this illustration to the genres of the Bible. First, though vocabulary and grammar can play important parts in genre, neither is a defining mark of genres in the Bible. Even in brief, statement-oriented genres like certain kinds of laws and proverbs—where one might expect vocabulary or grammar to be important—such aspects alone cannot be guarantors of the presence of particular genres. It is tempting, for example, to say that case law by definition uses the Hebrew particle ki "if/when," and that a case law cannot be constructed without this particle. The problem with this is that case law *can* be presented using alternate forms.

Second, in certain genres efforts must be made to read between the lines and make some postulation as to the social context that was concurrent with the spoken context, though this is not the same as the original oral setting (see above). For instance, Isaiah may issue a statement of judgment against a king of Judah. The deviance that elicited the prophetic intervention may not be known. The location where the statement was delivered may similarly be unknown, as well as who was present aside from the prophet and the king (perhaps not even the king was present but an intermediary). Perhaps even the identity of the king is in question. Based on the genre of other passages in Isaiah, however, ones in which more background information is available, a reader could put forth a reason (or reasons) for the inclusion of this statement by whomever compiled Isaiah's oracles. For instance, a reader could ask, "To whom is the collection of prophecies (the canonical form) addressed?" It may still be a king of Judah (or kings of Judah in general), or it may be both the court and the people of Israel. The point is that readers need to use a broader written context to formulate reasonable conclusions about the social setting of a particular written text in question (in the same way that if we had more written record of various conversations between the two basketball players, we could draw conclusions about the relationship of the two that would help greatly in determining the genre of the one statement above). In sum, genre as defined here does not refer to stages before or after canonical inclusion, nor can it be determined by vocabulary (though this may help).

What *Literary Form* Does Mean

If literary forms, or genres, are not defined by vocabulary or grammar, then what does define them? The three marks of genre are form, content, and function (or intentionality). Often *forms* or *structures* mark genre immediately, as with verse (in contradistinction to prose). Though there is debate about the well-known statement, "Verse is language in lines" (whether phrases such as "with meter" should be added), the definition remains a good one. [5] Line length matters in poetry, or better yet a regularity or system of line length matters in poetry, whereas it is given minor attention in prose composition. In terms of literary *structures*, a lament psalm must have a request or petition that follows a description; a narrative must have a plot. One should keep in mind that the word *must* is usually too strong a word for genre studies. A lament psalm may conclude with a praise section, and usually does. Using the New Testament for illustration, a Pauline letter may include an opening thanksgiving, and usually does. But this does not mean that once an opening thanksgiving is found, one is necessarily in a Pauline letter, nor does it mean that the lack of such a section negates an identification with the genre of the Pauline letter. To take this a step further, producing a composite of a Pauline letter is possible, even desirable. Such a composite would include an introductory greeting, an opening thanksgiving, transitional formulas throughout the body, an autobiographical section, parenesis (exhortation), and closing formulas, with several of these sections containing subpoints (such as vice or virtue lists under parenesis). However, it may well be that, when turning to the Pauline corpus, not one

---

5. The statement comes from C. O. Hartman, *Free Verse: An Essay on Prosody* (Princeton: Princeton University Press, 1980), 11.

letter would fit this composite point for point.[6] The idea of producing and using a composite is not flawed, though, since it alone is not used to determine genre, and in fact does help to identify Pauline letters. Furthermore, it helps to note what is unique within any given letter in comparison to other letters.[7]

Knowing the genre that a passage belongs to may or may not reveal something significant about content. However, *content* is still the second mark in determining genre. Though "psalm" tells us practically nothing about what specific topics will be encountered (suffering, joy, friendship, romance, etc.), once formal features lead us into a guess of psalm, a read for content helps greatly in confirming this, since psalms deal with brief, personal experience. This necessarily excludes narrative and epic poems as well as contrived or imagined experiences.[8]

The third mark is *function* (how the text is intended to function, therefore sometimes called intentionality). Just as with the brief statement, "I'll be there," pericopes rely on surrounding contexts for their proper interpretation. Setting the parable of Nathan and its interpretation (see 2 Sam. 12:1–14) within the context of all of 2 Samuel 11–12 and even the larger context of the Succession Narrative of 2 Samuel 9–20 is of paramount importance.[9] The *placement* of the passage, as well as *details* of the events surrounding the adultery and resultant confrontation by Nathan (in contrast with less-detailed pericopes within 2 Samuel), set the stage for other disgraces experienced by David. Function is very different from

---

6. For a non-biblical example of a composite, see the structure of a non-solicited business letter attempting to sell a service to businesses in Vijay K. Bhatia, "A Genre-Based Approach to ESP Materials," *World Englishes* 10 (1991): 157.

7. Form is used, in part, to identify Galatians as a letter, and then a Pauline letter. When unique traits are observed, such as the lack of an opening thanksgiving, labels for subgenres come into play, such as calling Galatians an "apologetic" letter or "deliberative" letter (see David E. Aune, *The New Testament in Its Literary Environment* [Philadelphia: Westminster, 1987], 206–8).

8. Woodard and Travers in this book discuss the interrelatedness of form and content (as does the article by Devitt they refer to, in contradistinction to many studies in the mid-twentieth century in which form was the only consideration).

9. This is Eugene Merrill's case study in chapter 5.

form or content. For most pericopes, one can take the same form and topic, even the same words, that comprise the passage, yet change the function by placing this same passage in a different broader literary context; and a different function usually means a different genre.

The broad genre of "junk" mail is a good example of the interrelatedness of form, content, and function. There is a minimum amount of information that I need before I will throw a piece of junk mail away. Sometimes there is enough information on the envelope to tell me this, and the piece can be discarded unopened. But more often I end up opening the mailing. At this stage I do not read through the cover letter, but look for several telltale signs which will help identify the genre and help formulate a response to the genre. Signs such as a reproduced signature and highlighted words and phrases in the letter (through bold, italics, colored ink, etc.) are formal features of a mass mailing. I also skim the letter or, more usually, the brochure or glossy promotional that accompanies it, for content (e.g., a credit card offer). Finally, I read a few sentences to determine function. Knowing that the form is a mass mailing and that the content is an offer from a long-distance phone company still falls short of the minimal amount of information I need to form a response. If the *function* or *intention* of the genre is to steal customers away from their present long distance phone company, for instance, I am willing to read the letter in greater detail to weigh the strengths and weaknesses (of dollars and cents as well as services) of each company.

How Different Genres Are Recognized

Recognizing genres generally begins with an unconscious identification with the kinds of literature that readers are already familiar with. When we read for the first time a sample of prose or poetry in English literature, we intuitively pick up on certain marks that gradually inform our subconscious thoughts about the literary form we are reading. Because of previous exposure to the various genres common in English literature, we are prepared to accept a new piece of literature into one of the genre categories already existing in our minds, even if we do not realize we are doing so.

Some people, however, who are especially interested in the specific marks of certain genres may consciously note the genre of any literature they read. Editors of anthologies of English literature, for example, often group the pieces of literature in their anthologies together by genre, including an introduction to each of the groupings describing the marks of the genres. They do this because they know that the better their readers grasp the distinguishing characteristics of genres the more they will appreciate and understand the significance of what they read. With some guidance these readers begin to recognize different genres more consciously, even taking note of new genres not encountered before or the uniqueness of a blending of genres.

Similarly, Bible readers unconsciously identify what they encounter in the Old Testament with literary categories already in place in their minds. The problem is that our preparation for the genres of Scripture is largely limited to our exposure to genres in English literature. Readers can handle some of the differences between poetry and prose, and are familiar with the general purposes of historical writing. But when they turn to the genre of wisdom in Proverbs, or law in Exodus, or apocalyptic in Daniel, they are faced with a common form of communication in the biblical world that is very uncommon in today's world. For instance, the prophetic genre is a category for which modern readers are quite unprepared. Readers struggle to find a plot in a genre that is really not meant to be a story; they often struggle to find an immediate blessing in what is really not meant to be a praise psalm. Even more perplexing than prophecy is the narrower genre of apocalyptic. How many Christians report being baffled by the books of Daniel and Revelation! Rather than wait to discover how forms like prophecy, apocalyptic, and proverbs work, many Christians move right on to interpretation and application. Since such a move gives priority to the readers' opinions over a contextual meaning of Scripture, unhealthy results can usually be expected.

Accurate interpretation hinges then on recognizing the genres used in the Bible to communicate God's revelation. There is nothing wrong with readers taking advantage of the genre distinctions they are already familiar with; this in fact should be encouraged. Readers should seek to grow in their knowledge of contemporary literature, literatures of other cultures, and literatures of the ancient world (annals from Assyria, mythologies from Canaan, love poetry from Egypt, heroic tales from Greece, or histories from Rome). But readers must not depend solely on previous exposure and present occasional reading in ancient literature to give them the framework for understanding the genres of Scripture. Since correct interpretation hinges on context, especially the middle level of context, interpreters must begin to compile a working knowledge of the genres in the Bible.

The process of overcoming the differences in time and culture has been described with different metaphors: building a bridge, filling a gap, meeting a horizon, looking through a window into another world, and learning rules to play a game. But the skill of interpretation is perhaps best illustrated by a tool belt. The belt has many slots, some of which are already filled by common sense tools such as a general knowledge of when to take expressions as figurative or literal (we know that God is not literally a "rock"). Every time an interpreter comes to a basic understanding of how a biblical genre works, an important tool is added to the belt. When several of these tools hang comfortably in the belt, the builder is enabled to use them to work on various projects (developing a proper view of God, deepening relationships with others, etc.). Without a knowledge of genres, an interpreter looks at a proverb and reaches for . . . what? There is no tool waiting in the correct holder. Which in turn forces the interpreter, consciously or subconsciously, to reach for a different tool, one not designed to deal with a proverb. Perhaps it is the tool for how to analyze the parts of speech of a sentence, or the tool which describes how to do a topical study using all of Scripture. Whatever the tool is, the interpreter's work will be parallel to the work of a carpenter without a saw, or a roofer without a hammer.

How do interpreters go about compiling this working knowledge? Insight into the genres of the Bible comes from internal data and from external parallels. The most important information about biblical genres comes from the Bible itself. Noting differences in content, form, and function, as well as what such differences mean, is the best guide for readers to understand correctly the various genres of Scripture. Also important are the many examples of parallel genres preserved in writings from the ancient Near East and from the writings of the Jews that were not considered canonical (see "Recommended Reading" at the end of the chapter). Such writings help to determine aspects of form, content, and function. They also help determine the uniqueness of the biblical genres, that is, when a biblical author is departing from or modifying a genre that was common in his world.

Though identification of biblical genres with their distinctive features is indispensable to interpretation, genres are not absolute, mutually exclusive categories. Genres are distinguishable, but as literary groupings there will be some pieces of literature that have the marks of more than one genre. Therefore, the process of distinguishing literary genres is not a hard science:

> The most important fact about genre is that *genres are generalizations*. As such they are both true and false. They are not natural objects like animals, vegetables, or minerals. They are made by humans out of the mind's penchant for observing similarities and differences in things, to provide order to understanding (italics his).[10]

We are familiar with this qualification. Any public library is divided into genres such as fiction/nonfiction, with numerous groupings under each of these categories: novels, history, children's books, business books. Some books, even if only one in ten, fit more than one category of topic. An autobiography can also be a part of history, poems can also be put to music and called lyrics.

But the existence of works which cross generic lines would never cause a librarian to say, "Forget about the groupings, from now on put books back on the shelves wherever you want." Such a response treats all books as if they were the same genre, when we know this is not true. Great harm would result from this kind of response: Library patrons desiring guidance for a particular concern would not know where to look, and would end up receiving information from books which really do not address the subject.

---

10. Walter R. Fisher, "Genre: Concepts and Applications in Rhetorical Criticism," *Western Journal of Speech Communication* 44 (1980): 290. See also Tremper Longman III, "Form Criticism, Recent Developments in Genre Theory, and the Evangelical," *WTJ* 47 (1985): 57.

In the same way, users of the collection of genres called "the Bible" must be careful not to treat all passages in Scripture as if they were the same genre. To avoid doing this, readers must constantly be developing and fine-tuning their skills of distinguishing, identifying, and describing different genres.

Listing the Literary Forms

Though the walls between genres may not be rock solid, it is possible to talk intelligently about specific literary forms in the Old Testament. The most basic forms are prose and poetry (the term *verse* is also used as an antonym for prose). Prose is well known to us as a means of communicating information. Histories, biographies, contracts, letters, and announcements fall within this category, even the more entertaining movement through a plot found in novels or even many children's stories. Poetry, or verse, is different. It can be distinguished by its form, content, and function. One definition of *form* is that verse is "language written in lines."[11] Definitions of *content* such as "experience related by the use of imagery" and definitions of *function* such as "to transfuse emotion—not to transmit thought but to set up in the reader's sense a vibration corresponding to what was felt by the writer"[12] —join with definitions of form to help distinguish verse. But within both prose and poetry, the diversity of form, content, and function calls for subdivisions of these two broad genres into more precise literary forms.

---

11. I would add "language written in lines with rhythm," rhythm which may or may not be metrical, that is, observable on the level of the line (Ronald L. Giese, Jr., "Strophic Hebrew Verse as Free Verse," *JSOT* 61 [1994]: 29–38).

12. A. E. Housman, *The Name and Nature of Poetry* (New York: Macmillan, 1933), 8. Combining topic and intentionality later, Housman cautions against overreading poetry (a caution not necessary for prose): "Even when poetry has a meaning, as it usually has, it may be inadvisable to draw it out. 'Poetry gives most pleasure,' said Coleridge 'when only generally and not perfectly understood'; and perfect understanding will almost extinguish pleasure" (p. 36 [for similar cautions about overreading, see chapter 9 on apocalyptic]). Such a caution is similar to Robert Frost's well-known definition that poetry is what gets left out in a translation.

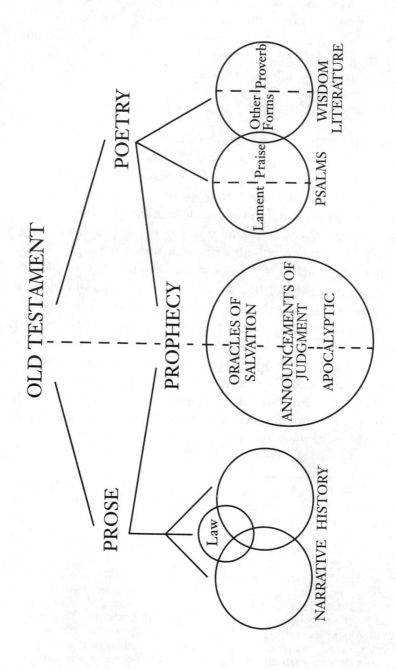

The Old Testament is often divided up into five genres. Prose is divided into narrative and law, poetry into psalm and wisdom, with prophecy falling somewhere in the middle since it is often a mix of prose and poetry. These categories are certainly helpful, but there is still an immense amount of diversity within any one of these five forms. It is difficult to formulate a rule or guideline for understanding prophecy when, even within the same book, there are different genres of prophecy used for very different purposes. Hence, a further division is necessary to make genre analysis more of a user-friendly tool that will adjust to different kinds of passages even within the same biblical book.

The categories of genres necessary to function effectively in the text of the Old Testament are ten. Prose is best seen as three different genres: narrative, history, and law. Prophecy, which typically is a combination of prose and poetry, is best seen as three different genres: oracles of salvation, announcements of judgment, and apocalyptic. Poetry is best divided into psalms of lament and psalms of praise. And wisdom is divided into proverbial and non-proverbial wisdom. The chart on page 18 shows how these genres relate to one another. While it is possible to subdivide these ten genres even further, the list of literary forms appears almost endless the further one travels down the hierarchy of forms. Less frequent genres would include genealogy, love poetry, court tales, conquest accounts, and various kinds of non-prophetic speeches. But the larger the list the more unmanageable the Old Testament becomes. The primary goal in genre criticism is to grasp different principles of interpretation for each genre within a given set of genres. If that list of genres is too long, it is unrealistic to expect students of the Bible to internalize all of the unique principles at work in each of the genres, especially when some of the genres are very foreign to begin with. Furthermore, many of the subgenres do not have separate guidelines for interpretation, whereas there are significant differences between all of the ten genres listed here.

Genres of the Old Testament

The ten genres discussed in this book can be briefly distinguished as follows.[13]

---

13. Some of the wording is summarized from the wording of the authors.

Narrative. Studying narrative as a genre involves examining features of *form* as the layout of scenes (the dividing of the action into sequences) and the development of plot. Issues of *content* include how characters are portrayed (often with God himself as one of the characters). This is often seen in what the narrator relates of their words and actions, as well as what he relates of their thoughts and emotions. A key issue in content analysis is the critique, direct and indirect, that an author places within the text. As with stories today, narrative can serve a variety of primary *functions* such as teaching kinship obligation or personal morality.

History. Narrative (sometimes called regular narrative) and history (sometimes called historical narrative) need to be distinguished. Narrative always involves individual characters, whereas history, because of its nature as a blend of genres, can easily move in and out between groups and various individuals who are only superficially described. History *form* is a unique genre in that it is a collection and organization of other genres. The *content* of history in the Old Testament focuses on the nation of Israel and not on a specific individual, family, or tribe. History often includes narratives, but unlike narrative, history's primary *function* as a genre is to present a chronicle of Israel's relationship with God, often seen through Israel's relations with its pagan neighbors as well as through the response that her kings gave to the word of the LORD as uttered through the prophets.

Law. Legal portions of the Bible include covenant, law, and ritual legislation. Covenant was the establishment and expression of a relationship (more far-reaching than a mere contract). Covenant was the basis for law in the Old Testament, since law provided the stipulations for the covenantal relationship. The covenant's *form* included a proposal, stipulations, and a solemnization. The *content* was not based in emotion as with much of poetry but in practical outworkings of the covenantal relationship: defining of interpersonal relations, rights and responsibilities, and ceremonies. The *function* was thus to have a real-life, everyday effect on personal and community life. Covenant was not static, but alive, something to be reaffirmed daily.

Oracles of Salvation. Prophecy in the Old Testament utilizes a mix of prose and poetry, but the prose sections mostly set the stage for the poetical sections. It is important to distinguish between the poetry of prophecy and that of psalms. Whereas the music of the psalms can be read as poetry by either a community or an individual, and generally read with an ignorance of historical background (occasion for writing) and authorship, such is not the case for the prophets. The prophets addressed nations, not individuals, though often the nation was addressed through addressing the court. In addition, the prophets also must be understood in their historical context. Though we may not have information about the original oral setting, gathering all that we can discern about any given prophet as well as the spiritual, economic, and social environment in which he lived is paramount in reading his work. An oracle of salvation, the first genre of prophecy, is a word from God that assures the people of the validity of God's promise and often of his deliverance from crisis. The *form* contains a word from the LORD (oracle), reassurance that God has heard the cries of his people, and an affirmation of God's commitment to his promises. This is often framed in a messenger formula at the beginning ("Thus says the LORD") and a concrete point of fulfillment at the close. In terms of *content*, the meaning of these promises, which begin in the book of Genesis, overlaps heavily with the sense of terms such as *salvation* and *blessing*. The *function* is eschatological, to produce a knowledge of God's victory at the end of time as well as to produce hope based on the final consummation and present extension of blessing.

Announcements of Judgment. Judgment is often a visual experience for readers since it is usually this genre that includes "sign acts" that often supplement the spoken word such as the wearing of sackcloth, the shaving of one's beard, or the wearing of a yoke. Whereas the poetry of the psalms is highly personal, the prophets proclaim a message that is not their own but is rather a message from God that they are called and compelled to share, even if counter to their own goals and lifestyle. Similar to the *form* of the oracle of salvation, announcements of judgment often begin with a messenger formula ("Thus says the LORD"), but differ in that they contain an accusation followed by an announcement of judgment. In terms of *content*, just as salvation can be described in very concrete terms with the oracle of salvation, here the judgment is often very specific. The *function* of announcements is either to inform the king or people of the impending wrath of God (where the king has stepped over the line) or to warn him in an effort to produce repentance (he is stepping over the line and must withdraw his foot immediately). Included in the function of this form is its necessity: God must speak through a prophet if a king is breaking the covenant since there is no natural judicial process against a king.

Apocalyptic. Apocalyptic is part of prophecy but a distinct form within it. Prophecy presents God's message in bold and explicit terms, calling people to change their ways and do what God wants; apocalyptic presents God's perspective in graphic visions filled with unexpected and often mysterious scenes of heaven and the future. The *content* of prophecy focuses on immediate, impending judgment, which can be averted if the people of God will simply return to following the LORD. The primary focus of apocalyptic is distant judgment and restoration: The final solution for the problems of this age is in the age to come, when God will reign and be recognized as the LORD of all. Though for prophecy the *function* of pronouncing God's hatred of disobedience and harsh judgment of those who disobey is a call to repentance, in apocalyptic the coming judgment is written to encourage the saints who are caught up in the crises of living in an evil world; they are encouraged to persevere and not give up hope, for God is truly in control and will "soon" intervene into world events in the person of the Son of Man.

Lament. Laments include as part of their *form* an invocation and plea to God, a complaint, a request or petition, and a statement of confidence in God's response. Lament refers to sorrow or grief, hence telling us something about the *content* of this genre. A lament psalm seeks to convey a response to a crisis. Though many Christians think that the Book of Psalms is filled with praise and uplifting emotions, there are more lament psalms than there are praise psalms. Lament can be directed toward the enemy of the lamenter, the lamenter himself, or God. Hence the *function* can be a call for God's justice, or a cry for help, or repentance on the part of the author.

Praise. Most psalms are either psalms of praise (security, orientation) or lament (distress, disorientation). The *forms* of praise psalms vary since there are several subgenres: hymn, enthronement psalm, song of Zion, and royal psalm, for instance. In terms of *content*, praise psalms, instead of asking for deliverance, seek to share primarily one emotion or experience, one response to a celebratory event, act of deliverance, or truth. The *function* is to complement God for who he is (sometimes called descriptive praise or hymns) as well as what he has done (sometimes called declarative praise or thanksgiving).

Proverb. Proverbs in *form* are brief, usually timeless pieces of advice which commonly have some literary devices to aid in memory. *Content* includes morality, finances, work ethic, interpersonal relations, conduct for leadership, and treatment of the poor. Advice that focuses on these areas *functions* to help devotees of wisdom develop the skill of handling everyday decisions. Many of these kinds of decisions are not clear-cut as in the legal forms of the Old Testament and thus require skill versus simple obedience. With many kinds of proverbs, what proverb fits in what social context is paramount, a skill that cannot be easily taught. Due to the form of a proverb, which is a statement often without a clearly related context, the kind of authority that each proverb exercises is a key issue.

Non-Proverbial Wisdom. In *form* non-proverbial wisdom encompasses units longer than single-statement proverbs such as parables, wisdom poems, and dialogues, as well as shorter units such as riddles. Not all of these need be in the form of poetry, an example of why the chart in this chapter is in some cases a generalization. In *content*, though many of the topics are similar, proverbial literature is often more direct and practical, non-proverbial forms are more reflective or speculative, sometimes even called "counter-wisdom." The *function* is similar to proverbial literature but again more reflective in that help is offered to the perplexing questions of life.

Conclusion

Genre, though often ignored completely, is actually the level of context to which an interpreter should give the most attention.

Everyone engages in genre criticism, or classification, at some level. Audiences simply cannot help but classify communications; even if they deem a speech or writing as unworthy of attention, they are classifying it. Though we bring a knowledge of English literary forms with us to the biblical text, and this is helpful, in some cases this will mislead us, and in other cases it is simply not enough since the modern forms are so different from the ancient ones. It is therefore of primary importance that we understand the major literary forms of the Old Testament. We must understand what makes them unique and how they relate to parallel forms outside of the biblical literature. Only then can we formulate principles or guidelines for each genre. These principles will serve us again and again, for it is impossible to read the Bible without reading a literary form.

To take us back to the way genres functioned for the biblical authors and audiences, and to bring these genres up through time for present-day application, is the reason for this volume.

Recommended Reading

Introductions to Form Criticism

Hayes, John J. *Old Testament Form Criticism*. San Antonio: Trinity University Press, 1974. This is the standard introductory work on the history of research in form criticism up to about 1971. There are six chapters: the study of forms, narrative, law, prophecy, psalms, and wisdom.

Knight, Douglas A., and Gene M. Tucker, eds. *The Hebrew Bible and Its Modern Interpreters*. Chico: Scholars, 1985. Though this is not a book on form criticism per se (there are chapters, e.g., on Israelite religion, archaeology, and theology of the Hebrew Bible), most of the book deals with genres. Seven of the fifteen chapters deal with genres proper (titles such as "The Historical Literature," "The Wisdom Literature," "The Lyrical Literature"), and some of the remaining chapters deal with form criticism ("The Ancient Near Eastern Environment" has headings on law, wisdom, covenant, love poetry, etc., and a chapter on literary analysis has a ten-page section on "form").

Tucker, Gene M. *Form Criticism of the Old Testament*. Philadelphia: Fortress, 1971. This short paperback (less than 100 pages) is part of Fortress' "Guides to Biblical Scholarship" series (which covers different hermeneutical methodologies). The book includes a brief history of form criticism, introduction to broad genres (the two broad genres included are narrative and prophecy), and representative texts of such genres with commentary (the two broad genres included are narrative and prophecy).

Ancient Near Eastern Parallel Literature

Beyerlin, Walter, ed. *Near Eastern Religious Texts Relating to the Old Testament*. Translated by John Bowden. Philadelphia: Westminster, 1978. This text is set up in the same format as Matthews/Benjamin (below); that is, it is a collection of texts (translations) with brief introductions. The difference is that Beyerlin is more technical: More texts are included and more secondary sources are cited (though of course key works since this publication are not included).

Matthews, Victor H. and Don C. Benjamin. *Old Testament Parallels: Laws and Stories from the Ancient Near East*. New York: Paulist, 1991. This book is intended to get an interpreter into reading parallel texts right away. This concept of only the briefest amount of introduction or commentary to each text, combined with the affordability of a paperback, puts *Old Testament Parallels* within the same genre as the abridged version of *Ancient Near Eastern Texts* (see below). The chapters are organized around books and collections of books in the Old Testament rather than genres (hence titles like "The Book of Genesis" or "The Books of Samuel and Kings"). Before each translation is a helpful introduction to the text, and more than one hundred illustrations are interspersed among the texts. If a line from one of these texts is similar to a verse from the Old Testament, the Old Testament reference is given in parentheses right after the corresponding line in the translation (i.e., throughout the translation and not collected at the end).

Walton, John H. *Ancient Israelite Literature in Its Cultural Context: A Survey of Parallels Between Biblical and Ancient Near Eastern Texts*. Grand Rapids: Zondervan, 1991. This is a helpful library resource tool for students working in biblical studies. Chapters are organized around genres, hence titles such as "Legal Texts," "Historical Literature," and "Prophetic Literature." Each chapter has: (1) a "materials" section, which includes a listing of manuscripts, translations and notes, and a brief description of content; (2) a "discussion" section, which includes comments on form and content (with recommended secondary literature in footnotes); and (3) one or two pages of bibliography. Excurses and sections entitled "cases of alleged borrowing" appear where applicable. The book is both an introduction to parallel genres and a bibliography. Since it does not include examples of parallel literature, as does Matthews/Benjamin, its usefulness depends upon one's access to a research library.

Pritchard, James. *Ancient Near Eastern Texts Relating to the Old Testament.* 3d ed. Princeton: Princeton University Press, 1969. Often abbreviated *ANET*, this is found (often in multiple copies) in any library that cares about biblical studies, but the work is too expensive for students to purchase for themselves (it totals more than 700 pages). *ANET* includes translations with brief introductions and bibliographies. *ANET* has been abridged (in a combined format with *ANEP, The Ancient Near East in Pictures*) in an affordable, two-volume paperback version (both volumes total about 700 pages, but the size is much smaller).

Hermeneutics Books that Include Sections on Genre

Fee, Gordon D. and Douglas Stuart. *How to Read the Bible for All Its Worth.* Grand Rapids: Zondervan, 1982. After two introductory chapters, every chapter covers a different genre.

Greidanus, Sidney. *The Modern Preacher and the Ancient Text: Interpreting and Preaching Biblical Literature.* Grand Rapids/Leicester: Eerdmans, InterVarsity, 1988. This book combines interpretation with sermon preparation, and contains chapters on preaching Hebrew narratives and preaching prophetic literature.

Klein, William W., Craig, L. Blomberg, and Robert L. Hubbard. *Introduction to Biblical Interpretation.* Dallas: Word, 1993. Two chapters are devoted to genre criticism: One deals with general rules for prose and poetry, and the other works through various genres such as narrative, law, prophecy, and wisdom.

Longman, Tremper III. *Literary Approaches to Biblical Interpretation*. Grand Rapids: Zondervan, 1987. After a section on the theory of literary analysis, there are two additional sections, one on prose analysis and one on poetic analysis (each with examples).

Osborne, Grant R. *The Hermeneutical Spiral: A Comprehensive Introduction to Biblical Interpretation*. Downers Grove: InterVarsity, 1991. Part II of the book is on genre analysis, with chapters on narrative, poetry, wisdom, prophecy, and apocalyptic.

Ryken, Leland. *Words of Delight: A Literary Introduction to the Bible*. 2d ed. Grand Rapids: Baker, 1992. Part I of the book is on biblical narrative, part II is on biblical poetry, and part III covers other literary forms such as proverb, drama, and satire.

Ryken, Leland, and Tremper Longman III, eds. *A Complete Literary Guide to the Bible*. Grand Rapids: Zondervan, 1993. This book is largely an evangelical response to Alter and Kermode's (editors) *The Literary Guide to the Bible* (Harvard University Press, 1987). The chapters work through most of the biblical books, hence chapter headings like "Genesis" and "Ruth." There are more general chapters on the Bible as literature, the value of a literary approach for preaching, and also chapters on narrative, poetry, and prophecy as broad genres (Richard Patterson, in whose honor the present volume is dedicated, contributed the chapter on prophecy).

The commentary series entitled The Forms of Old Testament Literature (Eerdmans) should be mentioned. Various commentaries in this series contain introductions to literary forms (e.g., Genesis has an introduction to narrative literature) that can be very helpful. The multivolume *Anchor Bible Dictionary* also has helpful articles on various literary forms.

2

LITERARY FORMS AND INTERPRETATION

Branson L. Woodard, Jr. and Michael E. Travers

Long ago as the Israelites prepared to enter the promised land, they heard a pointed reminder: "I am setting before you today a blessing and a curse—the blessing if you obey the commands of the LORD your God that I am giving you today; the curse if you disobey the commands of the LORD your God and turn from the way that I command you today by following other gods, which you have not known" (Deut. 11:26–28). All the repetition aside, here Moses cautions that if God's words are acknowledged as *law*, as commands to be obeyed, the Hebrews will enjoy God's favor. But if the congregation ignores what God said to Moses on Mount Sinai—treating God's words simply as *advice*, a sort of nice idea—chastisement will come. The difference between law and advice is partly a matter of genre.

A genre is a group of things with common characteristics. Like dinner at a fine restaurant (hors d' oeuvres, salads, entrées, desserts), the things that people write can be categorized. Genre criticism is the process of identifying in a text the range of literary-rhetorical features that make the text one type of writing and not another—that determine where on the literary "menu" a text should be listed. A personal letter is not a business letter, and a novel is not a short story, though each pair of these examples has internal similarities. Genre is an important aspect of how an author creates meaning in a text, and genre criticism is a vital part of interpreting that text afterward. Effective use of genre criticism depends upon two primary factors: (1) distinguishing clearly between genre criticism and other critical theories, and (2) recognizing generic analysis for its advantages, its limitations, and its relationship to hermeneutics.

A Strange Word, A Familiar Idea

Why should anyone be concerned about determining the genre(s) of an Old Testament text as a part of biblical interpretation? What does genre have to do with the meaning of a verse or passage? These and other questions continue to create suspicion among some students of Scripture. While genres are as old as time itself, only since the 1970s have biblical scholars returned to a serious consideration of the subject. Much productive research has been done in this short time, though literary criticism—and genre criticism in particular—continues to be refined. Various pitfalls do await the unwary critic, as has been noted in the larger context of literary criticism and biblical studies.[1]

Nevertheless, genres inform our everyday lives. They are the form-and-content models by which we understand different things, literature being only one of them. Our nation's labor force is sometimes classified as white-collar, blue-collar, salaried, hourly, self-employed, professional, technical, and unskilled. Genres are everywhere, used each day in different settings, often perhaps unconsciously, and they enable us to recognize patterns or groups of things and to communicate about them. The word *genre* still may "stick out in an English sentence as the unpronounceable and alien thing that it is," as the leading critic Northrop Frye said years ago, complaining about the lack of a consistent theory of genre.[2] Nevertheless, we know the concept well.

---

1. See Tremper Longman III, *Literary Approaches to Biblical Interpretation* (Grand Rapids: Zondervan, 1987), 47–62.

2. "The Function of Criticism at the Present Time" (1954), in *Literary Criticism and Theory*, ed. Robert Con Davis and Laurie Finke (New York and London: Longmans, 1989), 662. This volume is a handy collection of works on literary criticism.

Discussions about genre must consider how form and content interrelate. Obviously, ideas in communication differ from the vehicle. The thoughts of a preacher or a novelist are not the same as either the sermon or the written narrative. Moreover, certain content is expected within a particular form. Good sermons may contain a humorous word occasionally, but they consist mainly of exegeted passages and related principles from Scripture—not at all the material in a Saturday morning cartoon on television. Content and form are different.

Still, communication cannot be discussed in depth according to neat and simplistic dichotomies of ideas and words or of messages and methods. Shakespeare wrote some tragi-comedies, mixing seriousness with humor, and Saturday morning cartoons convey some serious principles for living. Further, effective communicators are sensitive to such matters as their medium, their audience, and how best to express their ideas. The medium may be writing a chapter for a book or for a magazine or acting on stage or in front of a television camera, or speaking before a large audience or face-to-face. The audience may be educated or general, affluent or poor, teens or retired people. The best way to express ideas involves what to say, what to imply, and when. These dynamics of form and content must be kept together—an idea *and* a form support a genre. Accordingly, genre criticism is the process of relating a literary form-and content model with a text.

What Genre Criticism Does

The best way to understand genre criticism is to relate it to other ways of studying a text. Genres have a historical dimension, but genre criticism is not the same as historical background. Epic, lyric poetry, and tragedy are ancient forms, and each has contributed in different ways to historiography: The historian approaches the *Iliad* seeking to recover a sense of the Homeric world as a context for understanding the poem. That is essential, but the genre critic focuses more on the different features of the poem, looking for correspondence to one or more genres, and eventually uses the genre(s) to describe the poem.

Literary criticism, a broad discipline, encompasses such issues as plot, theme, structure, characters, word choice, point of view, and tone. Here the text is treated as an artifact; the analysis focuses upon specific parts, both in isolation and in relation to the text as a whole. The genre critic goes beyond this to seek authors' intended meanings through their choice of literary features.

Genre criticism can also be distinguished from the older *form criticism* in biblical studies. The genealogy in Genesis 5, for example, is seen by the form critic as a distinct segment, to be isolated from the surrounding material, examined on its own terms, and related to earlier genealogies in other texts. This entire process leads to some generalization about possible influence of the earlier text upon the latter. To the genre critic, the genealogy in Genesis 5 has internal features worthy of examination as well as a larger purpose within the entire Book of Genesis. Assuming Genesis is a unity, its sections are connected either thematically or in some other way. For this reason the genealogy in chapter 5 is significant in the local and global context.

In recent years biblical scholars have paid increasing attention to another theory, *rhetorical criticism*. Rhetoric (as defined by Aristotle) is the art of using all available means of persuasion and is distinct from genre but related to it. Both genre criticism and rhetorical criticism begin with a written text, but the rhetorical critic presupposes an earlier spoken discourse, one whose content and format resemble the written version. The written text is examined as if its audience were listeners to a speech rather than readers of a scroll or book. This oral dimension in the criticism of Genesis or Samuel or Isaiah is all the more appropriate in light of the Israelites' oral tradition and the dominance of speech over writing in ancient rhetoric. For the genre critic, interpretation is based ultimately and finally upon the written text and its form, not upon preceding oral expressions of it.

The contrast in focus of genre and rhetorical criticism may be illustrated by a dramatic moment in Elijah's dialogue with the prophets of Baal (see 1 Kings 18). Within that historical account lie details that must be examined generically and rhetorically, mainly because communication occurs in a context and that context is informed by values.[3]

---

3. The subject of values in the communication process is examined at length but in a nontechnical way in Peggy Rosenthal's *Words and Values* (New York: Oxford University Press, 1984).

The exchange between Elijah and the false prophets is potentially harsh and confrontational. The language may sound civilized, but at times Elijah's zeal for the LORD of Hosts is overpowering. At one point the Baal worshipers call out to the idol but receive no response. Then comes Elijah's reaction to the prophets' appeal to their god: "Shout louder! . . . Surely he is a god! Perhaps he is deep in thought, or busy, or traveling. Maybe he is sleeping and must be awakened" (1 Kings 18:27). Though Elijah speaks as if he assumes the existence of Baal as a god, to conclude that a prophet of Yahweh is asserting a personal belief in Baal misses the whole point of the dialogue. The irony here is transparent: Elijah believes the opposite of what he says.

The power and intention in this text grab our attention through the functions of genre and rhetorical criticism. As a genre it is a good example of Hebrew narrative[4] with its multifaceted nature, characterized by (1) short, pungent sayings, (2) greater emphasis upon the actual dialogue than upon background information about it, and (3) clever use of irony and wordplay.[5] From a rhetorical viewpoint, if we "listen" to the text (as well as read it), it becomes clear that Elijah's words were a taunt to his immediate hearers. They would not have understood Elijah to be admitting belief in Baal. The irony of Elijah's words is confirmed by genre and rhetorical criticism.

Though for some students of Scripture there is a hesitancy to examine God's inspired words generically or rhetorically—therefore, any discussion of genre, audience, or artistry (irony, in the case of 1 Kings 18) is a threat to biblical authority—the judicious use of genre and rhetorical criticism helps to illumine the meaning of Scripture. Elijah was fighting to rid Israel of idol worship, and the author of Kings—under divine inspiration—is writing Elijah's mocking rebuke of the false prophets to show the folly of their

---

4. See chapter 4 below. Highly readable analyses of Hebrew narrative appear in Robert Alter's *The Art of Biblical Narrative* (New York: Basic Books, 1981) and in the chapter on narrative in Gordon Fee and Douglas Stuart's *How to Read the Bible for All Its Worth*, 2d ed. (Grand Rapids: Zondervan, 1993), 78–93.

5. Helpful explanations about irony in Scripture appear in Edwin Good, *Irony in the Old Testament* (Sheffield: Almond, 1965) and Robert Chisholm, *Interpreting the Minor Prophets* (Grand Rapids: Zondervan, 1990).

powerless religion. Moreover, Elijah's devastating irony is no more significant than the genre in which that irony is expressed. While on one level Old Testament narrative expresses the plot of the incident, on a higher level the narrative is one way to structure and explain history itself. So Elijah's derisive words within the larger narrative meant that there was no God but Yahweh.

All in all, genre analysis occurs within a broader range of critical process, an approach that some recent critical theorists have unfortunately made its own end. Only since 1975 has critical theory become its own reason to exist. Traditionally, genre criticism has intended to enable readers to understand better the meaning of primary texts.

What Genres Have Looked Like in the Past

The ancient Near East had no formal treatises on genres, though writers displayed considerable literary sophistication. Collections from Ugarit, Sumer, Egypt, and elsewhere show a variety of form-and-content models: prayers, omens, epics, hymns, satires, and royal inscriptions. While no formal cataloguing of genres has been discovered from that era, the biblical authors used some of the conventions of an epic or a tragedy in what they wrote. Descriptions of different genres come later in Greek literature: In Plato's *Republic* (2.9) the proper teachings about God are conveyed through literature, whether "epic, lyric [ode or hymn], or drama." And Aristotle's *Poetics* (6) lists the features of tragedy in order to compare it with epic, another genre well known around the Mediterranean (as well as in India and elsewhere).

Centuries later, theological commentary would lead to a renewed interest in allegory and the dichotomous worldview that it implies. In *Summa Theologica* Aquinas theorized about two senses of words—the *historical*, for words that refer only to objects (e.g., tree), and the *spiritual*, for words that have additional signification beyond mere objects (e.g. cross, blood). This latter sense, in turn, was divided into the anagogical (i.e., whatever points to the eternal glory of God), the moral and the allegorical. Such categories help to explain why medieval literature had different levels, especially the so-called literal and figurative or the earthly and heavenly.

During and after the Renaissance, the epic, tragedy, comedy, and satire continued to appear, while new genres—the essay, novel, and other prose works—gave writers new opportunities both to explain discoveries from science and world exploration and to tell stories about people's experiences and situations. While the traditional genres appeared in new combinations (e.g. tragi-comedies), the newer genres quickly assumed clear, fixed formulas.

Our era is perhaps a time to itself. With the advent of radio, television, film, videotape, audiotaped books, and CD-ROM, genre distinctions have been blurred, not from any change in the fundamental dynamics of the tragic, the comic, or the romantic but from many radical changes in communication itself.

Today genre criticism still lacks a formal theory accepted by a majority of literary critics. Since Northrop Frye's complaint about the lack of a consistent theory of genre, researchers have attempted to follow Frye's lead and to define genre from a rhetorical perspective. As a result, the old idea of genre as a static classification system of different literary forms is giving way to a new model.[6] Here the writing process is emphasized rather than the process of reading, and the situation involving a speaker, listener, and discourse is the starting point. Because each communication event is part of a recurrent pattern of events over time (e.g., an acceptance speech by a newly elected politician, a commencement address, a funeral oration), the speaker can determine content, tone, structure, and other matters according to the rhetorical exigencies of the situation, with an eye to how the address has been done before. Genre thus becomes a mediator between form and content; it "constructs and responds to recurring situation. . . . Genre is truly, therefore, a maker of meaning . . . a dynamic rather than a static concept."[7]

This concept of genre, strongly oriented toward writing theory, may be helpful in biblical studies. Certainly the older idea of genre as form—a definition of genre according to a catalogue of literary types, each with its own set of features—works well in interpreta-

---

6. Amy Devitt, "Generalizing about Genre: New Conceptions of an Old Concept," *College Composition and Communication* 44 (Dec. 1993): 573–86.

7. Ibid., 578–80.

tion because the interpreter's primary task is not writing but reading. Yet the newer model, like rhetorical criticism, can add perspective to understanding biblical texts that originally were presented orally.

The *oracle* of Nahum, for example, communicates additional force and life when studied as a spoken discourse. The genre assumes a vibrancy and timeliness not apparent if the book is simply catalogued as an oracle and then analyzed according to the prescribed list of features that appear in other oracles. No doubt this work should be done but in the context of the prophet's proclamation of divine condemnation upon an impenitent city—impenitent despite Jonah's warning a century earlier.[8] In other words, a rhetorical basis for genre enables us to recapture at least some of the immediate sense of authorial purpose in the text. Genre is both dynamic *and* static, and we need to "hear" the text, not simply read it. The new model of genre—with careful use of history, theology, and the context of the text—can equip us better to hear as well as read.

Why Genre Analysis Is Essential

The Old Testament is written in a wide variety of literary genres (see chap. 1), each demanding its own rules of interpretation. Modern readers who ignore the genres of the Old Testament do so at their peril, for genre criticism helps readers to see the similarities among various texts within a genre and the differences among various genres, thereby alerting readers to important considerations in interpretation. The purpose of genre criticism "is not so much to classify as to clarify such traditions and affinities, thereby bringing out a large number of literary relationships that would not be noticed as long as there were no context established for them."[9] To Frye, the process moves inductively, the reader discovering similarities in various texts and ascribing them to appropriate genres. For others, however, genre criticism moves deductively. It

---

8. See R. D. Patterson and Michael Travers, "Literary Analysis and the Unity of Nahum," *GTJ* 9 (1988): 45–58, and Patterson's exceptional synthesis of literary, linguistic, historical, and theological scholarship in his commentary on Nahum in Wycliffe Exegetical Commentary (Chicago: Moody, 1991), 1–115.

9. Northrop Frye, *Anatomy of Criticism: Four Essays* (1957; reprint Princeton: Princeton University Press, 1971), 247–48.

"does not assert that authors should or should not do so-and-so. Rather, it poses a question: What can we say about the way structures like narrative organize themselves?"[10] Genre is a means of understanding how a work of literature is structured. Either way, genre criticism is an interpretive tool that helps the reader to understand a text more fully.

Recognizing generic affinities in literary texts, even unconsciously, prepares a reader to respond appropriately to the text, a process that E. D. Hirsch calls the "socializing" of the writer's expectations;[11] it is part of the common ground between the author's intentions and the reader's understanding. Perhaps the best contemporary illustration of author/audience "socializing" is television. As soon as viewers recognize a program as a sitcom or a drama, for instance, they watch with different, often unconscious, expectations. In sitcoms, characters are usually stereotyped and do not develop as individual persons; plot conflicts are resolved at the end of the program, often conveniently with an unexpected solution. Dramas, on the other hand, often present individualized characters who develop in the course of the action; plots in dramas turn on more complex conflicts and, in modern dramas, are often not resolved neatly at the conclusion. Though TV viewers are not conscious of genre, they know tacitly what conventions to anticipate and how to enjoy or understand the specific TV genre they watch. If they did not—if they approached drama with sitcom expectations, for instance—they would be frustrated and turn off the program. Genre is a "socializing" influence in which readers/viewers respond to particular types of literature with appropriate expectations.

Old Testament genre criticism in its broadest sense is an analysis of the historical, literary, and theological dynamics that draw attention to the communication between author and reader as established in and limited by a text. When an author chooses to write a poem, for example, rather than a narrative, he chooses to work within certain formal parameters (though they may vary in partic-

10. E.g., Seymour Chatman, *Story and Discourse: Narrative Structure in Fiction and Film* (Ithaca: Cornell University Press, 1978), 18.

11. E. D. Hirsch, *Validity in Interpretation* (New Haven: Yale University Press, 1979), 81.

ular details from one culture to another); in turn, readers must agree to understand the work within those same parameters. Correct understanding depends on readers' knowledge of the author, his culture, and the genre of literature. To read generically is to sign a rhetorical contract with the author to understand his work in the terms that he shared within his intended audience. The task of hermeneutics is "not to develop new procedures of understanding but to clarify the conditions in which understanding occurs."[12] One of these conditions is the rhetorical interplay of an author with his intended audience; genre criticism helps to define this rhetorical dynamic, thereby clarifying the conditions of understanding, particularly for later readers.

Furthermore, the recognition of common features in a variety of texts does not force the reader to reduce all texts in that genre to just the common elements; in fact, generic criticism facilitates the recognition of idiosyncratic features of a particular writer. Without a knowledge of the common features of a genre, it would be impossible to distinguish specific variations that a certain author typically employs. Knowledge of the particular in the conventional might help the reader to locate a text historically and culturally.[13] By providing an understanding of conventions, genre criticism allows a reader to perceive in a text the individuality of the author and the conventions within which he worked.

Identification of genre is important for another reason. Generic conventions are closely related to meaning; they are not gratuitous decorations minimally relevant to the meaning of a work. On the contrary, they are necessary to a full understanding of the themes of the piece, or the history and theology of a book in the Bible. Readers come to understand the propositional truths of a text in its generic terms; each genre communicates meaning within its own conventions, not in spite of them. In the Old Testament narratives the theological truth is communicated in the chronological

---

12. Gerald Bruns, "The Horn of Midrash," in *The Book and the Text: The Bible and Literary Theory*, ed. Regina Schwartz (Cambridge: Basil Blackwell, 1990), 189.

13. Meir Sternberg, *The Poetics of Biblical Narrative: Ideological Literature and the Drama of Reading* (Bloomington: Indiana University Press, 1985), 249.

development of the events of the story; the reader does not just understand the truth—he experiences it. In Old Testament poetry the truth is expressed in the emotional intensity of a speaker's particular situation, prompting the reader to empathize with the speaker, not just to understand him. The theology and history of a given pericope are not the paraphrasable kernel, which a reader finds by stripping away the literary (and generic) frills.[14] Rather, theology and history are to be understood in the experiences in the text—specifically the situation in which the speaker of the poem or the protagonist in the narrative finds himself. In Milton's *Paradise Lost*, for instance, Milton does not preach free will but shows Adam and Eve to have adequate resources to choose wisely, even if they choose otherwise. The reader understands the theology and history in narrative and lyric by experiencing that theology and history along with the protagonist. Genre, then, is integral to exegesis, as well as to theology.

Still another value of generic criticism is the focus on a text as a whole, rather than as a fragmented subject for dissection. While the work of form and redaction critics has been an important part of biblical scholarship, many researchers have tended to overemphasize these approaches, failing to return to the text as it is in its extant, canonical form. The result has been an unfortunate atomizing of the biblical texts into specimens, rather than a larger holistic study of the texts as complete works. Genre criticism depends upon a proper understanding of the whole text, achieved in part by knowledge of the conventions used. Therefore, attention to details is vital to the larger, global view of the text.

This sense of the whole is easy to appreciate in analysis of poetry. Each psalm, for example, is a self-contained unit that invites, even demands, understanding of the parts in terms of the whole. Many fine literary analyses of the Psalms have drawn attention to such psalmic types as lament, imprecation, and praise, showing how genre provides appropriate parameters for understanding. Narrative, however, is in some ways more difficult to examine holistically. Take, for instance, the accounts of David's life in 1 and 2 Samuel, 1 Chronicles, and 1 Kings. The reader may easily lose

---

14. Paul Ricoeur, "Interpretative Narrative," in *The Book and the Text*, ed. Regina Schwartz (Cambridge: Basil Blackwell, 1990), 238–39.

the sweep of the whole narrative in the details of its parts, appearing as they do in several different books. Considered as a whole, however, not only does the chronology become clear, so does the theology. With God's announcement of the Davidic covenant (see 2 Sam.7:8–16), the reader is given a normative starting point to the narrative of David's kingship; David is to have a son who will build a temple for God, and he is to have descendants on the throne forever (vv. 12–13, 16). The reader knows that the pericope is complete when it fulfills its promises; David has a son, Solomon (12:24), whose line completes the covenant. The story is similar to Abraham's, to be sure, where again the reader is given a normative introduction (see Gen. 12:1–3) that sets the limits on the narrative pericope in the birth and survival of Isaac (see Gen. 21–22). In Old Testament narrative, then, an understanding of genre is not only helpful but vital to a proper understanding of theology.

Clearly there are significant advantages to a sensitive use of generic criticism in Old Testament studies and in literature in general. Genre study helps to clarify conventions in a culture's literature, defining the rhetorical interplay between an author and his intended audience. In turn, this knowledge helps clarify proper understanding of a given text. At the same time, knowledge of conventions frees a reader to appreciate the idiosyncratic features of a text, further extending comprehension. Finally, genre criticism preserves the unity of the texts in the canon—a necessary antidote to the atomizing of some types of twentieth-century biblical criticism. Alongside genre criticism, however, lie some disadvantages.

Can Genre Criticism Be Misleading?

To begin, readers must remember that genre criticism is not a Semitic idea. As noted earlier, the ancient Hebrews did not theorize about genres, and the idea of genre within literary criticism was not elaborated until Aristotle in the fourth century B.C. Though they wrote in a great variety of genres, the Old Testament writers did not possess a fully-developed aesthetic of genre criticism. Consequently, modern readers must not force Old Testament texts into detailed generic codes when those texts clearly do not correspond.

Even so, non-Hebrew genre distinctions in literary criticism can help the modern reader to understand the Old Testament texts. When we think of a full-blown definition of epic, for example, we bring a non-native designation to Semitic literature. The exodus and the David narratives clearly have epic affinities, such as their vast scope and the unifying heroes of Moses and David. Of course, significant variations from the standard epic genre exist as well, notably the biblical hero who glorifies God, in contrast to the Greek epic hero who glorifies himself. A knowledge of epic helps in understanding the exodus and David stories, but readers must remember that Moses and David did not model their stories on Homeric epics. The latter genre becomes a purely heuristic device, not a formal prescription. Even though we cannot establish native genres with certainty, it may be appropriate to use non-native genres with caution to aid analysis.

A second concern, related to the first, is that readers not impose modern Western aesthetics upon ancient Hebrew writings. Misappropriation of Greek conceptions of genre is no less problematic and misleading than misuse of modern conceptions of genre, those conceptions developing along European lines. For instance, for today's readers the prototype of narrative is the novel, a form that originated in the eighteenth century and was wholly foreign to ancient Semitic writers and even to European authors until the late Renaissance. It seems inappropriate, then, to understand Old Testament narratives in terms of the European novel. Complicating matters still further is the fact that the novel has evolved over the years from the epistolary structure of eighteenth-century writers Samuel Richardson and Tobias Smollett, through the linear chronologies of nineteenth-century writers such as Jane Austen, Charles Dickens, and George Eliot, to the stream-of-consciousness form of James Joyce and Virginia Woolf. The self-conscious artistry of many modern novels has no parallel in the Old Testament literature; however, narratives in the Old Testament do demonstrate implicit psychological analysis, as in the Jonah and Daniel narratives, to cite two obvious examples.[15] Of course, modern novels can help readers understand such narrative elements as plot, conflict, and character. Ultimately, then, genre analysis must function within two aspects of history: the actual time and place underlying the primary text and the actual development of literary criticism itself.

Third, we should remember that genres are convenient, reader-designed constructs that are helpful in understanding literary texts, but they are not rigid final forms into which a writer must fit his ideas. As Wittgenstein put it, genres are "family resemblances,"[16] formal qualities that individual texts share with other texts—characteristics that suggest affinities. There are no categorical imperatives in genre study. Accordingly, we must acknowledge two caveats. Because genres are "composites of features,"[17] we must remember that some features occur in more than one genre and are, therefore, not markers for a particular genre. For example, figurative devices such as metaphor and imagery occur in prose and poetry and in narrative and exposition. Poetry uses figures of speech more intensely than does any other genre; however, the presence of figures of speech in nearly every form of writing means that they cannot be used to differentiate among genres. Not only are some features anything but markers of specific genres, some works contain elements of more than one genre; they are "mixed."[18] This reality should caution readers not to be too dogmatic in classifying a text as a particular genre. There is a second caveat: while the "general tendencies [of genres] . . . form the subject of rational inquiry,"[19] such inquiry begins but does not end with generic considerations. The study of literary texts by genre is not an exclusive method of literary analysis but a supplement and complement of other valuable and necessary procedures. Close exegesis and historical and biographical theologies are necessary

---

15. These two books are discussed in Branson Woodard, "Jonah," in *A Complete Literary Guide to the Bible*, ed. Leland Ryken and Tremper Longman III (Grand Rapids: Zondervan, 1993), 348–61; and idem, "Literary Strategies and Authorship in the Book of Daniel," JETS 37 (March 1994): 39–54.

16. Ludwig von Wittgenstein, *Philosophical Investigations* (New York: Macmillan, 1953), 32.

17. Chatman, *Story and Discourse*, 18.

18. Ibid.

19. Ibid.

corollaries of generic criticism; one without the other would provide an imbalanced, imprecise understanding of a text.

Conclusion

In many respects genre analysis itself carries both a blessing and a curse. Attention to genre, combined with other critical methods, can enliven the reading and study of a biblical passage, showing the unity of that passage within the entire book as well as within a smaller and more immediate framework. This approach, in turn, could counteract some of the intellectual, ethical, and cultural fragmentation in modern life. Once the Old Testament is seen as far more unified than may have been imagined, one piece of groundwork is laid for a more coherent view of life, with different situations fitting into a larger, identifiable pattern.

On the other hand, genre criticism can become problematic in two respects, both leading either to misapplication or to no application of Scripture at all. Generic analysis must not be neglected or become a law unto itself. It should serve a higher purpose, that of contributing to the reader's knowledge of God's Word and relationship with God himself.[20]

---

20. Such has been the conviction of R. D. Patterson for many years. Indeed, the main ideas in this chapter appear throughout his scholarship. His research, unlike that of many other biblicists trained in grammatical-historical exegesis, has displayed a particular sensitivity to literary criticism and as such has served as a model of interdisciplinary thinking and theological integrity. In sum, R. D. Patterson has beheld a new land for traditional evangelical biblicists and has led the way into it. The following chapters reflect some of his vision.

3

LITERARY FORMS
AND INSPIRATION
John S. Feinberg

Accurate identification of literary genres affects many issues, even some we might not suspect. The complaint about teaching the theory of evolution as scientific fact in public schools is common among Christians. If evolution has a right to be heard in the science class, then so does creationism. Evolutionists reply in disgust that creationism does not deserve equal time. Evolution is science, but creationism is not.

Though this is a familiar debate, what is not clearly understood is that a major point at issue is the proper identification of the literary genre(s) of Genesis 1–11. Did the author intend these chapters as a scientific explanation of the world's origins? Is creationism science? Or are these chapters the author's way of expressing the theological concept that God is the one in control of the origin and development of all things, including man? Do theologians and students of the Bible need scientists to help explain the processes God used, or are the processes revealed in the text of Scripture? What did the author of Genesis intend?

Though it would be wrong to interpret Genesis 1–11 as irrelevant to science and history, trying to interpret Genesis as just science, history, or any other type of literature without understanding the genre(s) is like trying to play a game of baseball before learning the rules that govern it. All the equipment is present, but it is hard to know what to do without knowing the rules. And if we try to figure it out for ourselves, we may invent a game that would not even be recognized as baseball.

Though exegetes of all theological persuasions are prone to overlook the significance of identifying the genre of a piece of biblical literature, some contend that this oversight has had especially negative results among evangelical exegetes. Evangelicals tend to interpret the sentences of Scripture as simply descriptive and informative, each with its own separate truth value. As a result, errors in genre identification can lead interpreters to make interpretive errors such as understanding literary embellishments as scientifically true assertions.[1] Think, for example, of Jesus' claim that the kingdom of heaven is like the mustard seed, which is the smallest of all seeds. Is Jesus making a point about botany? If so, he is wrong since scientists know of smaller seeds. Or is he using the device of hyperbole (exaggerating to make a point) to teach the theological concept that the kingdom of heaven, though very small at its outset, when it has spread throughout the world is a large and all-encompassing kingdom? Jesus' listeners would be familiar with the mustard seed so they would catch his theological point about the kingdom of heaven. Or is Jesus doing something entirely different by making this comment about the mustard seed? Clearly, the need to understand the literary genre of parables and the literary device of hyperbole is crucial to answering these questions.

Genre identification is indeed critical to proper interpretation of the Old Testament. As the writer of Hebrews says, during the Old Testament era God spoke *through* the prophets at many times in various ways (see Heb. 1:1). Surely, this refers not only to the prophets' oral communication (their preaching), but to their writing as well. As we read the Old Testament, it also becomes evident that God spoke *to* the prophets in various ways. Theologians and exegetes have not always taken seriously enough these two facts: (1) God spoke *through* the prophets in many ways and (2) he spoke *to* them in many ways. However, both facts have great significance

---

1. James Barr, *The Bible in the Modern World* (London: SCM, 1973), 125.

for a proper understanding of the genres of Scripture. Clearly, recognizing the various genres of biblical literature is absolutely central to understanding how God accommodated his thoughts to written language and to proper interpretation and theological reflection.

In discussing genre theologically, while there are many issues that could be considered,[2] the *general* theme of this chapter is that genre is a crucial concept at all points of the revelatory and interpretive endeavor (i.e., it is central to communication), and thus, we dare not ignore it when doing exegesis or theology. The *specific* purpose is to ask and answer four key questions:

1. Is genreless communication possible so that God could have communicated his word without using genres?

2. What part in communication do genres play, and does God know our genres so as to know how to use them to communicate with us?

3. To what extent did God use genres in his revelatory acts and in his inspiring of the written documents of Scripture?

4. What are the implications for biblical interpretation and systematic theology of God's use of genres in accommodating his thoughts to human language?

---

2. For example, the major issues handled in Kevin J. Vanhoozer's article "The Semantics of Biblical Literature" (in D. A. Carson and John Woodbridge, eds. *Hermeneutics, Authority, and Canon* [Grand Rapids: Zondervan, 1986], 94–103) are not my primary focus. Vanhoozer treats the nature of propositions and how the notion of propositions relates to the sentences of Scripture. He also contends, invoking a speech act analysis of language, that one must be careful to discern the illocutionary force of biblical sentences (i.e., what the writer is trying to say in writing what he writes). Hence, when scriptural sentences assert something, they are true, but when they perform some other function (e.g., warn, command, express delight), even though such sentences may be neither true nor false, they still infallibly accomplish the goals the divine and human authors intended. One could also discuss genre theologically along the lines that continental philosophers like Gadamer and Ricoeur have followed or that structuralists have taken. These discussions have introduced both epistemological and ontological dimensions into genre study. For discussion of the epistemological and ontological dimensions of genre, see Grant Osborne, "Genre Criticism—Sensus Literalis," *TJ*, n.s., 4 (1983): 9–16.

Is Genreless Communication Possible?

In order to answer this question we must first be clear about the definition of literary genre. As defined in chapters 1 and 2 above, genre is widely understood to be a classificatory tool for grouping together series of texts.[3] Texts in such a group "exhibit a coherent and recurring configuration of literary features involving form (including structure and style), content, and function."[4]

In addition to the notion of genre, it is helpful to introduce the concept of literary conventions. Certain conventions, or ways of doing things, are associated with each genre group. A convention "refers to any arbitrary device or rule of conduct which we agree to accept."[5] For example, though not all poetry rhymes, poets often adopt the convention of making their poems exhibit some rhyme scheme. Likewise, we accept the convention that when writing a letter one begins with a salutation, and depending on the culture, that salutation will be of a certain sort (e.g., beginning a letter with the salutation "Dear . . . .").

Each genre has its rules and conventions, but those rules are not so rigid as to be a straitjacket. Writers can blend genres and conventions, and they can even develop new genres. As a result, it is extremely hard to find an example of a piece of literature that illustrates any given genre in its pure form. In fact, the idea of a pure form of a genre may be mistaken. Rather than having distinct boundaries between genres, characteristics of genres typically overlap.

This does not mean that it is impossible to differentiate one genre from another.[6] Writers and readers usually know the basic

---

3. For those who think otherwise, see Osborne's excellent treatment of these discussions in his *Trinity Journal* article cited in note 2.

4. David E. Aune, *The New Testament in Its Literary Environment* (Philadelphia: Westminster, 1987), 13. John J. Collins, "Introduction: Towards the Morphology of a Genre," *Semeia* 14 (1979): 1, defines genre as "a group of written texts marked by distinctive recurring characteristics which constitute a recognizable and coherent type of writing."

5. Marlies K. Danziger and W. Stacy Johnson, *An Introduction to Literary Criticism* (Boston: D.C. Heath, 1961), 67.

6. As philosopher Ludwig Wittgenstein says about boundaries of concepts in general, inexact "does not mean "unusable." Ludwig Wittgenstein, *Philosophical Investigations* (New York: Macmillan, 1953), sec. 88, p. 41e.

characteristics and conventions of existing genres. Because readers/hearers know the basic rules for saying a given message in a particular way, they can also understand what a writer means when saying something new or saying something familiar in a new way.

Because writers know the basic rules of genres, they know the cues that will "tip off" their readers to what they want to say. Hence, they know that if they want to teach something, express joy, make sarcastic or satirical remarks, or whatever, there are certain linguistic conventions associated with various genres that are the way humans express those things with words. Literary critics, whether working with biblical or non-biblical literature, can describe those cues and thereby differentiate genres from one another.[7]

With this understanding of genre, we can now ask whether it is possible to communicate something without using genre and conventions. The answer is no. Even the simplest piece of verbal or nonverbal behavior incorporates some genre—some verbal (and/or nonverbal) way of saying something.[8]

Perhaps the easiest way to support this claim is to offer examples of language which one might consider genreless and show that even these examples incorporate genre. Consider first a grocery list. Some might think this is genreless. After all, grocery lists are not usually written in complete sentences. They are lists of words or phrases with an occasional number here and there. How could such lists have a genre?

Despite our initial intuitions, even a grocery list incorporates genre. Unless one understands the features of a grocery list, one

---

7. Of course, what those cues are in each genre may be a matter of debate. How does one determine the genre of a given piece of literature or part thereof? See Tremper Longman's excellent discussion of this issue, including his proposal of criteria for genre identification in "Form Criticism, Developments in Genre Theory, and the Evangelical," *WTJ* 47 (1985).

8. Tremper Longman makes the further significant point that there is no such thing as a culture-free genre system. In other words, not only are genres inherent in communication, as I am arguing, but also the shape of any particular genre at any point in history is determined to a large extent by the culture in which the genre is used. Ibid., 54.

might misidentify what the list is. Someone might think it is simply a list of words chosen at random from a dictionary. Others might think it is a list of someone's favorite foods. If the list is short, someone might think it is a recipe for some main dish to be served at a dinner party. Someone else might think it is not a list at all but a poem in which each word has a symbolic meaning. Other options are possible as well, including the possibility that it is nothing but gibberish, actual words and numbers arranged in random order, signifying nothing. And, of course, some might identify it as a grocery list.

This example illustrates three main ideas. First, unless there were such things as genres (a genre for poetry, for grocery lists, for recipes, and even for gibberish), that is, if there were not specific forms and conventional ways of writing a grocery list (as opposed to a recipe or a poem), anyone who looked at the document could not identify it as anything other than writing on a paper. In order to identify it as one of the things mentioned above, there must be genres, ways of expressing each of the things mentioned, and the person trying to identify what the document is must know what those genres are and how writers use them to communicate one thing or another.

A second point stems from the first. Even this apparently genre-less writing cannot be identified for whatever it is unless it incorporates some genre (genre for writing up grocery lists, genre for poetry, etc.). Just because the document does not exemplify one of the standard genres we think of when we think of a work of literature, that does not mean it is entirely devoid of genre. As mentioned, if it were totally devoid of genre, there would be no way to identify it as anything other than writing on paper.

Third, in order for a reader to identify the document as one thing or another, there must be enough verbal clues in it to let the interpreter know that it is a grocery list rather than a recipe, or gibberish, or a list of words one plans to use when playing Scrabble. The writer may not include enough cues and clues for the reader to identify the document as one thing rather than another, but it is doubtful that a reader would look at the document and say it gives equal evidence of being any of the things already mentioned. Something about the content and form of the document will help the interpreter eliminate certain possibilities, even if it does not allow him to settle on just one.

Perhaps one might agree with the conclusions drawn from this illustration, but argue that the points would not apply to some communication in a primitive language where there are only a few expressions. For example, imagine a society of construction workers with a primitive language in which there are only a few words like *block, slab, here,* and *there.*[9] Surely, in such a society communication would be genreless.

But even in this primitive setting communication incorporates genre. It might well be nonverbal behavior and the context in which the words are uttered that tip off what someone means when he utters "block" or "slab." In other words, both the utterer and the hearer have learned that when constructing a building, if a builder wants his helper to bring him a block of wood, he can communicate that by uttering "block here" and by pointing to the spot by his feet when he says "here." Within the "language" of this society, there is a genre that uses verbal and nonverbal cues to convey intent. And both speaker and listener understand the genre and conventions for saying this rather than something else.

Someone might respond that it may be true that ordinary languages incorporate genres, but it is not true of technical languages. For example, someone who writes his thoughts using symbolic logic surely does not employ a genre. However, even in this case a genre is used. Symbolic logic consists of various symbols and various rules for combining those symbols to communicate one idea rather than another. Thus, if a written document contains nothing but the symbols of symbolic logic, the marks on the paper will communicate nothing unless they are arranged according to the agreed upon rules for communicating something by means of those symbols. Anyone reading it will not be able to understand it. So, there is a genre that identifies even a technical language, like symbolic logic, as a language and allows us to understand what the writer is trying to say. To use this language one must know the

9. This is precisely what we find in the early sections of Wittgenstein's *Philosophical Investigations.* See Wittgenstein, secs. 8, 19–21, pp. 5e, 8e–10e.

rules and conventions by which it operates; one must know its genre.

In sum, regardless of whether a society's language is very sophisticated or very simple, it is impossible to communicate anything either verbally or nonverbally without incorporating the rules and conventions of genres. If that is so, then it follows that if God is to communicate anything to the human race in a way humans can understand, he must know and use our genres and literary conventions to do it. There is no genreless communication.[10]

Does God Know How to Use Our Genres?

God *must* know how to use human genres in order to communicate with us. But *does* he? To see that God does know how to use our genres we need to introduce the notion of a language-game, or form of life. This idea comes from the later philosophy of Wittgenstein.

Wittgenstein came to see language as a complex of what he called language-games. These language-games are distinct from one another and yet interdependent. He offered perhaps his fullest definition of a language-game when he wrote, "I shall also call the whole, consisting of language and the actions into which it is woven, the 'language-game'."[11] In other words, language is more than mere words. Language is always used in a context, a context that includes behavior (nonverbal). "The term 'language-*game*' is meant to bring into prominence the fact that the *speaking* of language is part of an activity, or of a form of life."[12]

By form of life Wittgenstein means a complete way of doing a certain activity, whether the activity is playing a game, teaching a skill, exhibiting religious devotion, expressing pain, or whatever. As such, a form of life includes both verbal and nonverbal behavior. How many of these forms of life are there? Think of the different contexts in which language can be used and it becomes clear

---

10. I would contend that this is so even for God. That is, even within the Godhead the members of the Trinity must have various ways to communicate to one another, ways that typify divine communication, even if human beings do not know what those genres and conventions are.
11. Wittgenstein, sec. 7, p. 5e.
12. Ibid., sec. 23, p. 11e.

that language may be used in many different ways. Thus, there are multiple forms of life, many language-games.[13] If a language-game is a form of life, whose form of life is it? Forms of life relate to human beings. This simply means that human beings are language users—one of the ingredients of being human. Language use is as natural to humans as activities like walking, eating, drinking, and playing.[14]

How do language-games/forms of life relate to literary genres? There is a close relation between them, but they are not exactly equivalent. Since a language-game is a complete way of doing a particular activity, including verbal and nonverbal behavior, it should be clear that a literary genre helps to define and clarify the *verbal* aspect of a particular language-game. Of course, to play any specific language-game, one must know *all* the rules and procedures for that game, not just the verbal rules.

For example, if one plays the "language-game of praying," one must know what kind of ideas are appropriate for prayer, plus the appropriate words and styles of expressing those words in sentences when praying; that is, one must know the literary genre of prayer. In addition, there are certain nonverbal cues that let an observer know that someone is praying. Those who pray often bow their head and close their eyes; they may also kneel and fold their hands together. We could speak roughly of a genre of these behaviors associated with praying, but strictly speaking, such behaviors are not what we mean when we refer to a *literary* genre—a literary genre can and usually does relate to text on a page, even if that text is never audibly uttered or used amidst various nonverbal behaviors. Both the verbal behavior with its genre and the nonverbal behavior with its "genre" make up the language-game of

---

13. As Wittgenstein says, "There are *countless* kinds: countless different kinds of use of what we call 'symbols,' 'words,' 'sentences.' And this multiplicity is not something fixed, given once for all; but new types of language, new language-games, as we may say, come into existence, and others become obsolete and get forgotten." Wittgenstein, *Philosophical Investigations*, sec. 23, p. 11e. Given this understanding of language as a complex of language-games, Wittgenstein adopted a use theory of meaning, that is, "the meaning of a word is its use in the language" sec. 43, p. 20e).

14. Ibid., sec. 25, p. 12e.

praying. A *literary* genre deals with the verbal part of a language-game.

Now that the relation of language-games/forms of life to literary genres is clarified, it should be clear whether and how it is possible for God to know our genres. If language is part of our forms of life, who would better understand the ways humans do things than the one who created them, especially when that creator is omniscient? It is unthinkable that God who created us should not know everything there is to know about us. Since that is so, he clearly should know how we communicate with one another, and that means he knows both the appropriate verbal and nonverbal behavior in any context and on any occasion to say one thing rather than another. He must know what our literary genres (the verbal part of our language-games) are and how to use them. And he does.

J. I. Packer has argued that the various ways language is used in ordinary communication can be grouped into five main categories:

1. Language may be used to *inform* people of what the speaker assumes they do not know.

2. Language may be used *imperatively*, i.e., to command and call people to action.

3. Language may be used *illuminatively* to help us understand and gain deeper insight into facts which at one level we already know.

4. Language has a *performative* use. By uttering certain words, the speaker performs an action. By saying "I promise," one commits himself to a given course of action. When the minister says "I now pronounce you husband and wife," he actually marries the two people before him.

5. Language also has a *celebratory* use which focuses "on a shared apprehension of things in a way that confirms that it is shared and so binds together more closely those who share it."[15] Much ritual and ceremonial language falls in this cate-

---

15. J. I. Packer, "The Adequacy of Human Language," in Norman Geisler, ed., *Inerrancy* (Grand Rapids: Zondervan, 1979), 209. See Packer's complete discussion of these functions on pages 206–10.

gory, as typically do exclamations of enthusiasm in the face of some event, action, person, or object.

Clearly, God has done all five of these things in Scripture with human language. And he has done even more. Language may also be used to question, to express doubts, wishes and dreams, to warn, encourage, comfort, and exhort. Language is put to all of these uses in Scripture, and all of these functions presuppose literary genres that relate to the verbal part of the language-games God and the human authors of Scripture are playing. God definitely knows our language-games (and the genres and conventions that go with them), and he knows how to use them.

To What Extent Did God Use Genres in Communicating His Word?

The answer to this third question is that God used genres at every stage of transmitting his word to us. Normally, discussions of God's accommodation of his thoughts to human language focus only on the biblical text. Likewise, discussions of the literary genres of Scripture (OT and NT) invariably address the written text of Scripture. However, genre consideration also involves God's activity prior to inspiring the writing of Scripture. Thus, we should begin with God's revelatory acts to the biblical writers. Before God ever communicated his word *to us* through the biblical text, he communicated to the biblical writer what he wanted him to say. Hence, our recognition of the significance of genre must begin with God's actions prior to the text.

Daniel recorded in the language of Scripture the contents of Nebuchadnezzar's dream (see Dan. 2). In Daniel 9 he recorded his vision of the seventy weeks. In Ezekiel 37 Ezekiel speaks of his vision of the valley of dry bones. God revealed this information to them. How did he do that? Originally, he gave Nebuchadnezzar a dream as the king slept. Later, he may have communicated that dream and its interpretation to Daniel while Daniel slept or while Daniel was awake. We simply do not know. But God performed some revelatory act in each case. Did the dream include language, or was it solely pictorial? Again, we are not told, though we are surely safe in saying that whatever God did in revealing this dream and its interpretation to Daniel included the possibility that the content of the revelation could be expressed in language, even if the revelatory act itself did not originally contain language.

As for the vision of the seventy weeks, we do not know if it was purely a vision of images or whether it also included language. Most likely it included the latter (even if also the former), since Daniel tells us that God mediated the vision to him through the words of an angel. It is also possible that God revealed the content of the message through the words of the angel and then inspired Daniel to use a visionary genre as he wrote the message for us. In that case, Daniel would not necessarily have seen a vision of images.[16] As for Ezekiel's vision (see Ezek. 37), we may say the same things. However, it seems likely that this revelatory act of God included both language (at points of the vision Ezekiel records what is spoken to him) and images, for Ezekiel explains that he was taken in the spirit to a valley that was filled with bones. If he did not actually *see* something, questions arise about the truthfulness of his claims to have seen something.

In addition to these revelatory acts, there were occasions when God evidently revealed something by direct speech (rather than indirectly through a dream or a vision). See, for example, passages such as Genesis 1:28–30; 3:9–19; Numbers 12:8; 1 Samuel 3:1ff. These instances of direct communication to various people (most of whom did not write Scripture) show that God, despite not having a body, a literal mouth, or a voice box, could also speak to biblical writers.

Though in many cases it is easy to identify God's revelatory act, in some cases it is very hard. A good example is Ezekiel 37:15ff. In this passage Ezekiel records that God told him to take two sticks, write something on each, and cross them while holding them. God told him that once this was done the two sticks would become one in his hand. God also ordered Ezekiel to explain the significance of the symbolic act to the people, a meaning which God revealed to Ezekiel. In this passage, we can distinguish three

---

16. I owe this point about visionary genre to Brent Sandy. The point is not that we know God didn't actually give the writer a vision of images. In many cases, it is likely that he did do that. The point is that when we understand the nature of a visionary genre, it is at least possible in some cases that the writer using that genre saw no vision of images at all.

things. First, there was God's revelatory act (whatever it was) by which he told Ezekiel what to do and what it would mean. Second, there was Ezekiel's act of picking up the sticks, writing on them, crossing them in his hands, and having them become one, plus Ezekiel's explanation of what this meant. And third, there is the biblical account of both God's instructions to Ezekiel (however they were revealed) and the meaning of this act. That biblical account is, of course, revelation to us.

All of this underscores the need in reading Scripture to differentiate God's revelatory act to the writer from his revelatory act to us through the words of Scripture. But what is the relevance of this to our discussion of genre? The point is that if no one can communicate without using some genre(s) and conventions, then it stands to reason that God's revelatory acts (whether they be miracles, direct speech, dreams, visions, or whatever) incorporate some genre. There are certain clues and cues that mark off an apocalyptic vision from a dream, and others that distinguish both of those revelatory acts from direct speech. Moreover, there are genres and conventions distinctive to each of these revelatory acts that enabled biblical writers to understand what God wanted them to say and how to say it.

This point is important, because it reminds us that even though we may tend to confuse the genre of God's revelatory act to the writer with the genre of the inscripturated word, we really have no right to do so. In fact, since the genres of the inscripturated word all pertain to written language, those genres may differ from the genres of God's revelatory acts. In some cases, of course, there may be overlap. For example, if God moves the writer to use some already existing written document or portion of a document, the genre of the document need not necessarily differ from the genre of the biblical text the writer produces. Of course, whatever God did to move the writer to use this material will not likely be equivalent to the literary genres of the source material or of the biblical text itself. Moreover, if God by direct communication gives a prophet a message that he then writes in one of the biblical books, presumably the genres of God's revelatory act and the biblical text will be similar if not identical. So, there may be overlap in the genre of God's revelatory act and the genre of the text of Scripture, but not always.

The main point from this discussion of God's revelatory acts is, however, a simpler one. It is that anyone who thinks it proper to discuss the manner or content of biblical revelation without appeal to the notion of genre is misguided. He/she is misguided because all communication invokes genre, regardless of whether that communication comes in written form (Scripture) or in God's revelatory act. God's accommodation of his thoughts to human language did not begin with the written word. It began with his revelatory act to the prophet, and God revealed himself to the prophets in many ways. That required his knowing and using many genres even at that stage of bringing his message to mankind.[17]

While God's revelatory acts to the biblical writers involved using genres, it is equally true that his inspiration of writers to transfer his revelation to writing involved not only giving them ideas but also the way to express those ideas. What Paul says (see 1 Cor. 2:13) about the Holy Spirit's activity in regard to New Testament apostles surely happened as well when he superintended Old Testament prophets as they spoke from God (see 1 Pet. 2:21). Of course, all of this means that inspiration of Scripture extends to the very choice of the words and sentences of Scripture, and that means it extended to and incorporated the various genres of biblical literature.

This should not surprise us in light of the need to use genres and literary conventions to communicate anything. It should not surprise us as well, because a common literary device in all kinds of literature is to communicate content in part through form. The chapters of this book explain the various genres of Old Testament literature, and they offer examples of how Old Testament writers, writing under divine inspiration, used literary form (genres) to communicate content.

---

17. Do *we* miss anything by not getting in on God's revelatory act to the writer? Not really. There is nothing we need to know in order to understand what God is saying to us that was included in his revelatory act to the writer but not included in his inscripturated word. The reason is that God moved the writer to record the content God wanted us to have in the manner (genre) he wanted so that we got the message he wanted.

While it should not surprise us that there are genres for the inspired texts of Scriptures, what may surprise us is the particular genre God chose for a given passage. For example, many psalms teach doctrinal truths about God and man, but they do so in a poetic genre. God could have communicated those same truths through different genres. In fact, in other Old Testament books they are taught through prophetic literature or the wisdom literature of Job, Proverbs, or Ecclesiastes. The New Testament also teaches many of the same truths through the epistolary genre.

Since content seems the same in each case, why not simply use the same genre in each passage? Perhaps God's reason in part is that by using different genres, he shows his understanding of our different ways of using language (sometimes even to say the same thing) and his understanding that people differ so that some people more readily catch a point made in a poetic form than in a more prosaic form (and vice versa for others).

Perhaps the reason is also that there is a certain content God can communicate by means of the poetic form, the aphoristic form of Proverbs, the narrative form of the historical books, or the apocalyptic form of some of the prophetic literature, a content that goes beyond the mere meanings of the words in the sentences. For example, it is surely possible for us to write a biblical theology of Job or to incorporate its content into a broader systematic theology or philosophy text. But to do that would lose something. In Job, we do not find reflections about God written in the third person by an uninvolved writer as we might if we were reading a theology or philosophy text. Instead, through the direct speeches of Job and his friends, we feel the emotion that attaches to the ideas they discuss and the events they experience. This is not some abstract theological treatise. It is the deepest emotional expression of a man in the midst of an existential crisis of faith. By using this form, the biblical writer not only informs us that evil is an intellectual problem for theistic belief. He shows us that in real life it can precipitate a personal crisis of faith. The author could have simply told us this, but instead, he *showed* us exactly what it means by *showing* us Job's raw emotions as he experienced evil and interacted with his "comforters." The genre and style of the book communicate so much more than the mere content of the words themselves. Of course, if God had chosen, the intellectual answers the book offers could have been communicated in a different genre. But it is hard to see how Job's feelings and his religious crisis could be so clearly and effectively communicated through another genre. Anyone who has experienced significant affliction, thought Job's thoughts, and felt his emotions will understand how much would be lost if, for example, Job's writer had written in the genre of philosophical discourse or systematic theology.

Indeed, we must analyze the genres of biblical literature not as incidental and accidental to the authors' message but as part of the very substance of what they are saying. Of course, because genres can overlap, because authors can create new genres, and because genre identification of any portion of a book (or of the book as a whole) can be difficult, genre analysis is not always easy. But we dare not shun the task just because it is hard in some cases. After all, the Bible is what God has said to us—we dare not ignore it. But we may not know exactly what he has said until we discover the genre that he used to say it. Anyone familiar with the debate over the genre of a book like Jonah will immediately understand this point.[18] Attempts to discern the message of this book by merely analyzing the meaning of individual words and sentences apart from the genre of the whole work can easily mislead us. Even if it is easy to identify the genre of a book or of a portion of it, once we understand not only the words and sentences but the way the writer uses them (i.e., once we understand the work's literary genre[s]), the book communicates God's message contained both in the words of the text and in the form used to express those thoughts and words.

---

18. See, for example, T. Desmond Alexander, "Jonah and Genre," *Tyn-Bul* 36 (1985); Michael Orth, "Genre in Jonah: The Effects of Parody in the Book of Jonah," in William W. Hallo, Bruce W. Jones, and Gerald L. Mattingly, eds., *The Bible in the Light of Cuneiform Literature* (Lewiston, N.Y.: Edwin Mellen Press, 1990); and Gerda Elata-Alster and Rachel Salmon, "The Deconstruction of Genre in the Book of Jonah: Towards A Theological Discourse," *Journal of Literature and Theology* 3 (March 1989).

What Are the Implications
of Genres in the Biblical Text?

The implications of genre criticism for evangelicals are many and too important for us to ignore them or be insensitive to them. In addition to the impact of genre criticism on our understanding of God's revelatory acts, genre criticism has profound implications for other theological doctrines such as inerrancy. And of course, it is crucial for proper interpretation of Scripture.

As already noted, God's accommodation of his thoughts to human beings involved using our genres. God not only used human genres in his revelatory acts to the writers, but he inspired the writers to use various genres as they wrote Scripture. That suggests something important for interpretation. If form conveys content, then the interpreter cannot fully understand what is said without genre identification. Furthermore, without proper understanding of the conventions and styles appropriate to each genre, one might entirely mistake the point of a portion of Scripture. It makes a world of difference, for example, if one thinks the Book of Jonah is basically a history or biography, as opposed to a mythological way to teach some theological point.[19] A similar point is true with respect to genre identification of the first eleven chapters of Genesis.[20] Misunderstanding genre in those cases would obviously be detrimental to accurate interpretation, but it is also significant (as other chapters in this book show) in lesser debated and discussed passages.

A further point about interpretation stems from the distinction between the genre of God's revelatory act and the genre of the biblical text. In interpreting God's Word, that distinction suggests that the interpreter must be careful not to confuse the genre of the revelatory

19. Also, if one adopts Michael Orth's suggestion that Jonah's genre is parody of the prophetic genre, then the chances that traditional interpretation has badly misunderstood the point of the book are very high. See Orth, "Genre in Jonah: The Effects of Parody in the Book of Jonah."

20. See, for example, Walter C. Kaiser, Jr., "The Literary Form of Genesis 1–11," in J. Barton Payne, ed., *New Perspectives on the Old Testament* (Waco, Tex.: Word, 1970), and Bruce K. Waltke, "The Literary Genre of Genesis, Chapter One," *Crux* 27 (1991).

act with the genre of the written text. For example, an interpreter might be misled if he forgets that even though a writer received and describes a vision, what the reader has is not pictorial or visual in the same sense it was when the writer received the vision. What the writer says about the vision may or may not evoke pictorial images for us.

Daniel's vision in chapter 7 of the four beasts likely will elicit images in the interpreter's mind, whereas the vision of the seventy weeks in Daniel 9 is less likely to evoke images—it can hardly evoke images of weeks since it is hard to imagine what a visual image of a week would be. However, what the writer tells the reader does convey a message. In reading Daniel 7 we see that the vision of the beasts made a major impression on Daniel. He says so and shows so by asking the interpreting angel to explain the vision, especially the particulars about the fourth beast. As we read Daniel 7, what Daniel says may elicit an image of each beast. But, of course, we cannot interpret the meaning of the beasts in terms of any pictorial images aroused in our minds, but in terms of the particular elements in the literary description of this vision, including its apocalyptic genre. The angel's explanation to Daniel informs everyone that the beasts are symbols. Placing this chapter within the genre of apocalypse informs us that the chapter is about the end times and God's consummation of his program with the world.

The implications of this study on genre also touch the doctrine of inerrancy. In contemporary discussions, inerrancy has been defined in terms of truth,[21] and truth has been defined in terms of an assertion's correspondence to reality.[22] Obviously, whether a sentence is true depends in part on what it says and how it says it. Only assertions are capable of bearing truth, so sentences that are questions, commands, and exclamations do not bear truth and are neither errant nor inerrant.[23] This in no way damages inerrancy; it merely clarifies which sentences of Scripture are being defended

---

21. See Paul D. Feinberg, "The Meaning of Inerrancy," in *Inerrancy*, ed. Norman Geisler (Grand Rapids: Zondervan, 1979).
22. See my "Truth: Relationship of Theories of Truth to Hermeneutics" in Earl Radmacher and Robert Preus, eds., *Hermeneutics, Inerrancy, and the Bible* (Grand Rapids: Zondervan, 1984).
23. I argue this point in "Truth: Relationship of Theories of Truth to Hermeneutics."

whenever an inerrant Bible is claimed. But, of course, what a sentence says and means depends in part on its literary genre. Hence, it is premature to claim that a given sentence is inerrant before seeing whether its form is that of sentences that do bear truth. Moreover, it is premature to claim that a particular idea supposedly conveyed by a biblical sentence is inerrant until one analyzes the genre of the literature where the sentence appears, to be sure that the author is saying what the interpreter supposes.

Consider again suggestions for the genre of Jonah. There is a world of difference between saying the writer relates historical facts about Jonah's life (and does so inerrantly) and saying the writer is making a theological point to which matters of history are inconsequential. In the former case, one is likely committing oneself to the truth of the claim that Jonah was swallowed by a great fish. In the latter case, no such commitment need be made at all. The implication of all of this is obvious. Do not judge the inerrancy of a passage until you understand what it means. In searching for the author's meaning, be sure to consider the literary genre he uses.

A second point about inerrancy must be made. Implicit in this chapter is the idea that genres are dependent on culture and time. Hence, they can change from time to time and culture to culture, and new genres can even be created. We must be careful, however, not to conclude that this means Scripture's truth is dependent on time and culture (which, in essence, means it is changing). Just because literary genres and conventions can fluctuate does not mean there is no changeless, binding truth in Scripture. One must be careful not to confuse the form for saying something (the genre)—which is changeable, and the content being communicated—which is timelessly true, if presented as a timeless truth. Of course, form also communicates content. But the point here is that if form does change, that does not make the content communicated by that form no longer true; it only means that the author chose not to communicate the content conveyed by the older form and decided to replace the content communicated by that form with the content expressed by a new form. If the author of Job had written the message of Job in the form of a philosophical treatise, that would in no way negate what the Book of Job in our canon conveys about the existential crisis of faith that accompanies the intellectual problems that beset the sufferer. The author simply would have chosen to present the basic intellectual message of the book in a different form—a form that would likely omit a portrayal of a man amidst a religious crisis.

In regard to the changeable nature of genres, we must also remember that the Holy Spirit who inspired the biblical writers is omniscient. The Bible was written over a vast number of years and amid varying circumstances. In each era and culture the Holy Spirit knew how to communicate his timelessly true message truthfully and understandably using the genres and conventions of that day.

A final caveat about inerrancy cautions theologians and exegetes not to mistake a case of bad hermeneutics (e.g., genre misidentification or ignoring altogether the genre of a passage) for a theological defection (rejection of biblical inerrancy). That is, we must be careful not to call an unusual interpretation of a passage a rejection of the passage's inerrancy.

Several examples illustrate the point. Consider the Book of Jonah, Genesis 1–11, and Daniel 11. If someone does not believe Jonah was swallowed by a great fish, or if someone does not believe God created the world in six literal twenty-four-hour days, that does not mean they have rejected inerrancy. Likewise, if someone says Daniel 11 is a carefully written history after the fact, we should not assume that person has rejected inerrancy. If an interpreter believes Jonah is completely historical, but denies that there ever was a fish, or if someone says Genesis 1–11 is accurate history and careful science, but then says it is wrong because everyone knows evolution is correct, then they *have* denied the inerrancy of those texts. But suppose some really do not think the genre of either of these passages has anything to do with history or accurate science. However, whatever the passages do mean, they are true. In that case, we might disagree with these interpreters' hermeneutics (beginning with disagreement over genre identification), but we surely would be wrong in accusing them of denying inerrancy.

Some, of course, may reply that in cases like this, the writer *obviously* intends to speak history, so the interpreter's identification of the genre as something else just shows he rejects the truth of the *obvious* meaning of the text. Indeed, misidentifying literary genre may be a clever ploy to avoid the apparently clear meaning of a text; but maybe not. At least we must carefully avoid question-begging in this matter. What appears as *obvious* to us may not be so obvious to others. Some people may misinterpret the clear (in our opinion) meaning of a passage not because they see it as a clever way to avoid what the passage teaches. They may in fact just be bad hermeneuts and exegetes. In that case, their exegesis needs critique, not their theology.

The same point pertains to Daniel 11. Some may claim it is history after the fact rather than prophecy before the events, because they are driven by an antisupernaturalistic bias that rejects the possibility of prediction of the future. On the other hand, bad hermeneutics and exegetical skills may be what drives them, not any Bible-denying theological or philosophical presupposition.

Anyone acquainted with the different interpretations that have been offered for the Book of Revelation will immediately see the point. Though there are surely some biblical skeptics and antisupernaturalists who interpret that book in a preterist mode, not every preterist is such because of rejecting inerrancy or some other doctrine. Throughout the centuries godly exegetes, orthodox on all cardinal doctrines, have still taken a preterist approach to Revelation. If it is wrong to say that those people have rejected inerrancy because their interpretation of that book differs from ours, it is likewise wrong to say that others have a low view of Scripture because we believe they have misidentified the genre of Daniel 11. The error may well be bad hermeneutics and exegesis, not theological defection. Hopefully, understanding this point will cause us to exercise extreme caution before labeling someone who claims to hold inerrancy a rejector of it.

Two other implications of genre are noteworthy. The first concerns the perspicuity of Scripture. Perspicuity of Scripture was a doctrine greatly emphasized by the Reformers as they argued that Scripture's interpretation was not the private domain of the clergy. According to this doctrine, Scripture is understandable to the average person for salvation and for basic principles of godly living. This is true, at least in part, because Scripture comes in various literary genres. Scripture is not written in technical language or as a technical treatise; it is written in ordinary language. But both technical discourses and ordinary language have their genres. In inspiring Scripture God had to accommodate himself to, among other things, our literary genres in order to communicate with us. Since this is so, it should be clear why Scripture is perspicuous. If God used ordinary language, and if the average person understands what ordinary language means and knows how to use it (thereby knowing how to use its various genres), then it is understandable that Scripture will be perspicuous to the average person.

The final implication of this study on genre concerns the enterprise of systematic theology more generally. Careful exegetes often scold theologians for supporting their doctrinal conclusions by prooftexting. They argue that Scripture may teach the doctrine the theologian proposes, but not in the passage(s) the theologian cites. Unfortunately, theologians have too often been guilty of proof texting. The answer of course is for theologians to base their theological formulation on careful exegesis of the text. It should be obvious then that recognizing and identifying the different literary genres of Scripture are crucial for the task of theology, because they are crucial for the task of accurate exegesis. Put another way, even though this essay is a *theological* discussion of literary genres, that does not mean that the only theological implication of genres is that one can write an essay such as this about genres. It means as well that when theologians turn to the task of accurately reflecting the doctrinal content of Scripture, they dare not ignore the genres God used in revealing his message to the biblical writers and through their texts.

Even if Scripture were written as a systematic theology, theologians and exegetes alike would have to understand the defining characteristics of that genre in order to understand God's Word properly. Just because Scripture is not written as a systematic theology, theologians are not excused from genre analysis. On the contrary, it all the more necessitates awareness of the many genres of scriptural revelation and careful identification of the genre of any given text as essential to the exegetical work that is foundational to evangelical theological formulation. It also underscores the point suggested at the outset of this chapter that one should

not even enter debates like those between evolutionists and cre-
ationists about whether Genesis 1–11 belongs in the science class-
room until one identifies the genre(s) of those chapters as a way
to clarify what the author intended to reveal about science and history.

4

NARRATIVE
Walter C. Kaiser, Jr.

Most of us have enjoyed hearing a good story since we were small children. Though the characters of a story may belong to an altogether different time and culture, children listen with fascination while the characters take on a life of their own. As the plot unfolds, children sit spellbound (well, most of the time), even if they have heard the story before. Questions are common as children interact with the action taking place. Through stories the lives of young (and old) are enriched, as concepts and values are grasped, often more readily than if those same concepts and ideas were presented merely as propositions.

Since both the Old and New Testaments are largely written in story form, narrative is the essence of biblical revelation. The long narrative corpus of both testaments forms the heart of the story and message of the Bible. That makes understanding narrative essential for all interpreters of the Bible.

To the frequent question of why so much narrative material appears in Scripture, the most obvious answer is that no form of communication is more vivid. How many people seem to have their interests revived in a Sunday morning sermon when an anecdote is interjected into what may otherwise be a dreary experience! In addition to being vivid, narratives employ concrete realities. Given the vivid depiction of concrete persons and events, the listener is drawn into the actions, struggles, and solutions by a process of identification.

Though narrative is common in our experience, the stories in the Bible are sometimes misunderstood. Rarely does the author of a text state what the point of the story is; that is left to interpretation. With so much of the Bible written in narrative form, correct interpretation of narrative must be the concern of all who are serious students of Scripture.

In recent years the number of studies dedicated to investigating the literary features of biblical narratives and the number of voices in the discipline have risen to a cacophonous level. The previous attention of scholars to questions about the authentic form of the narratives and the original shape of the text—supposedly restored by peeling off alleged additions and disposing of alleged alterations—has largely been drowned out. Although the present enthusiasm for analyzing literary narratives is related to form-critical methods (called *Formgeschichte*), the form-critical method occupies itself more with questions of fairly fixed literary forms and their setting in life (referred to as *Sitz im Leben*). Form criticism focuses on *repeated* social conventions that typically called forth stereotypical phrases and forms such as in a wedding ("Who gives this woman to be married?") or in a sermon ("Dearly beloved . . .").

Current literary method is more concerned with individual narratives. It seeks to highlight the narrative's artistic qualities, its rhetorical characteristics, its inner organization, and other structural and stylistic features. Thus, a real paradigm shift has taken place for many biblical scholars—a shift from a preoccupation with the search for the historical aspects of a text, or lack thereof, to what is now a search for the literary aspects of the text. Each of these aspects is important to the interpreter.

What Are the Components of Narrative?

Every story has a package of literary devices. They are scene, plot, point of view, characterization, setting, dialogue, structural levels, and stylistic or rhetorical devices. These are the aspects of form that are most significant if one is to unravel the thread of meaning from the narrative forms in the Bible.

Scene

"In Old Testament prose the scene is about the most important unit in the architecture of the narrative." [1] In the scene, the action of the story is broken up into separate sequences, each scene representing something that took place at a particular time and place. Within the scenes, the emphasis is put on the deeds done and the words spoken. Thus the scenes function much like the frames in a movie that make up the total film. Each one contributes to the whole, but each may be analyzed in and of itself in order to discover how the parts contribute to the whole. Each scene is usually made up of two or more characters. In those cases where a group is present in one of the scenes, they function as one of the characters.

For biblical narrative, one of the most distinguishing features is "the pervasive presence of God."[2] Often God is one of the two "characters" in the scene. In the early chapters of Genesis, it was God and Adam (chap. 3), God and Cain (chap. 4), God and Noah (chap. 6), and God and one of the three patriarchs in the rest of the Book of Genesis. Even when God was not directly mentioned as being one of the participants in the scene, his presence often was implied from the point of view taken by the narrator, writer, or the prophet who spoke on his behalf.

It will be the task of the interpreter to identify each of the scenes, just as one would break up a long prose passage into paragraphs. Once the divisions have been made, a brief synopsis of what is in each scene is most helpful. That summary, statement, or synopsis, focuses on the words and deeds of the main characters as presented by the writer or narrator of the scene. By using the author or the narrator's point of view as the basis from which to

---

1. J. P. Fokkelmann, *Narrative Art in Genesis: Specimens of Stylistic and Structural Analysis* (Amsterdam: Van Gorcum, 1975), 9.

2. Sidney Greidanus, *The Modern Preacher and the Ancient Text: Interpreting and Preaching Biblical Literature* (Grand Rapids: Eerdmans, 1988), 199.

judge, the divine point of view should be in the forefront of interpretation.

Plot

All stories have a beginning, a middle, and an end. This sequencing is generally called the plot, for it traces the movement of the incidents and episodes as they revolve around some type of conflict. As the plot thickens, the narrative moves toward a resolution or a climax. Plots may be developed either in a single or a complex format. The stories in the Bible prefer the single plot, for they "exhibit the classical pyramid pattern. From a peaceful initial situation the action rises towards the climax where the decisive step determining the outcome of the conflict is taken, and from there it drops again to a more or less tranquil situation at the end."[3] This type of pyramid pattern is evident in Genesis 22 where God's quiet request to sacrifice Isaac rose to the climax of the sudden halt to what was almost the sacrifice of Isaac, and then settled down again to Abraham and his son returning back down the hill to the servants who were awaiting their arrival before they set off again for Beersheba.

The story of Isaac's blessing in Genesis 27 is an illustration of a complex plot. "The narrative . . . reaches its climax when Jacob comes very close to the suspicious Isaac and is subjected to bodily examination. A resting point is reached when Isaac, apparently satisfied, gives Jacob his blessing. But when immediately after Jacob's departure Esau enters his father's tent the story flares up again. A new resting point is reached only after Jacob departs from his home and a physical distance is created between the hostile brothers."[4]

Another aspect of plot is pace. The pace of a plot can be accelerated by the use of short sentences (something the Hebrew language enjoys doing), the omission of detail, and the avoidance of lengthy character descriptions (such as one is accustomed to finding in Russian stories or many modern novels). The point is that the narrator can direct the speed of the story. Verbatim repetition,

---

3. Shimon Bar-Efrat, "Some Observations on the Analysis of Structure in Biblical Narrative," *VT* 30 (1980): 165.
4. Ibid., 166–167.

for example, will deliberately slow down the action, as will direct speech and the infrequent interjection of the narrator's thoughts. "The significance of detecting 'retardation' in the narrative is not only that it helps one perceive the built-in suspense but, more importantly for preachers today. . . it helps one understand 'the structure of the narrative, its culminating points and consequently its significance.'"[5] Correct interpretation of narratives depends in part on an appreciation of the plot as it marks out the beginning, middle, and end of both single and complex patterns and an appreciation of the pace of the narrative.

Point of View

Another question that must be faced in the analysis of narrative forms is from what perspective or stance the story is told. Does the narrator side with the actions, deeds, or words of one or more of the characters he describes? Four planes of point of view can be distinguished for interpreting narratives in the Bible: spatial, temporal, psychological, and ideological.[6]

In the spatial point of view, the narrator identifies himself with a particular character, who quite often is set in a specified locale. But when that identification is not specified, the narrator is seen jumping from scene to scene. Thus, in Genesis 13 the narrator clearly is with Abraham, rather than Lot, as they decide where each will graze his flocks.

There may also be a temporal limitation or lack thereof placed on the narrative. Here we must ask if the narrator limits himself to telling the story as it happened. Or does he interrupt his story with information that comes from a later point in time? And what about the psychological point of view used by the storyteller? Did he dare give some of the thoughts and emotions that ran through the heart and mind of the character he is describing?

---

5. Greidanus, *The Modern Preacher and the Ancient Text*, 205, quotes in part from Shimon Bar-Efrat, "Literary Modes and Methods in the Biblical Narrative in View of 2 Samuel 10–20 and 1 Kings 1–2," *Immanuel* 8 (1978): 25–26.

6. Tremper Longman III, *Literary Approaches to Biblical Interpretation* (Grand Rapids: Zondervan, 1987), 87 n. 24, where he cites Boris Uspensky, *A Poetics of Composition* (Berkeley: University of California Press, 1973), 55–56.

Finally, there is the matter of ideology. What evaluations, estimates, and analyses did the writer place on the narrative either directly or indirectly? If the writer is God's chosen instrument for revealing the narrative at hand, one must carefully note that the point of view adopted by the narrator is the one that God would take, and therefore the one that we must give credence to as well.

Characterization

Since Hebrew narrative does not describe characters in much detail, the interpreter must pay special notice to the details that are given in the Bible. For example, Esau's ruddiness and hairiness, Rachel's beauty, and King Eglon's obesity place us on notice that these somewhat scarce descriptions in typical Hebrew narrative will probably figure prominently in the plot, theme, or consequences soon to be told.[7]

Even though the Old Testament rarely describes its characters, occasionally it will give a brief physical, gentilic, or professional designation like "a head taller than any of the others"—referring to Saul in 1 Samuel 9:2—or like Hittite, Amalekite, prophet, prostitute, or shepherd, referring to others. This allows us to locate the characters in terms of their place in society, their outstanding traits, or even to discern the types of persons they were.

Characters are often contrasted in Hebrew narrative. Thus, as they are played one off the other, a better idea of each is gained. Rahab stands over against Achan; Samuel against the sons of Eli; David is pitted against Saul; Ruth is seen as opposite to Orpah. In some of these cases, one acts as the foil for the other.

The characters in biblical narrative may be analyzed in a threefold categorization: round (or full-fledged), flat, and as an agent.[8] A round character has many traits, is more complex, and therefore less predictable, but more real. A flat character usually only has one trait and thus is single-dimensional. An agent has no personality at all, but simply functions to move the story along.

---

7. Robert Alter, *The Art of Biblical Narrative* (New York: Basic Books, 1981), 180.

8. Adele Berlin, *Poetics and Interpretation of Biblical Narrative* (Sheffield: Almond, 1983), 23–33.

Setting

The setting of a story in the Bible functions in several ways. For one thing it locates the plot and the characters in a space/time world. Biblical narrative is closely related to history, for that is one of its categories: historical narrative.

But setting will also function as another clue in the interpreting process. The fact that Abraham is on Mount Moriah in Genesis 22 is not a mere appendage and useless detail to the narrative; instead, it prepares us for the fact that it will be on this same spot where the temple mount will be built. Finally, setting can add atmosphere and character to the story as it stirs up associations that were already attached to a particular site because of the past history of revelation connected with that locale.

Dialogue

While detailed characterization is fairly rare in biblical narrative, there is a high proportion of dialogue in the stories of the Bible. "Everything in the world of biblical narrative ultimately gravitates towards dialogue. Quantitatively, a remarkably large part of the narrative burden is carried by dialogue, the transactions between characters typically unfolding through the words they exchange, with only the most minimal intervention of the narrator." [9]

So central is dialogue that it often carries the theme of the passage, that is, the point of view being expressed. Alter gives two helpful rules to use when interpreting dialogue:

- Note the place where dialogue is first introduced, for that will be an important moment in revealing the character of the speaker— perhaps even more than in the substance of what is said.

- Note also where the narrator has chosen to introduce dialogue instead of narration. There is a special rhythm of moving back and forth between narrative and dialogue. This focusing on the sharp exchange between the characters will help to see the relationship of the characters to God and thus to each other.

---

9. Alter, *The Art of Biblical Narrative*, 182.

When the dialogue occasionally appears in a stylized speech— where one character repeats a part or the whole of what another has said—it is well to pay very careful attention in these instances to any small deviations, differences, slight alterations, reversals of order, elaborations, or deletions. These may tip off the interpreter to key disclosures about the character or the events being described. In those extremely rare instances where the narrator does enter the narration directly, it is usually to give a summarizing speech at an especially critical point in the narrative. This is done to give some perspective on what has been done or said, to speed up the action, or to avoid excessive repetition.

Dialogue is almost always between two characters, and rarely between three or more. But it is always one of the telltale signs of distinctive biblical narrative. Dialogue adds the color, the vividness, and realism to biblical narrative. It makes for a most lively and memorable announcement of what God wants us to learn.

Structural Level

Hebrew narratives have structures that are a "network of relations among the parts of an object or a unit."[10] But what makes up a unit? While it is impossible to define in a rigid manner, the Bible's narratives are fairly easily recognized and link up to create larger literary units. Thus, in Job 1:13–19 the four messengers come to Job one after another with the sad news of a new catastrophe that had just occurred. The cohesiveness of this unit is further strengthened by the recurring phrase, "and I only have escaped to tell you," or "while he was yet speaking another came." Or in Ruth the two central scenes are chapters 2 and 3, describing the encounters between Ruth and Boaz in the field. These two central scenes were preceded by two brief scenes showing Ruth and Naomi at their home. Ruth 1 contrasted Ruth with Orpah, while the final chapter in the Book of Ruth contrasted Boaz with the redeemer. Moreover, in both the first and last chapter the women of Bethlehem act in the role of a chorus commenting on Naomi's condition, an unhappy one in chapter 1, but a happy one in chapter 4. Chapter 1 refers to people who died before the main action just as chapter 4 refers

---

10. Bar-Efrat, "Some Observations on the Analysis of Structure," 155.

to people who were born after the main action. The book forms a beautiful acrostic:

1: Ruth — Orpah

2:Boaz — Ruth

3:Boaz — Ruth

4: Boaz — Redeemer

Stylistic or Rhetorical Devices

The last major component of narrative texts is style. Though not easy to define, style is always easily recognized by its presence or absence. Basically it is the result of the choices that the writers and narrators made as they told their stories; it was the way of putting things that determined style. Five important devices that enhanced style are repetition, omission, inclusion, chiasm, and irony.

Repetition. While many have come to expect and to enjoy repetition in Hebrew poetry, it has rarely been appreciated or even recognized in prose until recently. Instead, scholarly reaction to repetition in prose in the past had been to think of it as redundancy that probably signaled clumsy editing of the sources used by the redactor. But scholars have now become accustomed to viewing repetition as a favorite rhetorical device of the Hebrew raconteurs. Repeated words, phrases, or even sentences were used to express a certain emphasis, meaning, or development of the text. There are five basic types of repetition in the Hebrew Bible: key word (*Leitwort*), motif, theme, sequence of actions, and type-scenes.[11]

Most significant of these repetitions was the *key word*. In this case a certain word or group of words was set in special prominence by the way it appeared frequently or most strategically in a text. A well-known illustration of this usage is the juxtaposition of the Hebrew words for *kid,* or *young goat* and the verb *to recognize* between the stories in Genesis 37:31, 33 and Genesis 38:17, 25–26. The subtle implication of these two key words in these two passages is this: Just as the kid had been used to deceive their father Jacob by saying that Joseph had died perhaps by an attack by a wild animal, so Judah (the one who suggested that the brothers

---

11. Alter, *The Art of Biblical Narrative*, 95–113.

sell Joseph to the Midianites) was himself deceived by his aggrieved daughter-in-law, which he too finally "recognized" in a most embarrassing moment.

The other most commonly used form of repetition is a *type-scene*. This term describes texts that are similar in content and structure, or "an episode occurring at a portentous moment in the career of the hero which is composed of a fixed sequence of motifs."[12] Thus, in the patriarchal era the type-scene of the barren woman who gave birth to boys who would become biblical heroes was a dominate example of such.

Repetitions are a most valuable part of the biblical text and are not to be seen as marks of sloppiness by the scribes or as an opportunity for excision of the material by modern critical scholars. Instead, they help direct our attention to things in the text that we might otherwise have overlooked.

Omission. Just as important as repetitions were the omissions, or "system of gaps," in a text.[13] A gap was an unstated piece of information that was essential for getting at the meaning of that story. Thus, an unstated motive, an unexplained cause for an action, an unstated purpose, and the like are all part of these gaps or omissions used as stylistic devices by the writers of the Old Testament. These omissions are examples of the writer's selectivity, but in some instances the "gapping" played rather important roles. At the very least the omissions created interest, curiosity, suspense, and surprise.

Inclusion. Another stylistic device is inclusion. Often the narrator deliberately indicated the beginning and end of either the whole narrative or one of the important scenes within the narrative by repeating the identical clauses or words, thus effectively bracketing off or enveloping the marked-off material.

Exodus 6:13 and 26–27 is a favorite example. Verse 13 declared: "Now the LORD spoke to Moses and Aaron about the Israelites and Pharaoh king of Egypt, and he commanded them to bring the Israelites out of Egypt." Verses 26–27 form the end of the inclusion by saying: "It was this same Aaron and Moses [note the chiasm

---

12. Ibid., 96.
13. Meir Sternberg, *The Poetics of Biblical Narrative* (Bloomington: Indiana University, 1985), 186.

from v. 13] to whom the LORD said, 'Bring the Israelites out of Egypt by their divisions.' They were the ones who spoke to Pharaoh king of Egypt about bringing the Israelites out of Egypt. It was the same Moses and Aaron." What intervenes between these two bookends, as it were, is an incomplete genealogy of Jacob's twelve sons: Only Reuben, Simeon, and Levi appear; the other nine sons are not mentioned at all. Since the three sons named here had been featured in the previous and informing theology of Genesis 35:22; 49:4; and 34:25–31 in a negative way for their gross violations of morality, and since Moses and Aaron's line stemmed from Levi, who also was implicated in these dastardly deeds, it is no wonder that the inclusion featured the emphasis that "this was that same Moses and Aaron [indeed!]." Therefore, the inclusion helps to emphasize that the gifts and calling of God for leadership had very little to do with heritage, lineage, natural endowments, or natural goodness.

Chiasm. Old Testament narrators often used a literary device called chiasm (after the Greek letter *chi* that looks and functions like our English letter *x*). Thus it is named for the inversion or crossing of related elements in parallel constructions. Chiasms may involve anything from words or clauses in parallel lines of poetry to a whole narrative. Chiastic patterns are found in dialogues as well as in whole scenes. Therefore, a chiasm often involves the use of an ordering principle within both verses, sentences, and even whole books.[14]

Irony. Irony is usually classified as a figure of speech, but recently it has received more attention and recognition as one of the tools in the narrator's literary basket. There are four characteristics of irony. First, it must be demonstrated that it was *intended* by the author. In that sense, the narrator said something in order to set it forth as being false and therefore subject to rejection. Second, irony is usually *covert*, for there is no explicit statement that the statement or passage is ironical in nature. In this case the surface meaning is deliberately misleading unless the reverse train of thought is picked up. Third, biblical ironies are *stable*, for there is a limit as to how far one can move from the surface meaning of

---

14. John W. Welch, "Introduction," in *Chiasmus in Antiquity*, ed. John W. Welch (Hildesheim: Gerstenberg, 1981), 11.

the text. And finally, ironies are *local,* or *finite;* that is, they are limited in terms of their scope. Only a portion of the surface text was meant to be ironic, not its entirety; otherwise nothing would remain steady while the reverse world was being depicted.[15]

How to Interpret Narrative

The principles for interpreting narrative texts are constantly being updated and revised, but the foregoing discussion of the literary aspects of narrative has suggested the main essentials for understanding narrative. The interpreter of Scripture is advised to master this method, which can be summarized as follows.

Guidelines for Interpretation

1. *Identify each scene of the narrative.* Since the focus of interpretation centers on the main character(s), summarize their words and actions so as to reflect the narrator's point of view and reason for recording these details.

2. *Analyze the plot of the narrative.* Note how the action rises toward a climax and how the author paces the plot and highlights the high points of the story, thereby marking the beginning, middle, and end of both single and complex patterns within the story.

3. *Determine the point of view from which the narrative is recorded.* How does the narrator tell the story? Which character in the story does the narrator focus on? Does the narrator reveal the thoughts and emotions of the characters or add a critique of the action? These are the key issues in isolating the meaning of narrative.

4. *Pay close attention to the details of the scene.* How the characters are described is usually important to understanding the story. Where the action takes place may also add to the significance of the events.

5. *Examine the dialogue that the author uses to narrate the story.* Where is it introduced into the narrative? How does the author move back and forth between dialogue and narrative?

---

15. Wayne Booth, *The Rhetoric of Irony* (Chicago: University of Chicago Press, 1974), 1–6, as cited by Longman, *Literary Approaches to Biblical Interpretation,* 98. Note also the pioneering work of E. M. Good, *Irony in the Old Testament* (Philadelphia: Westminster, 1965) [now available under the same title from Sheffield: Almond Press, 1981].

6. *Look at the units within a scene and their relationship with one another.* Understanding how the units were structured may contribute to the meaning of the scene.

7. *Study the stylistic devices the author used:* These include, among others, repetition, omission, inclusion, chiasm, and irony. For example, repetition expresses an author's emphasis on certain parts of the story.

Another important part of interpretation is understanding the biblical world and the writings preserved from that time period. Though there are well-known examples of narrative from the ancient Near Eastern world, there are a limited number that are close in genre to biblical narrative, such as in Genesis or Ruth. Even those examples often listed as parallel genres reveal key differences. The Egyptian works of Sinuhe and Wenamun are written in the first person, for instance. The Canaanite epics of Keret and Aqhat are not prose but a mix of genres called epic poetry. Biblical court tales, for example, are stories of individuals not associated with the royal court but who rise to a position of favor (such as the stories of Joseph, Esther, and Daniel). But there are only few parallels to these biblical narratives, namely the Aramaic story of Ahiqar and a few intertestamental accounts.[16]

Jacob Wrestles with God

Genesis 32:22–32 is a good example of biblical narrative that has raised many puzzled looks from modern readers. The story centers on the experience that Jacob had one night as he wrestled with a man until daybreak.

Plot and Setting

This episode is part of the broader story involving the disquietude of Jacob's heart: He faced the prospect of seeing his brother Esau for the first time after many years. They had been separated since Jacob's outrageous act of cheating Esau out of his inheritance

---

16. See Richard D. Patterson, "Holding on to Daniel's Court Tales," *JETS* 36 (1993): 445–454. For a more detailed discussion, see Lawrence M. Wills, *The Jew in the Court of the Foreign King*: Ancient Jewish Court Legends (Minneapolis: Fortress, 1990).

rights. Clearly, Jacob was extremely restless and apprehensive as the time for the confrontation of the two brothers approached.

The setting for the story is a ford of the Jabbok River.[17] While that is the geographical setting, there is an obvious play on words here, for "Jabbok" in Hebrew (*yabbok*) sounds like the very rare Hebrew verb selected to describe the fact that "he wrestled" (*ya'abok*). The meaning of the Jabbok would be something like the "wrestling, twisting" river. There is more, however, for the name of the man is Jacob (*Ya'aqob*).

The plot is fairly simple in that it has only one scene that takes place at the one setting, the Jabbok River. At the *beginning* of the plot, Jacob quietly sends his two wives, two maidservants, and eleven sons across the ford of the Jabbok along with all his possessions. Then the drama intensifies as he is left alone without his family or possessions and a man wrestles with him all night long until daybreak. When the man saw that Jacob could not be overpowered, he touched Jacob's hip so that his hip was "wrenched" (v. 25). Even then Jacob would not break off his hold on the man, but demanded that he bless him before he released him. So it happened that the man blessed him by saying, "Your name will no longer be Jacob, but Israel, because you have struggled with God and with men and have overcome" (v. 28). That was the *middle and the peak* of the action. The end of the plot follows immediately, for Jacob inquires what the name of the man was, but he refused to give it. Jacob concludes (and thus the plot comes to an *end*) by naming that place "Peniel," for he declared, "I saw God face to face, and yet my life was spared" (v. 30). The sun comes up, thereby closing the scene, but Jacob limped from that day on because of his hip. The plot in this single-scene story is a single plot with a definite pyramid pattern that begins quietly in the night at the Jabbok, builds to a crescendo, and then quietly comes back to where it started as the sunrise marks the end of the scene.

---

17. The Jabbok River is the *Wadi ez-Zerka*, "the blue," that is a clear mountain stream on the frontier of the land according to Allen P. Ross, "Jacob at the Jabbok, Israel at Peniel," *BSac* 142 (1985): 342, 352 nn. 20, 25.

Point of View

The narrator does not identify himself with Jacob (the spatial plane); instead, he concludes the narrative by introducing the ideological plane, thereby explaining why it is that Israelites do not eat the tendon attached to the socket of the hip to this day: it was because Jacob's hip was touched near the tendon (v. 31). This was a taboo that grew out of this story, but it was never part of the Law of Moses.

Surprisingly, the narrator never introduced the psychological plane, for he never let us know what thoughts and emotions were running through Jacob's mind when all of this was about to happen or while it was in progress. Only in the dialogue are we aware of all that was going on.

The perspective of the writer, and therefore of the divine intention, is captured best by noting what is told in the dialogue. Especially prominent is the speech of the man who wrestled with Jacob in verse 28. He gave Jacob a whole new identity and nature: He changed his name from Jacob to Israel. The change signaled the transformation from one who grasped the heel of his brother and who was twisting and wrestling to one whom God fought. Ever afterwards the nation would recall the time when Jacob contended with God successfully, yet the time when God won the battle. The fact that God had prevailed would be of significance for the future of the nation.

Characterization

Clearly this passage is about a change of character and a change of nature for one who had been accustomed to thinking that he could live by his own wits and might to get whatever he wanted. Had he not bested his brother Esau and his father-in-law Laban in a contest of wills? But then all of a sudden he had to confront his past—facing his brother with no idea how Esau might react.

The very name *Jacob* is a key word in this text; first of all, the name *Jacob* is a play both on the word for *heel* (*'qb*) and the verb *to wrestle* (*'bq*). Note the metathesis of the *q* and the *b* in the two words that play on Jacob's name. "Tripping his fellow-men by the heel (*'qb*) has for Jacob come to its extreme consequence: a wrestling (*'bq*) with a *man* which to Jacob is the most shocking experience of his life, as appears from the fact that thereafter he proceeds through life a man changed of name, and thus of nature, and under the new name he becomes the patriarch of the 'Israelites.' (This comes out even more strongly in Jacob's own confession in v. 31, [English v. 30]."[18]

But the Hebrew verb *yāqaʿ*, *to touch,* also implies a separation or dislocation from the *blow* or *touch* administered by the man who wrestled with Jacob. This same verb is again used figuratively in Jeremiah 6:8 and Ezekiel 23:18. Not only are the wordplays with Jacob's name and the Jabbok River strong (the sounds b/v and k/q forming strong alliterations at the beginning of the story),[19] but the twisting, beguiling, and crafty aspects of this wheeler-dealer Jacob are all too clear from both this narrative and the informing theology that laid behind this text and made up part of the context for Jacob's terrible fear of facing his brother.

The other character in this narrative is the *man* (Hebrew, '*îš*). The name alone suggests mystery with no hint of deity. He refuses to reveal his identity, and he insists on being gone before daybreak. We learn of this man's identity just as Jacob did: only by his words and actions. He remains a mystery. Our only clue comes in Jacob's statements at the end of the section where he declares he has seen God (v. 30). About a millennium later the prophet Hosea in the eighth century B.C. would refer to this same incident in Hosea 12:3–4 and draw the same conclusion that Jacob did—that man was God! Hosea wrote, "In the womb [Jacob] grasped his brother's heel; as a man he struggled [wrestled] with God. He struggled with the angel and overcame him; he wept and begged for his favor. He found him at Bethel and there he talked with us" (Not: "him," as some English translations incorrectly suggest).[20]

---

18. Fokkelmann, *Narrative Art in Genesis,* 210, as cited by Ross, "Jacob at the Jabbok," 352 n. 16.

19. Ross, "Jacob at the Jabbok," 344, quoting R. Martin–Achard, "Un Exegete Devant Genesis 32:23–33," in *Analyse structurale et Exégese Biblique* (R. Barthes, F. Bovon, F. J. Lâeenhardt, R. Martin-Achard, and J. Starobinski; Bibliothique Theologique; Neuchatel: Delachaux et Niestlé Éditeurs, 1971), 60.

20. For further detail, see Walter C. Kaiser, Jr., "Inner Biblical Exegesis as a Model for Bridging the 'Then' and 'Now' Gap: Hosea 12:1–6," *JETS* 28 (1985): 33–46.

Dialogue and Structure

Only four Hebrew sentences are used to describe the fight; no other details are given. But the fight served as an important preamble to highlight that which was central: the dialogue. Beginning with verse 26 with the man demanding, "Let me go, for it is daybreak," the dialogue practically structures the total scene. Jacob responded, "I will not let you go unless you bless me." That exchange served as an introduction for the main substance of this narrative.

The structure can be analyzed as follows:[21]

1. The demand of a name from God to Jacob (v. 27)	The response of Jacob (v. 27)	The result: name change (v. 28)
2. The demand of a name from Jacob of God (v. 29)	An indirect response (v. 29)	The result: decision name change Peniel (v. 30)

Obviously there is parallelism here: Jacob's direct demand for a blessing leads to his being renamed "Israel." But the indirect response of the assailant leads Jacob to name the place "Peniel," for he realized that it was God who had fought ("Israel") with him face to face ("Peniel"). Thus, the scene may be divided up into five movements: (1) the prologue, verses 22–24a; (2) the event itself, verses 24b–25; (3) the blessing, verses 26–28; (4) the evaluation, verses 29–30; and (5) the epilogue, verses 31–32.

We have already noted that the theme of this narrative appears in the key words of *Jabbok, Jacob,* and the verb *to wrestle.* That wordplay will be a perpetual reminder of what took place there and how the nation got the name it now has.

The name *Israel* both here in Genesis 32:28 and in Hosea 12:3 is interpreted to mean "to fight."[22] Thus, the name *Israel* would carry this meaning, "God contends," "God fights," or "may God contend, persist." If this is so, then the narrator used the Hebrew

---

21. R. Barthes, "La Lutte avec L'Ange," in *Analyse structurale et Exégèse Biblique*, 35, as cited by Ross, "Jacob at the Jabbok," 252 n. 18.
22. R. B. Coote, "Hosea XII," *VT* 21 (1971): 394; idem, "The Meaning of the Name Israel," *HTR* 65 (1972): 137.

root *Sârâ(h)* to explain the name *Israel*. This verb is rare, for it only occurs in connection with this incident.

Summary

In the story of Jacob wrestling with God at the Jabbok River, "Peniel" signals that God's face and presence was still with Jacob, even though everything that God had promised him at Bethel when he first left home, fleeing from the wrath of his brother Esau, seemed threatened. But God touched Jacob at the most sensitive point in his whole being: his rugged tenacity and self-confidence. He emerged lame and partially useless, for he now limped as a memorial to the fact that he had tried by his own carnal efforts to obtain what only could be granted in the grace of God. He was a changed man, for he had to be if he was to witness all that God had promised.

All of this took place at the Jabbok River, which is right on the border as one enters the land that God had promised to give them. Could anything be more emblematic? Israel's victory over the land would not come the usual way that nations gained control of other lands; it would come by the blessing, grace, and power of God, not by the craftiness, wisdom, power, or deceit of men. If necessary, God would cripple all who assumed differently in order to teach them to be bold in faith rather than to be bold in themselves.

Conclusion

Narrative texts are not only abundant and challenging; they are vivid and memorable as well. But all too frequently narrative portions of Scripture are the victims of abuse. In the rush to make legitimate applications and personal utilization of these texts, preachers, teachers, and general readers of the Bible hastily assume the *meaning* of a passage has been understood (or worse still, that determining the meaning of the story is a waste of time) and move on to make an inappropriate *application* of the narrative. Usually this is accomplished by allegorizing the story as a whole and/or allegorizing every single detail in the story, making everything stand for some so-called heavenly truth by assuming that for each earthly aspect of the story there is a heavenly analogue.

But the entire process is flawed from the start. There is no such interpretive principle. Even in interpreting parables, not every detail is to be pressed into service. And there is no law of correspondence that says that for every detail or type there is a heavenly archetype or analogue. Philo assumed this teaching, but the Bible does not.

There is simply no substitute for taking the time to determine the *meaning* of the narrative. Only after this has been secured, by the steps suggested above, will it be possible to ask how this text may now be *applied* in the times, culture, and situations that a present audience of readers and listeners faces.

While few stories explicitly attach a moral or explicitly state why the story is being told, that does not mean that no such purpose existed or that the listener or reader is excused from making any applications to his or her personal life and needs. On the contrary, the very reason why God felt it was necessary to record these details was to make us wise in correct doctrine, living, and thinking. Thus, rather than assuming that the story form relieves our generation from any personal involvement with the text, it does the opposite: The story makes the ultimate teaching or ethical point all the more memorable, thus increasing our accountability.

Recommended Reading

Alter, Robert. *The Art of Biblical Narrative.* New York: Basic Books, 1981. This has almost become a classic in its time.

Auerbach, Erich. *Mimesis: The Representation of Reality in West ern Literature.* Translated by Willard R. Trask. Princeton: Princeton University Press, 1953. This was one of the forerunners in the study of biblical narrative, with special focus on the comparisons and contrasts between Genesis and Homer.

Bar-Efrat, Shimon. *Narrative Art in the Bible.* Sheffield: Almond, 1989. One of the most up-to-date discussions of narrative.

Berlin, Adele. *Poetics and Interpretation of Biblical Narrative.* Sheffield: Almond, 1983. A very good source for definitions and practice in narrative.

Deuel, David C. "Suggestions for Expositional Preaching of Old Testament Narrative." *Master's Seminary Journal* 2 (1991): 45–60.

An application of some of the insights from narrative into the challenge of contemporary preaching by an evangelical.

Frei, Hans. *The Eclipse of Biblical Narrative*. New Haven: Yale University Press, 1974. One of the most important, if not controversial, books in the area of narrative.

Long, V. Philips. "Toward a Better Theory and Understanding of Old Testament Narrative." *Presbyterion* 13 (1987): 102–109. Another evangelical contribution to this field.

Kromminga, Carl G. "Remember Lot's Wife: Preaching Old Testament Narrative Texts." *Calvin Theological Journal* 18 (1983): 32–46. Insights carried over to the field of preaching by an evangelical.

Miscall, Peter D. *The Workings of Old Testament Narrative*. Philadelphia: Fortress, 1983. A much more technical work.

Pratt, Richard L., Jr. *He Gave Us Stories: The Bible Student's Guide to Interpreting Old Testament Narrative*. Brentwood, Tenn.: Wolgemuth and Hyatt, 1990. An extensive (500 pages) introduction for evangelicals.

Scholes, Robert and Robert Kellogg. *The Nature of Narrative*. London: Oxford University Press, 1966. Another early, but excellent and useful tool in this area.

Sternberg, Meir. *The Poetics of Biblical Narrative*. Bloomington: Indiana University Press, 1985. An Israeli literary critic whose book is well worth the effort, even if it is verbose.

5

HISTORY
Eugene H. Merrill

All persons and cultures reflect upon and recall the past. Families do it, passing on the stories of significant events in the lives of family members. Businesses do it, keeping records of production, sales, and customers. Governments do it, partially to have a basis for future decision making. All of these reflections of the past are in one way or another what we call history.

When people ponder even yesterday's events, they are indulging in historical reconstruction. When they seek to penetrate the more remote past and on a comprehensive scale, they are doing what historians describe as historiography: the recollection and recounting of persons, movements, and ideas that made a difference then and whose impact may still be felt.

Biblical history in general is no different in form, but in substance it is sacred history: a historical record of the outworking of divine intention and purpose in human affairs. Understanding the Old Testament without considering this quintessential element will misrepresent the method and message of Old Testament history.[1]

---

1. For a helpful discussion of this necessary distinction between history in general and Old Testament history in particular, see David Howard, Jr., *An Introduction to the Old Testament Historical Books* (Chicago: Moody, 1993), 41–42, 47–49.

History as a genre is predominant in the first half of the Old Testament and necessitates careful reflection on form and hermeneutical principles. What distinguishes history from narrative? Is storytelling an accurate way of recording history? May writers of history legitimately reconstruct historical scenes, for example, by creating speeches given by persons in the story? Is chronological accuracy expected of biblical historians? What are we to learn from the history of the Israelites—social and political trivia about God's chosen people, or something beyond this?

What Makes History Different from Narrative?

Is history a *record* or is it a *story?* The two approaches have characterized historiography from ancient times to the present but historians have commonly taken the former more seriously than the latter. Storytelling appears to lend itself more to fictional overtones than does the reportorial style of ordinary historical discourse, which presumably recounts the unalloyed facts (though hopefully with abundant documentation). The biblical record is, of course, replete with stories even in its most narrowly defined historiographical parts. For this very reason its historical reliability has frequently been challenged, a challenge shared by Herodotus, Thucydides, Hesiod, and other classical historians who also related their histories in story, poetry, or even biography.

Contemporary historians have begun to reassess the role of story as history and, far from disparaging it as a subscientific approach to recovering and retelling the past, have praised it as a worthy and reliable vehicle for the communication of past events.[2] Even biography, parables, and the like are now accepted as legitimate means by which the story of bygone days can be told and retold in ways that—precisely because of their liveliness and variety—are more easily understood and assimilated. The Old Testament is the major and oldest case in point, a vast historical record

2. See Karen J. Winkler, "'Disillusioned' with Numbers and Counting, Historians Are Telling Stories Again," *The Chronicle of Higher Education,* June 13, 1984, 5–6.

known and loved in great part because its message is both interesting and historically reliable.

What, then, makes history a genre that is distinguishable from narrative? There are two main answers to this question. In the Old Testament, history is *national* and not familial or tribal; it is recordkeeping and not storytelling (though the latter can be used for the former). Though the Davidic kings may be the framework of a particular history, the state of the court determined the state of the nation. Though Samuel-Kings is a history of Israel from the author/editor's viewpoint of the monarchy, it is still a history of *Israel*. For instance, we do not read of royal family matters that are irrelevant to the nation or to God's attempt to fulfill promises made to the nation through the person of the king. Second, history is a *series* of accounts (various subgenres, as outlined below), with *cause-effect sequences* given much more weight than plot (see 1–2 Kings below). History is a tapestry of accounts in which there is a place for each account and each account is in its place. This goal of a unified collection of accounts makes it more important to set an episode in Samuel-Kings within its broader context than it is with some of the episodes in Genesis. Two additional observations can be made about biblical history. *Commentary*, which is the voice of the author/editor in the text as he offers direct, subjective analysis of a person or act, is more common in history than in narrative. Commentary is, perhaps the most important difference between biblical history and modern history, since the latter is not supposed to contain any. Samuel-Kings as a history leaves no doubt whether a significant king was wicked or wise, odious or obedient. Explicit judgment pronouncements, reflecting God's point of view as well as the author's, are practically nonexistent in Genesis. Though commentary as a mode of narration is not very common in narrative *or* history, it is more evident in history. Finally, history in the Old Testament is characterized by God who acts through representation (see below on 1–2 Samuel) in the form of both prophet and king. In narrative forms God either speaks directly or is very much behind the scenes (as in Ruth).

How History Functions

While the genre of history appears in many places in the Old Testament, those parts that have always been regarded as historiographical in the strict sense—Samuel, Kings, and Chronicles—are the special focus here. An examination of these historical accounts reveals important ideas about biblical history as well as the variety of literary techniques employed to record history.

1–2 Samuel

Central to the books of 1 and 2 Samuel is the "History of the Succession to the Throne of David" of 2 Samuel 9–20. Most Old Testament scholars view it as genuine history by an author whose "portrayal of personalities and events breathes an atmosphere which must silence any doubts as to the reliability of his account."[3] Nevertheless, it is history of a theological or ideological nature, with the purpose not just to establish the legitimacy of Solomon's succession to David but to do so messianically.[4] The narrative seeks to demonstrate that Yahweh, though not breaking radically into history as in the stories of the judges, for example, is nevertheless sovereignly working within and through history to achieve his redemptive purposes. In addition to the key narrative in 2 Samuel, other important parts of the history in 1 and 2 Samuel include the "ark narrative" (see 2 Sam. 6:1–20a) and Michal's reaction (6:20b–23) as well as the story of Nathan's oracle (chap. 7) and the catalog of David's conquests and officials (chap. 8). All this follows the history of Saul (1 Sam. 8–15) and the long review of the rise of David to kingship (1 Sam. 16–2 Sam. 5). These are regarded by most scholars as authentic historical accounts, though many question the accuracy of some of the historical content.

Apart from major genres such as narratives and prophetic speech, Samuel exhibits a wide variety of subgenres:[5]

dirge	2 Sam. 1:19–27; 3:33–34
eulogy	2 Sam. 1:19–27
battle reports	2 Sam. 10:15–19
boasts	1 Sam. 18:7

---

3. Gerhard von Rad, "The Beginnings of Historical Writing in Ancient Israel," in *The Problem of the Hexateuch and Other Essays* (London: SCM, 1966), 166–204.

4. Ibid., 202.

5. These terms and categories are taken from Burke O. Long, *1 Kings*, FOTL 9 (Grand Rapids: Eerdmans, 1984), 243–64.

commissions	2 Sam. 11:18–21
dedicatory statement	1 Sam. 2:28
indictment speech	1 Sam. 15:17–19; 22:13
juridical parable	2 Sam. 12:1–4; 14:5–7
lists	2 Sam. 23:24–39
oaths	1 Sam. 3:17; 14:44; 20:3
official report	2 Sam. 11:18–25; 18:19–19:1
oracle	1 Sam. 28:6
oracular inquiry	1 Sam. 23:2, 4, 9; 14:37;
	2 Sam. 2:1
petition	2 Sam. 7:18–29
praise speech	1 Sam. 25:32, 33, 39;
	2 Sam. 18:28
prayer of dedication	1 Sam. 1:28
prophecy of punishment	1 Sam. 2:27–36
prophetic revelation	1 Sam. 15:10–11;
	2 Sam. 7:4–16
proverb	1 Sam. 10:11b; 19:24
prophecy of salvation	2 Sam. 12:13–14
taunt	1 Sam. 17:43, 44

All of these forms, whether originally existing independently or not, have been creatively woven together by the author(s) of Samuel to produce the brilliant montage of David's rise and succession.

1–2 Kings

The next great block of historical writings—the books of Kings—covers the period from Solomon's accession to the throne of Israel to its occupancy in exile by Jehoiachin in 562 B.C. This impressive work has the shape, form, and internal witness of being genuine history, though a history developed according to theological or ideological considerations.

The major genre of 1 and 2 Kings is history with "the intent to narrate and interpret events as they were presumed to have occurred, and with awareness of cause-effect relations among them."[6] Secondary genres of 1 and 2 Kings are texts that resemble royal inscriptions and contain the following:

---

6. Long, *1 Kings*, 30.

building activities	1 Kings 6:2–36; 7:1–12
military exploits	1 Kings 14:25–26
king (or administrative) lists	1 Kings 4:2–6
chronicles or chronistic	
material	2 Kings 12:6; 17:6; 18:9–15

various kinds of reports such as reports of the

death of a leader	1 Kings 2:1–12
commissionings	1 Kings 12:22–24; 21:17–19
throne conspiracies	1 Kings 15:27–30; 16:9–11;
	2 Kings 15:10, 14, 25
prophetic revelations	1 Kings 16:1–4
symbolic actions	1 Kings 11:29–31
dream epiphanies	1 Kings 3:4–15; 9:1–9
oracles	1 Kings 6:11–12; 20:13–14;
	22:5–6, 15–17.

Narrative or story occupies a major place in the literature of 1 and 2 Kings and focuses on prophets for the most part (see 1 Kings 20:1–34; 21:1–29; 22:1–38), though kings are central as well (1 Kings 2:13–25; 3:16–28); sometimes both appear together (1 Kings 22:1–38). Some distinguish between ordinary story and legend, the chief characteristic of the latter being its "lessened interest in aesthetic elements and its augmented concern with miraculous power and exemplary conduct of the main character."[7] Examples occur mainly with prophets (1 Kings 13:1–32; 17:17–24; 18:1–46; 2 Kings 1:2–16; 2:1–25), but also with the king (1 Kings 10:1–10). This distinction is necessary to those who find the overtly supernatural elements of the stories incredible or distasteful, but it cannot be maintained on form-critical grounds alone.

The historical narrative in 1 and 2 Kings incorporates a wide variety of subgenres:

petition	1 Kings 8:14–53;
	2 Kings 19:15–19
farewell speech	1 Kings 2:2–4
prophetic judgment speech	1 Kings 11:31–39
prophecy of punishment	1 Kings 13:21–22; 14:7–11
theological review	1 Kings 11:1–13;
	2 Kings 10:29–31;

---

7. Ibid., 31.

	17:7–23; 21:9–15
announcement of reprieve	2 Kings 22:18–20
boast	1 Kings 20:10
indictment speech	1 Kings 2:42–43; 22:18
itinerary	1 Kings 19:1–18
parable	1 Kings 20:39–40
letter	2 Kings 10:2–3; cf. 19:9–14
oath	1 Kings 1:29–30
oracle fulfillment	1 Kings 16:34; 17:16;
	2 Kings 1:17; 2:22; 4:44
report of oracular inquiry	1 Kings 14:1–18; 2 Kings 3:4–20;
	8:7–15
parenesis	1 Kings 8:56–61
praise speech	1 Kings 1:48; 5:21; 8:15, 56
prayer	2 Kings 20:3
prophetic announcement	
of sign	2 Kings 19:29–31; 20:9–10
prophetic battle story	2 Kings 19:1–37
regnal resumé	1 Kings 14:19–20; 15:1–5, 33–34;
	2 Kings 10:34–35; 13:10–13
schema of reprieve	1 Kings 21:27–29;
	2 Kings 22:19–20
summary of prophetic	
oracle	1 Kings 21:23;
	2 Kings 9:36; 10:30;
	14:25–27; 17:13; 21:11–15
theophany	1 Kings 19:9–14
throne conspiracy	2 Kings 15:10, 14, 25, 30, 21:23
vision report	1 Kings 22:17, 19–22;
	2 Kings 8:7–15

The occurrence of most of these forms in other Old Testament compositions and in similar, if not identical, patterns suggests that the historian(s) responsible for Kings was aware of and made use of a wide inventory of stock genres which were integrated to produce the final result. Recognition of these literary devices and forms and how they contribute to the historical narrative is crucial to the hermeneutical and theological study of Kings.

1–2 Chronicles

Chronicles is a *version* of Old Testament history, another way of looking at the ground already covered, especially by Samuel and Kings. Chronicles is synoptic to these books to a great extent, parallel in some respects to them, and either supplementary to or subtracting from them in other respects.[8] The major additions to the history are the prolegomena to Israel's nationhood, a comprehensive approach that traces its roots back to Adam himself, through the patriarchs, and on to David, the focal person of the Chronicler's account. Strangely absent, however, are the great elective and redemptive events such as patriarchal promise, exodus, covenant at Sinai, and the like. Even the conquest and judges are ignored and Saul, the first king, receives short shrift almost as an impostor on the road to legitimate kingship. The other added material is that which briefly traces the history of Judah from the exile to the edict of Cyrus, the last datable event in the book (539 B.C.).

The question of the relationship of the Chronicler (i.e., the anonymous author or compiler of the material) to all his various sources cannot receive attention here. However, it is clear that the Chronicler had Samuel-Kings (and Joshua-Judges, for that matter) before him as he wrote, drawing heavily upon those writings as a major source.[9] The canonical tradition that locates Chronicles at the end of the sacred collection presumes that Samuel-Kings were composed before Chronicles.

Most literary critics regard Chronicles as history, though certainly not in the sense suggested by the English title of the book. It is not a collection of chronicles as that term is defined form-critically but, in line with its Hebrew title, a book of annals (*dibrê hayyâmm*, lit., "book of the days"). This observation is in agreement with the understanding of annal as "a concise, year-by-year series of reports, arranged chronologically and designed to record events pertaining to a particular institution, such as monarchy or temple."[10] Chronicles generally are more selective than annals, containing

---

8. For the data, see James D. Newsome, Jr., ed., *A Synoptic Harmony of Samuel, Kings, and Chronicles* (Grand Rapids: Baker, 1986).

9. Tomotoshi Sugimoto, "The Chronicler's Techniques in Quoting Samuel–Kings," AJBI 26 (1991): 30–70.

10. Long, *1 Kings*, 243.

narrative accounts of events in isolation from each other and with no particular organizing or guiding principle. The books of Chronicles clearly do not reflect this kind of lapidary reporting but reveal a pronounced ideological framework and development characteristic of standard historiography.

As history, Chronicles nonetheless is made up of numerous subgenres most of which have been noted already in connection with Joshua–2 Kings. Unique to Chronicles, however, is the genealogical section of 1 Chronicles 1–9.[11] This differs from genealogy proper in that this table "lists individual positions or responsibilities within a given organization, relates these to one another, and assigns individual persons or groups to fill each position and carry out each specific responsibility."[12] The purpose of the section is to tell how Israel is organized and thereby who and what it is.

The second great section of Chronicles—1 Chronicles 10–2 Chronicles 36—is history writing in the strict sense of the term. In compiling his data the Chronicler makes use of more than thirty named sources and uses a wide variety of literary genres in the composition of his work, the most prevalent being some kind of narrative.[13] Space restrictions preclude an exhaustive list of forms and references, but the following are among the more common and important:[14]

accusation	1 Chron. 10:13–14;
	2 Chron. 25:15
address	1 Chron. 21:17; 28:2;
	2 Chron. 6:3–11; 7:12–22
admonition	1 Chron. 22:11–13;
	2 Chron. 13:4–12
anecdote	1 Chron. 12:16–18;
	2 Chron. 9:1–12
battle report	1 Chron. 4:39–41;

11. Simon J. DeVries prefers to see this section as a collection of lists he labels "Table of Organization" in *1 and 2 Chronicles,* FOTL 9 (Grand Rapids: Eerdmans, 1989), 15.
12. Ibid., 27.
13. For a full list and discussion, see Howard, *Old Testament Historical Books,* 238–42.
14. Most of these depend on the analysis of DeVries, *1 and 2 Chronicles,* 426–37.

	2 Chron. 15:19–16:10
birth report	2 Chron. 11:18–20
catalogue	1 Chron. 6:31–53
chronicle	2 Chron. 14–16
commission	1 Chron. 22:6–16
construction report	2 Chron. 3:15–4:10
dream epiphany	2 Chron. 7:12–22
farewell speech	1 Chron. 29:1–9
hymn of praise	1 Chron. 16:8–36
instruction	1 Chron. 28:11–21
oracle	2 Chron. 1:11–12
petition	2 Chron. 6:16–20
praise speech	1 Chron. 29:10–13
prayer	1 Chron. 17:16–27
prophetic speech	2 Chron. 15:2–7; 25:7–9
report of ritual	1 Chron. 15:25–16:6
roster	1 Chron. 6:16–30; 27:16–22
royal narrative	2 Chron. 1:2–17
story	1 Chron. 21:1–27;
	2 Chron. 10:1–11:4
taunt	2 Chron. 32:10–15
throne conspiracy	2 Chron. 23:1–15
vocation account	1 Chron. 22:6–16

All of these (and more) the historian has utilized to produce the fabric of his historical account. Because the Chronicler was a compiler, no doubt many of these existed independently in their present form, whereas others were edited and otherwise reshaped in order to suit the special purpose to which the author addressed himself. Despite (or perhaps because of) the multitudinous array of genres constitutive of the Chronicler's work, it stands in its canonical form as a magnificent example of historical truth being refracted through many prisms and for that reason being all the more beautiful and effective.

Is History in the Old Testament Unique?

Apart from Israel and Greece no civilizations in the ancient Near Eastern and Mediterranean worlds produced significant historiography contemporary with the Old Testament. And Herodotus, the

Greek author usually credited with being the "father of history," lived five hundred years after the time of Samuel. This does not suggest, however, that ancient Near Eastern peoples did not think reflectively and critically on their past nor even that they had no sense of history as an expression of transcendent purpose. To the contrary, most of Israel's neighbors had a sense of historical cohesiveness and destiny, and they expressed this sense in a wide range of literary forms and texts.[15] Like Israel, the surrounding cultures developed the capacity to interact with their world and its practical and theoretical concerns and did so in literary genres appropriate to the situation. The difference lies in Israel's creative assembly and integration of these forms into comprehensive histories.

Mesopotamian historiography in the strict sense covers only five hundred years—from Tiglath-pileser III (744 – 727 B.C.) to the thirty-eighth year of the Seleucid Era (264 B.C.).[16] The principal historiographical records of this period are in the form of chronicles that for the most part are written in a factual, objective manner and that betray no obvious biases toward or against the political structure they describe.

A much longer period is embraced by the lists of kings which profess to trace history from the moment the gods lowered kingship to earth from heaven. Besides listing kings and dynasties (allegedly in sequence), they contain at times brief narrative or episodic sections. (Examples of those are found in the eponym lists, synchronistic histories, date lists, year formulae, etc.) All of these leave a great deal to be desired in terms of objectivity but their clichés and stereotypes contributed much to the stock of language typical of other, more fully written historical texts.

Though records of the past were preserved in other forms, such as dedicatory inscriptions inscribed on votive objects or on objects that were incorporated into the foundations of buildings—identifying the donor, the object, and the occasion—none of this resulted in historical prose. Nevertheless, it is apparent that the Mesopotamian civilizations were aware of the need to record

---

15. Bertil Albrektson, *History and the Gods* (Lund: CWK Gleerup, 1967).
16. A. Leo Oppenheim, *Ancient Mesopotamia* (Chicago: University of Chicago Press, 1964), 144–53.

present and even past events, but they did so in largely independent documents that never found expression in a wholistic fashion characteristic of the biblical histories like Samuel, Kings, and Chronicles.

In Egypt there was little interest in a comprehensive understanding of the past or the present. "The Egyptians had no real sense of history in the classical or modern sense. There are no extant histories; even chronicles and annals do not extend beyond a single reign or lifetime."[17] That does not mean, however, that there are no Egyptian texts that at least approximate historical genres. Some detailed records appear in the Old Kingdom period (Dynasties 3–6) in the form of annalistic stelae or monuments.[18] These contain information about each year of a king's reign, focusing on such matters as accession rituals, feasts, cattle census, the founding and dedication of temples, and building projects, especially of reservoirs and canals. Other inscriptions of a historical nature from this and later periods were found even in distant places like the Sinai and Nubia. These were usually stone monuments erected to attest to the far-flung interests and power of the Egyptian ruler.

Texts of a historical nature also appear on the interior walls of burial chambers in the pyramids and other burial structures.[19] These list the names of the deceased, his family members, autobiographical data, and even the names of ancient and revered predecessors. Many of these persons, kings and commoners alike, are also named in song and saga long after they had died. In this manner poetry was integrated into the historical narrative much as in the Old Testament.

By the New Kingdom (Dynasties 18 and 19), the powerful rulers of Egypt commissioned stelae and wall inscriptions that exhaustively detailed their domestic and foreign accomplishments.[20] These obviously are of enormous historical value; however, like comparable Mesopotamian royal inscriptions, chronicles, and the

---

17. William W. Hallo and William Kelly Simpson, *The Ancient Near East: A History* (New York: Harcourt Brace Jovanovich, 1971), 191.
18. For examples, see Miriam Lichtheim, *Ancient Egyptian Literature* (Berkeley: University of California Press, 1973), 1:15–28.
19. Ibid., 1:29–50.
20. Ibid., 2:11–15, 25–29, 35–39.

like, they lack any clear sense of linkage to a larger historical panorama. They are indispensable to historical reconstruction but are not themselves part of an indigenous Egyptian historical synthesis.

The extent to which surrounding cultures affected that of Israel, especially in terms of ideological and literary structures, cannot be known. There can be little doubt, however, that Mesopotamia and Egypt provided an environment that facilitated the development of a historical consciousness among the Hebrews; yet the Hebrews were the first to compose comprehensive histories.

Questions About the Accuracy of Historical Narrative

Before turning to a list of specific hermeneutical principles, some unique elements concerning accuracy in historical narrative require careful consideration in the interpretive task. This is all the more the case in biblical texts versus nonbiblical, for the implications of factuality and authenticity for biblical truth claims are clearly of paramount importance. Whether so-and-so said such-and-such or did this-and-that may be interesting or even to some degree important in secular historical texts, but the degree to which biblical texts reflect reality is, potentially, a matter of eternal destiny.

A penchant of most modern historiography is the arrangement of events in chronological order, from the beginning of a sequence of events to the end. Though it is clear that the ancients also followed this natural procedure, there are glaring exceptions to this dictated by thematic or ideological concerns that outweighed all others. This is apparent in biblical historical narrative in a number of instances. Close study of Samuel-Kings as compared to the synoptic account in Chronicles reveals chronological incongruence of the kind even more frequently seen in the New Testament Synoptic Gospels.[21] In 2 Samuel alone there appears to be conclusive evidence that the historian has completely abandoned any notion of chronological sequence in his desire to promote the Davidic king-

---

21. A random survey of the headings in Newsome's *A Synoptic Harmony* will reveal reversals of narrative order in Chronicles in relation to Samuel-Kings. (see, e.g., pp. 27, 29, 63, 69, 73, 98–99, 108, etc).

ship and to bring glory to Israel's God.[22] Similar rearrangement is detectable in the Elisha narratives and in the accounts of the reigns of Judahite kings.

This method, of course, has nothing to do with the credibility of the accounts but only with their understanding. For a historian to depart from the convention of chronological sequence is to presuppose a special purpose on his part, a purpose that may or may not be perceptible or even important. Even if the modern reader can reconstruct events of biblical history in the order they actually took place, he or she is obigated to be sensitive to the text as it stands, for that order best reflects the author's own intentions.

Akin to the previous observation about chronology is the proposal that there is no such thing as objective history. The raw material of history is facts or events but these are irrecoverable to the modern reader except as they are filtered through the biases, opinions, emphases, and interpretations of their transmitters.[23] A fact is no better or more understandable than the process by which it crosses the centuries from its occurrence to its incorporation by the historian.

This is all the more the case with literature of a religious or ideological nature that, almost by definition, has surrendered claims to objectivity. But lack of objectivity is not necessarily tantamount to lack of credibility or authenticity. In the case of the Bible, it is important to recognize that facts are selectively included in or excluded from the sacred record in accordance with the theological as well as historical purposes of the record.[24] To disclose and even greatly emphasize events that on ordinary grounds would seem unworthy of historical attention should not disqualify those events as history, nor should the Bible's omission of other occurrences that dominated the contemporary ancient world's attention suggest that the biblical historians were less than trustworthy or competent simply because those occurrences did not fit their

---

22. Eugene H. Merrill, "The 'Accession Year' and Davidic Chronology," *JANES* 19 (1989): 101–12.
23. K. Lawson Younger, Jr., *Ancient Conquest Accounts, A Study in Ancient Near Eastern and Biblical History Writing,* JSOTSup 98 (Sheffield: Sheffield Academic Press, 1990), 32–35.
24. Howard, *Old Testament Historical Books,* 38–41, 46.

ideological purposes. The Old Testament history (or any other) must be allowed to dictate its own principles and parameters of matters considered newsworthy. To do less is to invite serious misunderstanding of the Bible's own approach to history.

The ideology and/or theology of a narrative may be addressed by asking several questions. First, is the account interrupted in any way by observations either made or recorded by the narrator concerning the events he relates? That is, does he merely narrate happenings or does he interject his own or Yahweh's judgment on them? Such comments obviously constitute interpretation of the events—theological conclusions based upon or drawn from them. Second, to what extent does the narrator allocate precious space to this or that person or event? The relatively detailed account of the reign of Saul in Samuel as compared to his near omission in Chronicles makes it clear that the chronicler has a quite different ideological perspective from that of the author of Samuel. This is not a matter of truth or accuracy but of emphasis. Third, to what extent are themes or motifs of a given pericope derived from earlier biblical revelation and transmitted to subsequent texts? When such threads are observable (e.g., the patriarchal promises) in historical texts (such as 1 Sam. 2:28; 1 Kings 8:21–58; 2 Kings 17:15), the very use of these elements is indicative of theological and/or ideological considerations at work in the purpose and even pattern of the narrative. Stories never appear in the Old Testament historical record for their own sake—they invariably are functions of an over-arching theological concern.

A perhaps greater problem for the interpretation of historical texts is the extent to which the historian was free to embellish the record. Was he at liberty to reconstruct the words of conversations he was not present to hear or even the thoughts of persons which presumably had never been shared? For history writing in general, one would have to concede that much creativity enters the process of determining and telling the facts of the past. Historians must frequently reconstruct settings in which events occurred, including conversations and introspections that *most likely* could or would have taken place.[25] This is almost always necessary in order to

---

25. Robert Alter, *The Art of Biblical Narrative* (New York: Basic Books, 1981), 63–87.

transform the raw facts of what happened into a good story. The raw facts alone often do not make a story that lives and breathes. To use Alter's terminology, ancient historians used conventional "type-scenes" to form matrices against which the past must be understood.[26]

Saying this, however, does not annul the integrity of the record, for facts in any case must be interpreted by the reader as well as by the historian. Every modern observer of the past is free and indeed obligated to "fill in the blanks," for no historical account can be complete. The Old Testament narrative may appear to be an exception to this inasmuch as it is revelation—inspired literature whose veracity is bound up in that dogmatic claim. But inspiration does not mean a sort of dictation where the human authors were simply automated writers. The biblical text consistently shows the marks of its human authors, with endless differences of literary technique and style. Thus, biblical history is not precluded from critical analysis nor even from the possibility that some imagination was at work in its composition.[27] But imagination is not synonymous either with error or lack of facticity. Though humanly unaware of all the ingredients of the original scene he described, the biblical historian, like any other, reconstructed the complex of events but, as evangelical tradition insists, in such a way as to reflect accurately the acts, words, and even thoughts of the protagonists.

How to Interpret
Historical Literature

Every literary genre calls for a uniquely appropriate set of hermeneutical guidelines so that its message may be properly understood. This is no less true of historiographical literature, but the problem is greatly exacerbated in the case of Old Testament history writing given its generically complex nature. The following

---

26. Ibid., 47–62. Alter defines type-scenes as "certain fixed situations which the [author] is expected to include in his narrative and which he must perform according to a set order of motifs . . ." (p. 50).

27. For this, some use the term "fictive imagination." See Burke O. Long, "Historical Narrative and the Fictionalizing Imagination," *VT* 35 (1985): 405.

guidelines are suggested for the historical literature in its synthesized, canonical form.

Guidelines for Interpretation

1. *Determine the scope of the historical narrative under consideration.* What are the literary boundaries of the passage? Who are the principal characters? What is the focus of the story? What is the cultural and historical environment of the story? Where is the narrative located in its larger literary and canonical context? As stated above, history is unique in that the individual accounts, or pericopes, are strung together with overarching theological and ideological issues in mind, so the larger context cannot be ignored.

2. *Recognize that the historical record is only that—a record and not the event itself.* Events are transmitted through filters of time, space, and interpretation of the original authors (human and divine) and sometimes those who have had a hand in its further literary shaping. Readers must be sensitive to how an event is recorded and interpreted in written form.

3. *Look for evidence of the author's purpose in recording the story.* Because the biblical historians are not simply recorders of events, interpreters should seek to determine the motive for the author telling a story and choosing the details he includes. What the author intended to communicate is one and the same with the meaning of what he has written.

4. *Examine the features of historical narrative carefully for the meaning that is usually implicit rather than explicit.* As with narrative in general, note each of the following: the plot of the story and how the action progresses; the characters in the story and the values their actions demonstrate; how the characters relate to one another and to God; the geographical and temporal setting of the story; the literary devices used by the author and how they impact the story; and how the story relates to the surrounding narrative and to the book as a whole. One or more of these features of a story will help guide the interpreter to a story's meaning.

5. *Do not suppose that what happened in a historical narrative is prescriptive for what should happen.* The Bible records examples of good and bad motives, godly and ungodly conduct, and appropriate and inappropriate speech. The characters described in the historical narratives often make mistakes and are not necessarily

intended as examples for us. Keeping in mind that Old Testament history is, for the most part, the recording of *national* versus tribal or family concerns should make readers think twice before making too many personal applications. The key is not whether we as readers wish to see a character as an example but whether (and in what way) the author *intended* a character to be an example. This can be discovered, in the text, through the steps presented here.

6. *Permit the details in historical narratives simply to be supporting facts for the main point of the story.* All stories are made up of individual details that enhance the overall impression the story creates. But those facts in themselves do not generally have a meaning of their own. A historical narrative should not be allegorized so that the details in the story take on special significance.

7. *Do not look for devotional or doctrinal content in every historical narrative.* Stories about people in the past are intended to shape values as readers identify with the struggles of characters as well as the characters' attempts to deal with those struggles. Most of the stories in the Old Testament will have meaning at least for some readers some of the time, but not necessarily for all readers all the time. Readers who demand something applicable to their lives on the particular day they happen to be reading a historical narrative are likely to find some meaning that the story never intended.

Adultery and Its Icy Fingers

The tendency of history in the Old Testament to represent a particular theological viewpoint is well illustrated in the narrative of David's adultery with Bathsheba, the consequent murder of her husband, and the sorrowful aftermath seen in the disintegration of the royal family. This story appears in the Succession Narrative of 2 Samuel 9–20 and provides the occasion for the turbulence of succession in the first place. The text of 2 Samuel 12:1–14 is central to the wider context in which David's sin and its immediate effects are spelled out (2 Sam. 11–12). The following analysis will show how (1) history as story containing (2) type-scenes of a most private and personal nature can (3) be related rhetorically or thematically, without the bondage of a chronological straitjacket. It illustrates well the principle of cause–and-effect and betrays the fact (4) that history, especially in the

Bible, is sensitive first and foremost to ideologically and theolog-ically interpretive concerns.

The centrality of 2 Samuel 12:1–14 to the entire narrative is obvi-ous from the concentricity of the elements that precede and follow it. The whole is bracketed by lists of David's public officials (8:15–18 and 20:23–26), the names of whom are not in every case identi-cal since they represent different periods of David's reign. Next fol-lows the story of David's kindness to Mephibosheth, the last surviving son of his friend Jonathan (9:1–13). This is matched by a similar interest in and restoration of Mephibosheth following Dav-id's own restoration to kingship (19:24–30). Thematically linked to this is David's grace toward Barzillai (19:31–39) and David's recep-tion by his own people (19:40–43).

The circle narrows with the account of David's disgrace at the hands of Hanun, king of Ammon, and the punishment that fol-lowed (10:1–19). This corresponds to an expansive account of dis-grace and punishment involving Amnon (13:1–29) and Absalom (13:30–19:15) and, within it, the story of Shimei's abuse of David (16:5–14) and eventual remorse (19:16–23).

Finally, there remains 2 Samuel 11–12, a unit that itself reveals an increasingly narrow focus. It begins with David's stay in Jerusalem in the Ammonite campaign (11:1) and ends with the successful prose-cution of that campaign many months later (12:26–31). Next follows David's adultery and Bathsheba's pregnancy with an unnamed child (11:2–5). This parallels the birth to David and Bathsheba of a named child, Solomon (12:24–25). To prevent Bathsheba's husband Uriah from standing in the way of his having Bathsheba, David arranges for Uriah to die in battle, a death Bathsheba mourns (11:6–27). The counterpart is the death of the unnamed child of adultery and Dav-id's mourning and then acceptance of the tragedy (12:15–23).

What remains at the center is the parable of Nathan (12:1–6) and its interpretation (12:7–14).[28] Not only is the message of Nathan to David clear in its own right, but its place at the heart of the Suc-

---

28. Fokkelmann shows convincingly that the parable and its interpreta-tion are also at the center of chapters 11–12 inasmuch as God is the subject only in this pericope, albeit in the person of his prophet Nathan. J. P. Fokkelman, *Narrative Art and Poetry in the Books of Samuel,* vol. 1, *King David* (Assen: Van Gorcum, 1981), 71.

cession Narrative puts beyond any question the real issue behind the struggle for the throne: David's flagrant violation of the two great commandments, "You shall not murder" (Exod. 20:13) and "You shall not commit adultery" (Exod. 20:14). The whole Davidic covenant relationship (2 Sam. 7) is in jeopardy because its first beneficiary has broken its terms in a highhanded manner. But his heartfelt repentance does not fall on deaf ears. "I have sinned against the LORD," says David, and Nathan responds, "The LORD has taken away your sin. You are not going to die" (2 Sam. 12:13).

The function of 12:1–14 is to articulate the reasons for the complication in dynastic succession as well as the forgiveness that enabled it to be resolved despite the difficulties. Besides paving the way for the emergence of Solomon—even under morally questionable circumstances—the passage anticipates the removal of more legitimate claimants such as Amnon, Absalom, and Adonijah (v. 10). It also accounts for the deterioration of David's family and political life (cf. chap. 13–20).[29] Theologically, the Succession Narrative flows out of the Davidic covenant passage (2 Sam. 7) as the account of how that covenant was fulfilled in Solomon despite opposition from within and without.[30] As the heart of that narrative, chapters 11–12 (and especially 12:1–14) provide a classic example of the sovereignty of God who is able to turn apparent defeat and disaster to triumph. "We must go through many hardships to enter the kingdom of God" (Acts 14:22). In the larger context of the Old Testament as the record of Yahweh's universal and eternal dominion, the Davidic covenant represents an aspect of that dominion which is accomplished in the face of almost overwhelming satanic opposition, but accomplished nonetheless in the fulfilling work of Christ, the second David (see 2 Sam. 7:11b–16; cf. Isa. 9:7; 49:8; Amos 9:11; Acts 15:16–18).

---

29. Gunn, in fact, argues that 2 Samuel 11–12 is a story not about succession but about David and the tensions between his public and private life. D. M. Gunn, *The Story of King David,* JSOTSup 6 (Sheffield: The University of Sheffield, 1978), 82–83.
30. This does not appear to be the case chronologically, however. For arguments that the covenant revelation followed the outbreak of the Ammonite wars, see Merrill, "The 'Accession Year' and Davidic Chronology," 111.

In approaching the central narrative (2 Sam. 12:1–14) according to the hermeneutical principles suggested above, it is necessary to establish that the pericope is indeed a self-standing unit. This is a matter of virtual consensus among scholars, a major clue being the reference to Nathan's arrival to and departure from David at the beginning (12:1) and end (12:15a) of the account. In the next place, its location in and relationship to its larger context also gives the story a twist or nuancing that is important to its deeper meaning. Its centrality to the entire history of the succession suggests that the adultery and murder addressed by Nathan were indeed the sins of David that set in motion the decline of his royal house. Finally, it is important to remember that the brief narrative of Nathan's encounter with David (only fourteen verses) is not likely to be an exhaustive record of all that transpired at that moment. Surely other words were spoken, other persons may have been in attendance, and there certainly were reactions in tone, timing, and body language that are missing in the present version. Furthermore, the question of original authorship of the pericope comes to the fore. Is this incident from the memoirs of David, of Nathan, or of an official scribe in attendance? Does it stand before us as initially composed or has it gone through a process of inspired redactionary activity to bring it in line with the ideological and theological purposes of the Succession Narrative (and indeed of Samuel) as a whole?

While many (if not most) of these questions cannot definitively be answered, these are the kinds of queries that should be brought to any Old Testament historical text, for these texts serve more than the function of merely imparting historical information—they do so in the setting of a distant and complex ancient world and with the grander purpose of communicating divine and eternal truth to all subsequent generations of seekers including our own. Before that truth can adequately be known, the texts that embody it must be taken on their own terms and allowed to speak out of their own life situation, one recoverable only by sensitive recognition of the nature and purposes of those texts, namely, theological history in story form.

Conclusion

The accounts, or subgenres, that are strung together to make up the histories of the Old Testament are extremely varied: biographies, parables, lists, oracles, taunts, proverbs, letters, speeches—the list goes on and on. History encompasses the use of virtually all other genres found in the Old Testament, and thus is a genre heavily defined by the aspect of editorship, collection, and organization. Ideological and theological interpretive concerns run throughout the histories in the Bible. So important are these concerns that they likely determined which accounts/subgenres were included and which were not.

The Israelites were not the first to write in many of the literary forms found in the Old Testament such as law, proverb, or psalm. History is the glaring exception, however, since the Israelites were the first among the people groups of the ancient Near East to compose comprehensive histories. This creation of a genre has not been given the credit it deserves among modern historians of Israel's literary traditions.

Exegetical mistakes lie waiting for interpreters and preachers of biblical history who are ignorant of its uniqueness as a genre. Among the most common errors are (1) treating a text as prescriptive (an example to follow) when it is merely describing what actually happened; and (2) searching for devotional or doctrinal meanings in details where there is no indication that an author intended such meaning. But for the interpreter who pays attention to both the principles needed for narrative in general (issues such as plot and characterization) as well as the principles needed for history in particular, there is no better teacher than history for such cause-and-effect topics as sin and its punishment, and obedience and its blessedness.[31]

---

31. There is a common epithet—"a gentleman and a scholar"—that is uncommonly appropriate, for few individuals deserve to be so designated. Dick Patterson is among that deserving remnant as all his friends and colleagues are most happy to testify. For many years I have been impressed with Dick's careful, painstaking, and reverent scholarship but only of late have come to know him "up close and personal." How delightful to discover that the man behind the pen is identical to the man with whom I have shared precious moments of face-to-face dialogue. He is the embodiment of another modern cliché: "what you see is what you get." It is an honor for me to offer this essay as an expression of my respect and admiration of my friend.

Recommended Reading

Berlin, Adele. *Poetics and Interpretation of Biblical Narrative.* Sheffield: Almond, 1983. The importance of this work for historical literature lies in Berlin's analysis of certain character types associated with the story of David, especially the women. She helpfully points out Bathsheba's role both as an historical figure and as a character in the plot.

DeVries, Simon J. *1 and 2 Chronicles.* The Forms of the Old Testament Literature. Vol. XI. Grand Rapids: Eerdmans, 1989. This work, part of a series devoted to form-critical analysis of the Old Testament, painstakingly examines Chronicles in terms of structure, genre, setting, and intention. With the other volumes it is indispensable to the interpreter who wishes to get a feel for historical literature and how its units and their boundaries are to be identified.

Fokkelmann, J. P. *Narrative Art and Poetry in the Books of Samuel.* Vol. 1. King David. Assen: Van Gorcum, 1981. Fokkelmann addresses 2 Samuel 9–20 and 1 Kings 1–2 as a collection of 32 scenes, each of which he subjects to careful and exhaustive literary-critical analysis. He operates from the assumption of the integrity of the text and offers remarkably helpful exegetical, hermeneutical, and theological insights.

Gros Louis, Kenneth R. R. ed. *Literary Interpretations of Biblical Narratives.* Vol. II. Nashville: Abingdon, 1982. For purposes of historical literature, the essays by M. Fishbane, R. R. Gros Louis, and J. Levenson are particularly helpful. They attempt to identify literary hallmarks of this genre and to do close reading of the elements that characterize the various selected pericopes.

Gunn, David M. and Danna Nolan Fewell. *Narrative in the Hebrew Bible.* Oxford: Oxford University Press, 1993. Of special interest here is the attempt to read "between words and stories" in connection with the house of David narratives. The approach is one that attempts to bring intertextual lines of investigation to the process of literary analysis and that also points out the theological drivenness of such literature.

Howard, David Jr. *An Introduction to the Old Testament Historical Books.* Chicago: Moody, 1993. Howard's special contribution here is his introduction to historical narrative in which he discusses the genre as prose, history, and literature. He is helpful in addressing the characteristics, elements, and stylistics of this type of biblical literature, doing so on the basis of a high regard for the historical and factual credibility of the sources themselves.

Long, Burke O. *1 Kings, With an Introduction to Historical Literature*. The Forms of the Old Testament Literature. Vol. 9. Grand Rapids: Eerdmans, 1984. Long, like DeVries (see above), sets out to identify all the literary units of the literature under his purview. This he does by exacting form-critical analysis. He adds to this his understanding of the original and redactionary functions of the texts both as compositions per se and also as parts of an eventual canonical whole.

Miscall, Peter D. *The Workings of Old Testament Narrative*. Philadelphia: Fortress, 1983. Miscall's contribution to approaches to the historical literature is most apparent in the second half of this book where he offers his "reading" of 1 Samuel 16–22. By "reading" he means personal analysis based on careful attention to style, form, structure, themes, plots, and the like. Such close reading affords insights into complexities of language and literature that otherwise remain elusive. Miscall is particularly sensitive to paradigmatic readings of texts, that is, to shared or parallel features that suggest a larger unity of perspective or even of ideas.

6

LAW
Richard E. Averbeck

Aside from its importance for the Hebrew Scriptures themselves, the implications of the Old Testament law extend through the New Testament and into modern church ministry and the Christian life. From beginning to end and in various ways, the Bible speaks of God's principles of right and wrong, moral and immoral, good and bad. In the Old Testament law God spoke in a particularly direct way about his standards for the lives of his people in ancient Israel. He said "Thou shalt" or "Thou shalt not" or "If someone does this, then you must do this." God's law has much to say about social ethics, justice, morality, personal holiness, and relational fidelity.

While some of the Old Testament laws seem applicable for all time (e.g., "You shall not murder," Exod. 20:13), others are difficult to comprehend or apply in our modern cultural context. After all, Moses wrote the Pentateuch in a very different cultural, historical, and redemptive context. That makes it essential to understand the Old Testament law from the perspective of its original context and purpose. The study of literary forms contributes significantly to this kind of study of the biblical text. Regarding the law in particular, genre analysis helps the student, teacher, or preacher understand

and apply the law lawfully (see 1 Tim. 1:8), with due attention to its goodness (see Rom. 7:12, 14, 1 Tim. 1:8, etc.), its weakness (Rom. 8:3 and Heb. 7:18–19), and its ancient Near Eastern cultural and historical context.

Important questions confront modern interpreters of the legal portions of the Old Testament. What specifically is the Old Testament law? How do the genres (or subgenres) of legal literature in the Old Testament reflect the literary, historical, cultural, and ideological conditions of the day in which they were composed? How would the people of that day have understood the law? What effect should the answers to these questions have upon the use of the law today in the church community and in someone's personal Christian life?

The ox laws in Exodus 21:28–32, for example, seem obscure to westerners who are not accustomed to seeing an ox on every street corner. But the nature of their culture made ox laws as necessary in that society as modern automobile laws are to our society. Slave laws (e.g., Exod. 21:1–11, 20–21, 26–27) seem unfair and offensive, but understanding their socioeconomic context and intention will give insight into why they were necessary in ancient Israel (see the treatment of Exod. 21:2–11 below). As important as they are in the Old Testament law, rituals often seem to be magical or superstitious (e.g., Lev. 12, the "sin offering" law for the woman after childbirth). Most Christians find such regulations uninteresting if not confusing, if they pay attention to them at all. No wonder most readers never make it through the Book of Leviticus!

How Law and Genre Analysis Are Related

Law is fundamental to all societies, but different societies in different times and places often have different legislative needs, even though there are certain concerns that virtually all societies hold in common. Moreover, different religious, cultural, social, and political conditions cause the same or similar concerns to be handled in different ways. Because of its interest in the real-life situation of the Old Testament laws, genre analysis pays careful attention to the social conditions that the laws assume and from which they originated. For example, marriage is common to all societies, but some of the biblical laws make it clear that this institution was viewed and handled differently from today's culture. A man could have more than one wife (Deut. 21:15–17 assumes this) whether they were slave wives or not (e.g., Exod. 21:7–10).

Similarly, a genre-sensitive approach to Old Testament law considers the many comparable collections of laws recovered from the soil of the ancient Near East in order to broaden the cultural base for understanding the biblical laws in their world. Although the ox laws might seem obscure, they are well documented not only in the Bible but also in other law collections.[1] A careful reader of the Old Testament law will be sensitive to these cultural and historical factors which lie within and behind the text.

The major concern of genre criticism focuses on the literary character, content, and function of the genre. The Old Testament laws themselves need to be studied in regard to their own literary characteristics. Though the genre of law is similar in form to narrative, some distinct conventions appear, such as the common "if . . . then" clauses. In the books of Exodus through Deuteronomy, three subgenres of legal literature are common: covenant, law, and ritual legislation (often referred to as cult). This extensive body of law in the Old Testament functions primarily to raise the standards of God's chosen people to his level. Furthermore, the genre as it occurs is not without a literary context in Scripture, making it unacceptable to treat the unit of text in isolation from that broader context.

The primary focus of this chapter is the legal literature of the Pentateuch (Exod. 20–Deut. 32) as legislated through the media tion of Moses at Sinai and in the wilderness (Exodus–Numbers), and as preached by Moses in his final speech to the nation of Israel forty years after the exodus from Egypt (Deuteronomy). There are two important features of this law that must be recognized from the start. The Mosaic law is imbedded within the Mosaic covenant (see Exod. 19:5; 24:7–8, Lev. 26:9; 42–45, Deut. 5:2–3; 29:1, 9), and the ritual legislation in Exodus 25 through Leviticus 16 is an integral part of the Mosaic law. A realistic treatment of Old Testament legal literature requires careful consideration of the three literary subgenres—covenant, law, and ritual legislation—and the relationships between them.

---

1. See J. J. Finkelstein, *The Ox That Gored* (Philadelphia: American Philosophical Society, 1981).

How a Covenant Functions

The word *covenant*, occurring 283 times in the Old Testament, first appears in Genesis 6:18 and 9:8–17 for God's covenants with Noah before and after the flood. There are four other major historical covenants in Scripture between God and humanity: the Abrahamic covenant (e.g., Gen. 15:9–18; 17:1–21); the Mosaic covenant—by far the largest number of occurrences and our primary concern in this essay (e.g., Exod. 19:5; 24:7–8); the Davidic covenant (e.g., 2 Sam. 23:5, Ps. 89:3ff; cf. 2 Sam. 7); and the new covenant (e.g., Jer. 31:31–37; cf. Ezek. 36:22–32).

The influence of covenant in the Old Testament is not limited to passages where the Hebrew term actually occurs. For example, the covenant lawsuit of prophecy is an oracle in response to Israel's violation of their Mosaic covenant relationship with the LORD. The LORD was hailing them into the cosmic court for judgment (e.g., Hos. 4:1; 12:2; Isa. 3:13–26; Mic. 6:2; cf. also Isa. 1 and Jer. 2). It is sometimes argued that the prophets were essentially "covenant enforcement mediators." Recent research shows that covenant pervades the Old Testament and its world on several levels.[2]

To capture the spirit of this legal institution is to realize that a covenant is best defined as a means of expressing and/or a method of establishing and defining a relationship.[3] Taking it from the realm of relationships between humans, God often used this well-known, human-to-human, relational institution as a metaphor for establishing and communicating his intent in divine-to-human relationships. Understanding this is important lest the Mosaic covenant—within which the Mosaic law is imbedded—be considered primarily a legal contract rather than a relational bond. Covenants

---

2. Publications on covenant have blossomed since the classic essay by G. E. Mendenhall, "Covenant Forms in Israelite Tradition," in *Biblical Archaeology Reader*, vol. 3; (1954 reprint, New York: Doubleday, 1970), 25–53. Before Mendenhall, however, W. Eichrodt, *Theology of the Old Testament*, 2 vols., trans. J. A. Baker (Philadelphia: Westminster, 1961, first edition published in German in 1933) suggested that covenant was the center of Old Testament theology and binds the two testaments together.

3. See R. Davidson, "Covenant Ideology in Ancient Israel," in *The World of Ancient Israel: Sociological, Anthropological and Political Perspectives*, ed. R. E. Clements (Cambridge: Cambridge University Press, 1989), 324.

were not the same as legal contracts: A contract was a business transaction; a covenant was about two parties relating to one another on a long-term basis.[4]

The basis for understanding the metaphor of covenant is clear within the Old Testament itself, though that understanding is confirmed by ancient Near Eastern parallels. People established well-defined relationships with other people, such as Jacob's covenant with Laban (see Gen. 31:44–54). That covenant linked stipulations with oaths (vv. 47–53; see esp. v. 53 "May the God of Abraham and the God of Nahor, the God of their father, judge between us"); it also linked eating a covenant meal (v. 54) with setting up a stone heap as a pillar to serve as a witness to the covenant bond (vv. 45–48; cf. Josh. 24:25–28).

The framework of Exodus 19:1–24:11 consists of a narrative account of the making of a covenant with the same structure, content, and procedure as Genesis 31:44–54. In this case, however, it was a divine-to-human covenant between God and Israel.

- The process began with the LORD's *proposal of a covenant* relationship with Israel (see Exod. 19:3–6; cf. Laban in Gen. 31:43–44).[5]

- Israel then proclaimed their *anticipatory acceptance of the covenant* relationship that the LORD had proposed (see Exod. 19:7–8; cf. Jacob in Gen. 31:45–46). Exodus 19 anticipates the relationship with an oath, but Genesis 31 with a meal instead. After Laban initially proposed the covenant (Gen. 31:43–44)—but before the detailing of the stipulations and swearing of the oath (31:47–53)—Jacob responded by setting up a pillar, giving instructions to create a heap of stones that would witness the relationship (31:45–46a; cf. vv. 47–48 and 51–52), and then eating an anticipatory covenant meal with Laban by or upon the witness heap (31:46b; cf. v. 54 for the concluding covenant meal). In this case the text seems to record the eating of two covenant meals (similar to the multiple oaths in

---

4. G. M. Tucker, "Covenant Forms and Contract Forms," *VT* 15 (1965): 500.

5. See F. B. Knutson, "Literary Genres in PRU IV," in *Ras Shamra Parallels,* vol. 2, ed. L. R. Fisher (Rome: Pontificium Institutum Biblicum, 1975), 187–198 for a covenant proposal text from Ugarit.

Exod. 19 and 24), one before the oath ceremony (see the same order in Gen. 26:30–31) and one after (31:54).[6]

- After the appropriate preparations had been made and precautions had been taken (see Exod. 19:9–25), the LORD declared *the stipulations of the covenant* (Exod. 20:1–23:33; cf. Gen. 31:49–52), albeit with a significant interruption (Exod. 20:18–26) which created a division between the stipulations of the Decalogue (Exod. 20:1–17; lit. the "ten words" Exod. 34:28, Deut. 4:13; 10:4) and the rest of the laws in the "Book of the Covenant" (Exod. 21:1–23:33; cf. Exod. 24:7 for this title).[7]

- Finally, Laban and Jacob *solemnized the covenant commitment* by proclaiming an oath (see Exod. 24:3–8; cf. Gen. 31:53) and eating a meal together (Exod. 24:1–2; 9–12; cf. Gen. 31:46, 54).

Thus, God and Israel established a covenant relationship that they enacted by eating a meal together on the basis of Israel's solemn commitment to keep the stipulations of the relationship as stated in the context of the oath ceremony.[8]

In the Old Testament and ancient Near East "to make a covenant" encompassed not one but two basic ideas: stipulation and oath.[9] This is evident in Exodus 24:1–11 where the recitation of covenant stipulations and oaths (vv. 3–8) is surrounded by the

---

6. N. Sarna, *The JPS Torah Commentary: Genesis,* ed. N. Sarna (Philadelphia: The Jewish Publication Society, 1989), 220–222.

7. For the importance of stipulations, see E. Gerstenberger, "Covenant and Commandment," *JBL* 84 (1965), 46.

8. The relationship between the ratification of the Mosaic covenant in Exod. 24:1–11 and the anticipatory ritual ratification of the new covenant in Luke 22:19–20 is noteworthy. The two main parallels are: (1) the wine representing Jesus, blood (Luke 22:20) compares with the blood oath ceremony (Exod. 24:6–8) and (2) the bread representing Jesus body (Luke 22:19) compares with the meal on the mountain (Exod. 24:11). The apostles, being pious Jews and fully acquainted with Exodus 24, certainly would not have missed the significance of this.

9. K. Baltzer, *The Covenant Formulary in Old Testament, Jewish, and Early Christian Writings,* trans. D. E. Green (Philadelphia: Fortress, 1971, first pub. in German 1964), 16; cf. D. J. McCarthy, *Treaty and Covenant,* AnBib 21A, rev. ed. (Rome: Biblical Institute Press, 1981), 140; and esp. M. Weinfeld, "Covenant Terminology in the Ancient Near East and Its Influence on the West," *JAOS* 93 (1973), 190.

preparation for and participation in the covenant meal referred to in Exodus 24:1–2 and 9–11. A biblical covenant is a "personal union pledged by symbol and/or oath."[10] The complementary relationship between the stipulations of the covenant and the two rites (oath and meal) reveal that God wanted Israel to live before him in a certain way (the stipulations). He also wanted them to be deeply committed on an individual and corporate level to living that way before him (the oath). But most of all he wanted a relationship with them, a bond of peace and harmony that would bring them together with him in meaningful fellowship reminiscent of kinship (the meal).

How Law Functions

All treaties and covenants in the Old Testament had stipulations that defined the agreement by laying out the obligations of one or both parties to the covenant. In essence, the Old Testament law is the set of stipulations for the covenant relationship between the LORD and the nation of Israel. "The Bible itself does not conceive of a law code without a covenant at its base."[11] The Mosaic covenant is like a picture frame surrounding the law, and the various law collections in the Pentateuch fit into the scene in their own peculiar way.

As the frame for the law, the Mosaic covenant defines the limits of the law's content and primary application. Moreover, the covenant frame stretches and hangs the canvas of the law so that those who look at it can see it well and become sensitive to the spirit with which God gave it to Israel. The spirit of the law is basically this: God expects the people whom he has redeemed (see Exod. 19:4) to take their covenant commitment to him seriously (Exod. 19:5a) because he takes his covenant commitment to them seriously (Exod. 19:5b–6a).

The first list of key words for the Old Testament law occurs in Genesis 26:5, where the LORD himself testified to Isaac that "Abraham obeyed me and kept my requirements, my commands, my decrees, and my laws" (Gen. 26:5). This combination of terms ap-

---

10. McCarthy, *Treaty and Covenant,* 297.
11. M. Weinfeld, *"běrîth," TDOT,* 2:273.

parently refers to the Mosaic law as given at Sinai (e.g., Deut. 11:1). True, Abraham did not live under the law. But Moses as the writer of the Pentateuch was already living under the law when he wrote Genesis. Since Abraham was a righteous man, Moses therefore described him in terms of the law which defined righteous living in Moses' day, that is, in his own mind and in the minds of his readers.

Any one of the terms in Genesis 26:5, or almost any combination of them, can refer to the Mosaic law in general, yet each of them also carries relatively distinct nuances even when they refer to the same body of laws. The Old Testament law is basically a combination of two types of law: divine decrees and divinely determined judicial ordinances or precedents, some of which were very similar to other ancient Near Eastern laws. Other words that refer to or describe the Mosaic law relate in various ways to these decrees and ordinances.

The analysis of Old Testament law has focused for several decades on the distinction between laws that unconditionally and categorically assert right and wrong (apodictic law) and laws that define specific cases and prescribed legal consequences (case or casuistic law).[12] The latter is the conditional ("If . . . then . . .") case law while the former expresses categorical affirmations or prohibitions such as those found in the Ten Commandments. Each commandment of apodictic law applies to every case that could possibly be covered by the word used. It refers to no individual cases and no punishments. This means, "It keeps the strictly legal purpose of the commandments in the background, thus making their moral import stand out more clearly."[13]

The study of the formal apodictic and case law styles has undergone considerable refinement and modification in recent decades. Case laws, for example, are sometimes divided into two main types: first, remedial laws in which the "if" clause described the vi-

---

12. For discussion of this distinction in Old Testament law, see D. Patrick, *Old Testament Law* (Atlanta: John Knox, 1985), 21–24. The classic study is A. Alt, "The Origins of Israelite Law," in *Essays on Old Testament History and Religion,* trans. R. A. Wilson (New York: Doubleday, 1967, first published in German in 1934), 101–171.

13. Alt, "The Origins of Israelite Law," 157–158.

olation of someone's rights and the "then" clause prescribed the appropriate compensation or retaliation (e.g., Exod. 21:20 "If a man beats his male or female slave with a rod and the slave dies as a direct result, then he must be punished"); second, primary laws governed rights and duties in which the "if" clause described a legal relationship (and/or its attendant circumstances) and the "then" clause prescribed the conditions of the relationship (e.g., Exod. 21:2 "If you buy a Hebrew servant, then he is to serve you for six years. But in the seventh year, he shall go free, without paying anything").[14]

Though some have attempted to identify decrees and ordinances with apodictic and case law, respectively, others take the decrees to be the regulations of sacrifices, priesthood and tabernacle requirements, and the like, as opposed to the ordinances, which were the civil laws of the nation.[15] Yet such precise lines of division do not reflect the way the terminology and the laws themselves are mixed in the various Old Testament law collections (esp. Exod. 20–23; Exod. 25–Lev. 16; Lev. 17–25; and Deut. 12–26).

How Ritual Legislation Functions

The law is a unified whole, yet the ritual legislation (or cult) within it are a subgenre of legal literature because of the distinctive concerns and content. Though recent research has shown that building narratives for the tabernacle, like those in Exodus 25–31 and 35–40, constitute a separate subgenre of literature in the ancient Near East and Old Testament,[16] the priestly and holiness legislation (see Lev. 1–25 and 27) uses forms very similar, if not identical, to the case laws and laws of categorical imperatives com-

---

14. D. Patrick, "Casuistic Law Governing Primary Rights and Duties," *JBL* 92 (1973): 180–181; idem, *Old Testament Law*, 23–24.

15. See the summary and critique in W. M. Clark, "Law," in *Old Testament Form Criticism*, ed. J. H. Hayes (San Antonio: Trinity University Press, 1974), 132–34; Alt, "The Origins of Israelite Law," 159 n. 106; H. Ringgren, "*ḥāqaq*," *TDOT* 5:143.

16. See especially V. Hurowitz, *I Have Built You an Exalted House: Temple Building in the Bible in Light of Mesopotamian and Northwest Semitic Writings,* JSOTSup 115 (Sheffield: Sheffield Academic Press, 1992); and idem, "The Priestly Account of Building the Tabernacle," *JAOS* 105 (1985): 21–30.

mon in law. In terms of content, if the law was for the judges (see Exod. 18:13–27; 24:14), then the ritual legislation was for the priests (see Exod. 28–29 and Lev. 8–10). But both were to have direct impact on the people individually and corporately as they sought to live out their covenant relationship with the LORD.

While Exodus 25 through Leviticus 9 explains and initiates the tabernacle and priestly ritual system, Leviticus 10–16 defines the internal and ritualistic structure of the priestly conception of things, and Leviticus 17–25 works out its social, religious, and nationalistic implications for Israel. The literary and theological center of this is Leviticus 10–16. As difficult as some parts of it are to understand, a proper and thorough comprehension of the theology embedded in Leviticus 10–16 is pivotal to understanding priestly theology at its most basic level. Animals, people, and things that are clean and unclean—as well as the elements and processes of physical ritual purification—are all dealt with at a basic level and are shown to be the foundation of the entire ritual system.

Though ritual uncleanness is foreign to modern minds, it helps us to think of it this way: The LORD was tangibly present with the Israelites in the tabernacle and, therefore, set up a corresponding physically focused ritual system to maintain the physical sanctity of his residence in their midst and their physical safety in his presence. So, in Leviticus 15:31 the LORD says: "You must keep the Israelites separate from things that make them unclean, so they will not die in their uncleanness for defiling my dwelling place, which is among them."

Leviticus 12–16 distinguishes and gives examples of three levels of uncleanness. *Regular* uncleanness requires that once a person is no longer experiencing a normal flow (e.g., seminal or menstrual, Lev. 15:16–24), that person remain unclean for a period of time (one and seven days, respectively), wash themselves, and become clean without offering sacrifices. Such uncleanness restricts a person from entering the tabernacle lest they defile it. *Irregular* uncleanness requires that when the discharge ceases, whether it is, for example, a male's abnormal flow (see Lev. 15:1–15) or a female's blood flow after giving birth (see Lev. 12), the person becomes clean by washing and offering sacrifices that atone for the uncleanness. In neither regular nor irregular uncleanness is the person expelled from the community or camp. But there is also *severe* uncleanness which does indeed require expulsion from the community. It also requires that once a person is no longer plagued with the condition, leprosy for example (see Lev. 13–14), he or she must wash in association with certain priestly rituals (see Lev. 14:2–9) and then offer sacrifices before he or she can be readmitted to the community.

The point is that sometimes clean and unclean conditions and purification procedures are associated not only with limiting access to the tabernacle (lest it be defiled), but also to the community which surrounded the tabernacle. Finally, the Day of Atonement rituals (see Lev. 16) deal with both: Removing defilement from the tabernacle and the community. The regular sin offering ritual cleansed the tabernacle. The scapegoat ritual cleansed the community.

How Old Testament Law Applies to Christians

The critical issue of the law's relevance today hinges partially on the answer to one question: Within the Mosaic covenant is there a valid distinction between law that is universal and timeless, and civil or ceremonial law that is culture-bound? This question has played an important role in debates over the application of the Old Testament law to the Christian life and modern ethics such as morality in law, politics, and medicine.[17]

Unfortunately, for what seems to be an attractive division of the law in the discussion of its modern application, the problems are insurmountable.[18] Though different parts of Old Testament law emphasize different legal concerns in ancient Israel, none of them

---

17. W. G. Strickland, ed., *The Law, the Gospel, and the Modern Christian: Five Views* (Grand Rapids: Zondervan, 1993), 30, 52–58, 99, 188–190, 240–276, and 336–337; also W. C. Kaiser, Jr., *Toward Old Testament Ethics* (Grand Rapids: Zondervan, 1983), 44–48; idem, *Toward Rediscovering the Old Testament* (Grand Rapids: Zondervan, 1987), 155–166; and C. J. H. Wright, "The Ethical Authority of the OT: A Survey of Approaches," *TynBul* 43 (1992): 205–20, 229.

18. S. E. Loewenstamm, "Law," in *Judges,* WHJP, ed. B. Mazar, vol. 3 (Israel: Jewish History Publications, 1971), 233–35.

do so in a way that suggests a clear-cut division into universal and absolute laws that are applicable today, as opposed to social, political and cultic laws that are not. Even the Ten Commandments in Exodus 20:1–17 (cf. Deut. 5:6–21), which appear to be moral and absolute, include at least one ceremonial law (i.e., the sabbath law), if not civil laws as well. The rest of the Book of the Covenant is a mixture of all three: The laws in Exodus 25 through Leviticus 16 focus largely on the ceremonial dimension because of the concern for the presence of God in their midst; the laws in Leviticus 17–25 and Deuteronomy 4–26 are a mix of all three.

This is *not* to suggest that we must choose between bringing the Old Testament law wholesale over into the Christian life, the church, and our culture, versus ignoring the law entirely. It is true that the law was given within the framework of the Mosaic covenant and was intended to function within that covenantal relationship, not ours. Yet the law continues to demonstrate God's expectations, though Christians live under the new covenant and have a different relationship to the Mosaic law (cf. Acts 15).

This seems to be the very point of the close connection between Jesus' proclamation of the good news of his kingdom (see Matt. 4:23), and his promulgation of the law of that kingdom in the Sermon on the Mount (Matt. 5–7). The law is applicable to Christians because we are to live it from our hearts (see Jer. 31:33). Thus, Jesus proclaimed the law in his sermons, summarized it in the two great commandments, and exemplified it spiritually, ethically, and relationally in the way he lived while sojourning here (see Matt. 5:21–26: not only do not murder, but also do not be angry with or speak angrily toward one's brother; Matt. 22:34–40; Rom. 13:8–10; Gal. 5:13–15: by loving one another, Christians are fulfilling the law).

With regard to the ceremonial law, although Jesus fulfilled the sacrificial requirements for salvation, that does not make the ceremonial law inapplicable. On the contrary, the ceremonial worship law is especially suited for defining the expectations of the Christian faith. When Paul urges the saints to offer their bodies as living sacrifices, holy and pleasing to God, he is using the expectations of relationship as defined in the Mosaic covenant (see Rom. 12:1). When Paul describes his commitment to his children in the faith, he phrases it in terms of the ceremonial law: He says that he is being poured out like a drink offering on a sacrifice (see Phil. 2:17). When believers are urged to do good and share with one another, this is sometimes referred to as a sacrifice to God (see Heb. 13:15–16). The issue then is not whether the Old Testament law is applicable today, but how it is applicable.

Where Legal Literature Is Found in the Ancient Near East

Covenant

International treaty patterns of the ancient Near East provide background for understanding biblical covenants, especially the Mosaic covenant. Although the form is flexible, the relatively unique shape of the Hittite treaties of the late *second millennium* B.C. is of special significance.[19] Note the correspondence with the shape of the Book of Deuteronomy. In general the pattern consists as shown on the following page.

The fourth element of this classic pattern is especially important in this essay because Deuteronomy 12–26 consists of stipulations of the Old Testament law. As in the Hittite treaties, the specific stipulations in the Book of Deuteronomy follow immediately after the statement of relationship (see Deut. 4–11).

Others have suggested that Deuteronomy corresponds to the category of a *first-millennium* B.C. loyalty oath and that this was the function of the covenant between God and Israel even at Sinai forty years earlier (see Exod. 19–24, etc.).[20] The Hittite loyal oaths involved primarily, if not exclusively, domestic affairs as opposed to the treaties which were international. On the one hand, in the domestic affairs of the kingdom the Hittite sovereign imposed completely unilateral loyalty oaths. On the other hand, on the in

---

19. See especially the discussion and citations in Mendenhall, "Covenant Forms in Israelite Tradition," 32–36; K. Baltzer, *The Covenant Formulary in Old Testament, Jewish, and Early Christian Writings,* 9–18; McCarthy, *Treaty and Covenant,* 51–81; and Knutson, "Literary Genres in PRU IV," 160.

20. M. Weinfeld, "The Loyalty Oath in the Ancient Near East," *UF* 8 (1976): 405–412.

ternational scene the Hittite king promised loyalty and protection to the vassal, suggesting a bilateral loyalty commitment.

Another type of ancient Near Eastern text important in the discussion of Old Testament covenants is the royal grant. In general "the grant is a reward for loyalty and good deeds already performed, the

Hittite Treaty	Deuteronomy
1.Preamble	1:1–5
2.Historical prologue recounting the previous history of relations between the two parties of the covenant	1:6–3:29
3.Statement of relationship[a]	4–11
4.Stipulations of the covenant	12–26
5.List of gods as witnesses[b]	27:2–3, 30:19; 31:19, 21, 26, 28, 30; 32:1, 46
6.Curses and blessings	27:11–16; 28

a. In the Hittite treaty this focuses the attention of the vassal upon the importance and benefits of continuing fidelity to the treaty. Similarly, Deuteronomy follows the historical prologue with chapters that some have referred to as "stipulations" but really are not specific enough for that designation (see Deut. 4–11). Instead, in these chapters Moses exhorted the nation to basic loyalty toward the LORD God and assured the Israelites of the LORD's loyalty and benefits in return (e.g., Deut. 5:29; 6:4–9; 17–19; 7:1–16; 11:8–12; 18–25, etc.).

b. This section normally included a list of the gods of both the suzerain nation and the vassal, as well as some that they both revered and some natural elements, which they probably viewed as gods in this context. In the Book of Deuteronomy no such list of gods occurs because the Israelite religion was monotheistic, and the true and only God was himself the suzerain of the treaty/covenant. Instead, some have suggested that the witnesses in the biblical world and specifically in Deuteronomy were the memorial stones (see possibly Deut. 27:2–3 and Josh. 8:32; cf. Gen. 31:45–52 and Josh. 24:26–27) or the song of Moses (see Deut. 31:19, 21, 30 in reference to 32:1–47) or the law-book (Deut 31:26 and 32:46 "solemnly declared" in NIV = "testify against") or the heavens and the earth (Deut. 30:19; 31:28, 32:1; cf. 4:26) or a combination of some or all of the above. "The heavens and the earth" also show up as witnesses in the prophetic controversy passages (e.g., Mic. 6:1–2) which are thought to be divine lawsuits against the nation of Israel because of covenant disloyalty.

treaty is an inducement for future loyalty."[21] The major distinction be-tween a treaty and a royal grant is that in a treaty the vassal obligates himself to the suzerain whereas in the royal grant the king obligates himself to his servant. The obligation goes in the opposite direction: superior to inferior versus inferior to superior: "the 'grant' serves mainly to protect the rights of the servant, while the treaty comes to protect the rights of the master."[22] Grants often concerned land or a house (referring to a dynasty), which was true of the Abrahamic and Davidic covenants, respectively. Thus, there are significant distinc-tions between ancient Near Eastern treaties and royal grants.

However, it is not true that grants are characteristically and strict-ly unconditional for the servant or vassal of the king. The kings of-fered royal grants to vassal rulers or court officials not only because of loyal service already rendered but also in anticipation of ongoing obedience and loyal service. At least theoretically, the grant was permanent even if one of the vassal descendants did not properly fulfill the expected services or obligations and, therefore, did not experience the benefits of the royal grant in his own day. But those who decreed the grants at least implicitly expected and often stated explicitly in one way or another that there were ongoing obligations associated with the grant. The same is true of the Abrahamic and Davidic covenants. The LORD expected Abraham to walk before him and be a blessing as well as fulfill other perpetual obligations (e.g., Gen. 17:1, 9–14). Similarly, David was fully aware that the LORD ex-pected the kings in his perpetual dynasty to rule according to the righteousness of the Mosaic law or suffer the consequences (e.g., 2 Sam. 7:14b; 1 Kings 2:4; 8:25; 9:4–9).[23]

In the Old Testament divine-to-human covenants, there was a pe-culiar confluence of the different relational emphases found in the *treaties, loyalty oaths,* and *royal grants.* The Book of Deuteronomy,

---

21. M. Weinfeld, "The Covenant of Grant in the Old Testament and in the Ancient Near East," *JAOS* 90 (1970): 184–203; idem, "Addenda" *JAOS* 92 (1972): 468–69.

22. Weinfeld, "The Covenant of Grant," 185.

23. B. K. Waltke, "The Phenomenon of Conditionality within Uncondi-tional Covenants," in *Israel's Apostasy and Restoration: Essays in Honor of R. K. Harrison* ed. A. Gileadi (Grand Rapids: Baker, 1988), 123–39; and R. W. Pierce, "Covenant Conditionality and a Future for Israel," *JETS* 37 (1994): 27–38.

in particular, has a shape that reflects most closely the second-millennium ancient Near Eastern treaty tradition known through the Hittite *treaties*. Moreover, the emphasis on loyalty to the divine sovereign in Deuteronomy 1–11 as well as other passages throughout Exodus and Leviticus suggests the ancient Near Eastern *loyalty oaths* which kings imposed on their court servants, officials, and sometimes even on foreign vassals (the latter especially in the first millennium). Finally, the absolute loyalty to which God commits himself by covenant, not only with Abraham and David but also with the whole nation, parallels the *royal grants* of the ancient Near East.

God was concerned to grant permanent promises that would assure the enduring nature of the covenant relationship no matter what might happen. He is not a fickle God. Conversely, God was also concerned that the people of Israel become loyal to him. He is a jealous God (Exod. 34:14). Therefore, to focus the attention of the people not only on the permanent promise but also on the importance of their faithfulness to him, he stipulated ongoing obligations by which they must live with him and one another. The promise was permanent (see Lev. 26:40–45; Deut. 30:1–10), but their experience of the covenant blessings (see Lev. 26:1–13; Deut. 28:1–14) as opposed to the covenant curses (Lev. 26:14–39; Deut. 28:15–68) in any particular generation depended upon their loyalty to the LORD and faithful fulfillment of the clearly stipulated obligations of the covenant (see Deut. 30:11–14).

Law

The major Mesopotamian law collections extant from the ancient Near East were not used as manuals but neither were they merely academic treatises or propaganda for the king's reputation of righteous rulership before the gods and the people. They were one of the means "whereby the Babylonians sought to preserve law and order as a living and continuing tradition."[24] Law and order was also an important concern in the Old Testament, and there are substantial parallels (both comparisons and contrasts) between the Old Testament law collections and the Mesopotamian ones.[25]

---

24. D. J. Wiseman, "The Laws of Hammurabi Again," *JSS* 7 (1962): 166.
25. D. J. Wiseman, "Law and Order in Old Testament Times," *Vox Evangelica* 8 (1973): 5–21.

The parallels between the laws of Hammurabi and biblical law are obvious and important, but not exact. When the LORD introduced the law for his people he often used categories and provisions of law that would have been very familiar to the people before the revelation at Sinai. Yet there are no ancient Near Eastern debt-slave laws that call for the kind of kinship and benevolence found in Deuteronomy 15:12–18 and Leviticus 25:39–43, 47–55. Though the Edict of Ammisaduqa (1646–1626 B.C.), an Old Babylonian successor to Hammurabi, has some debt-slave release laws, the style and function of this kind of document were very different from that of the law collections.[26] Edicts were not permanent law, but a temporary one-time selective righting of the disruptive economic imbalances of the society that had built up over a period of time, leading to oppressive circumstances and therefore public dissatisfaction with the system (a sort of periodic safety valve release). In other words, this was real law, but not a permanent monumental law-code like a collection of laws. Law collections were intended to be relatively comprehensive and to stand for extended periods of time. Edicts were not. Therefore, the slave release laws in this edict reflect the release of selected groups of people who had fallen into debt-slavery.

Ritual Legislations

The Hittite "Instructions for Temple Officials," for example, provide helpful background for cultic legislations of clean and unclean animals and other purity laws.[27] "Every bit of the loaves, the beer (and) the wine keep in the temple. Let no one appropriate for himself a sacrificial loaf of the god (or) a thin loaf. Let no one pour out beer (or) wine from the cup. Devote every bit of it to the god."[28]

---

26. See the discussion and bibliography for such edicts in Chirichigno, *Debt-Slavery in Israel and the Ancient Near East,* JSOTSup 141 (Sheffield: Sheffield Academic Press, 1993), 57–60; and H. Olivier, "The Periodicity of the *mēšarum* again," in *Text and Context: Old Testament and Semitic Studies for F. C. Fensham,* JSOTSup 48, ed. W. Claassen (Sheffield: Sheffield Academic Press, 1988), 227–235.

27. For discussion of details and bibliography, see J. Milgrom, *Leviticus 1–16,* Anchor Bible (New York: Doubleday, 1991), 349–56.

28. *ANET,* 208.

This quote applies to concerns of sanctity. What belongs to the god must not be taken from the god. This is basic to the understanding of the biblical guilt offering (see Lev. 5:14–6:7), where the issue is not contamination of the temple environment but the desecration of what is dedicated to God (i.e., taking something that is sacred and devoted to God and using it for common human consumption). Of course, there are also many differences between the ancient Near Eastern texts and the Israelites regarding sacrifice, especially the Mesopotamian focus on the care and feeding of the gods.[29]

How to Interpret Law

A genre sensitive approach to the interpretation of the legal texts of the Old Testament takes the following points into consideration. These principles of interpretation are arranged partially by priority and partially by logical procedure.

Guidelines for Interpretation

1. *Observe the context within the canon.* The canonical literary context is important. Understanding why the law being studied is located where it is may contribute to a better understanding of the law.

2. *Note the style of the law.* Is it a categorical assertion (apodictic law) or is it for a specific situation (case law)? What subgenre does it fit into with regard to form and content?

3. *Examine the grammar of the law* for that may carry further significance for the internal arrangement of the collection and categories of legal thought. This can help to distinguish one main sec-

---

29. See W. W. Hallo, *The Book of the People,* BJS 225 (Atlanta: Scholars Press, 1991), 64–65 and the literature cited there. For parallels to the biblical cult, see Milgrom, *Leviticus 1–16,* 1158–1163. For a survey of the rationale and moral standards of law and the cult in Israel as it compares to ancient Mesopotamian law and cult, see K. van der Toorn, *Sin and Sanction in Israel and Mesopotamia: A Comparative Study* (Netherlands: Van Gorcum, 1985).

tion of laws from another as well as subsidiary clauses from the others within a series.

4. *Compare laws in the biblical text with one another.* For example, the debt-slave laws in Exodus 21:1–11 have parallels in Deuteronomy 15:12–18 and Leviticus 25:39–43 and 47–55.

5. *Look for parallels with the ancient Near Eastern literature,* after paying close attention to inner-biblical parallels. The analogues in the biblical world are valuable especially when the laws assume that the reader is aware of this extra-biblical material. This is especially important for ritual legislation.

6. *Seek to determine the meanings of words, phrases, clauses, sentences, and paragraphs.* In some cases certain words or phrases are pivotal to the meaning of the passage.

Understanding the Laws for Debt-slavery

Exodus 21:2–11 is a good example of how Old Testament law can be foreign and at times even repulsive to modern standards. In this passage if a Hebrew owed a debt to a fellow Hebrew that could not be paid, he or she could become a slave in order to pay off the debt. The laws for debt-slavery stand at the beginning of the ordinances section of the Book of the Covenant and are representative of the legislative style of case law in the Pentateuch.[30]

The case structure of the law is clear and its organization explicit. Both verses 2 and 7 begin with the standard introduction to legislative main clauses. Moreover, each of the sections (21:2–6 and 7–11) is subdivided into subsidiary clauses where the conditions change but the main subject stays the same. The first section deals with the release of male debt-slaves, and the second section defines the issues of release for female debt-slaves brought in specifically for marriage purposes. Moreover, the laws are shaped into a chiasm with freedom at the beginning and end and permanent slave status in the middle (at the end of the first section and beginning of the second).

---

30. For recent discussion of research on this section of laws, see especially Chirichigno, *Debt-Slavery in Israel and the Ancient Near East,* 186–255; and J. M. Sprinkle, *"The Book of the Covenant": A Literary Approach,* JSOTSup 174 (Sheffield: JSOT Press, 1994), 50–72.

In the case of marriage to a slave woman, the commitment was clear, and the woman was not put in the position of automatic release in the seventh year for obvious reasons—it would dissolve the marriage. But the law also goes on to protect her from abuse and neglect. In other words, the main clause states the case if the marriage works out well, while the remainder of the section deals with situations that are less than ideal. The law in 21:2–6 falls into the category of primary law.[31] No remedy is being prescribed for a wrong, but the rights and duties of the slave are delineated.

The debt-slave laws elsewhere in the Pentateuch clarify further the intended spirit of debt-slavery in ancient Israel. Deuteronomy 15:12–18 points to its benevolent nature and Leviticus 25:39–43, 47–55 emphasizes the lack of harshness with which the institution was to be characterized in Israel. As it stands, the original law in Exodus 21:1–6 is very close to those in the laws of Hammurabi, except that Hammurabi has no exhortations to benevolence and lack of harshness such as in Leviticus and Deuteronomy.[32] Hammurabi's laws 115–116 deal with the natural or unnatural death of the debt-slave, and law 119 makes provision for the redemption of a slave-wife who has borne children to her original master. But this is not found in Leviticus 25:39–43, 47–55 and Deuteronomy 15:12–18. Furthermore, since Hammurabi limited debt-slavery to three years and Exodus 21:2 refers to a six-year period, claims about Old Testament superiority must be stated cautiously.

The distinction between native and foreign slaves in Leviticus 25:44–46 is also found in Hammurabi's laws.[33] It seems that in Babylonia one could have native property slaves (sometimes called chattel slaves), but for a Hebrew to own another Hebrew as permanent property is forbidden in Israel according to the Leviticus passage. The LORD was creating a covenant community in which the overall kinship mentality prevented this. As far as debt-slavery is concerned, it was to be handled in a way that amounted to a "bankruptcy" procedure for those with insurmountable finan-

---

31. In spite of arguments to the contrary, it is clearly casuistic (Sprinkle, *"The Book of the Covenant"*, 66–67); see Patrick, "Casuistic Law," 180–82.
32. See the full discussion of comparisons and contrasts in Chirichigno, *Debt-Slavery in Israel and the Ancient Near East*, 218–26.
33. See, e.g., *ANET*, 177 paragraphs 280–81.

cial problems. This was to be a productive, mutually beneficial, and benevolent way of resolving the situation.

Care needs to be exercised with the graduated penalty laws in Exodus 21:20–21, 26–27, 32. They apparently apply to property slaves, not debt-slaves.[34] The laws of Hammurabi also have graduated penalty laws for property slaves (as opposed to debt-slaves), but in that case the recompense was always paid to the owner of the slave, not the slave himself (cf. only Exod. 21:32).[35] The Israelites could own foreign slaves (either those from the nations around or from among the sojourners and aliens in Israel) and pass them on as part of their childrens' inheritance. However, in Israel even these slaves had certain rights that were to protect them from abuse and neglect. Under certain conditions they could receive recompense for injury (e.g., Exod. 21:20, 26–27). They were to have the full benefit of the sabbath rest (see Exod. 20:10, Deut. 5:14, Lev. 25:6) and at least most of the major festal offerings (Deut. 12.12, 18; 16:11, 14). Moreover, property slaves that had escaped from foreign masters and made their way to Israel were given sanctuary and allowed to live freely in the land (Deut. 23:15–16).[36]

The *placement* of Exodus 21:2–11 is striking. For the debt-slave laws to be at the beginning of this very important section of laws is conspicuous both historically and theologically. No other ancient Near Eastern law collection begins with slave laws. "Exodus 21 begins with servitude, just as does the prologue to the Decalogue in 20:2, in order to develop the central theme of the book of Exodus, deliverance from bondage."[37] The theme of the exodus shows up at the beginning of the laws, not just at the beginning of

---

34. Chirichigno, *Debt-Slavery in Israel*, 145–85.

35. See, e.g., the laws of Hammurabi (paragraphs 199, 213–14, 219, 252, etc.), and the surrounding laws for the contrasted treatment of a free man of standing or commoner (*ANET*, 174–76).

36. P. C. Craigie, *The Book of Deuteronomy*, NICOT (Grand Rapids: Eerdmans, 1976), 300–301.

37. Sprinkle, *"The Book of the Covenant,"* 62. If Craigie's view that the Israelites were previously under a slavery "covenant" to the Egyptians is correct, then this placement of debt-slave release laws might have carried even more impact for the first generation of the Israelites; see Craigie, *The Book of Deuteronomy*, 79–83.

the historical account in the Book of Exodus. Furthermore, the parallel debt-slave law in Deuteronomy 15:12–18 makes this historical and theological connection explicit: "Remember that you were slaves in Egypt and the LORD your God redeemed you. That is why I give you this command today" (v. 15). Since they were a nation of redeemed slaves, it would not be ethical for them to re-enslave one another (see the rebuke for this in Jer. 34).

While the debt-slave laws are no longer physically applicable, there is theological application for those attentive to genre. The exodus and the deliverance from slavery reappear throughout Scripture as reminders of the LORD's commitment to a *relationship* between himself and his people, as in a covenant. (Today, some underscore the importance of the exodus by calling it the "resurrection" of the Old Testament.) Since laws are part of the Mosaic covenant, Exodus 21 needs to be read in connection to parallel legal portions (such as Deut. 15) as well as to various speeches in Deuteronomy where the phrase "redeemed out of the house of slavery" appears.

In this light, the primacy of the slave laws in terms of their placement is a twofold reminder. First, it is meant to foster compassion for those in subservient positions (the Hebrews were not to forget what slavery was all about). Second, it is meant to encourage appreciation for the act of deliverance that freed the Hebrews from slavery. Such meditations on the imagery of the exodus were utilized by New Testament authors (see Acts 7:36; 1 Cor. 10:1–2; Heb. 3:16–17; 8:9; 11:29). Christians today will enhance their understanding of how the LORD works through the Old Testament imagery of the debt-slave laws as they relate to the Mosaic covenant.

Conclusion

Since the Mosaic law collections are a part of the Mosaic covenant, the study of the literary forms of law and ritual legislation must be preceded by a study of covenant. A covenant defines a relationship and has stipulations and obligations for one or both parties in the covenant. For correct interpretation of law, therefore, it is essential to recognize the connection between covenant and law: Without covenant there is no law. In the Old Testament, law consists of the stipulations of God's covenant with Israel. Though many laws may seem foreign and perhaps bizarre by modern standards, they served in a very real way to reinforce the Mosaic covenant by physically or visibly reminding the Israelites of their commitment.

The question, Do the laws in the Old Testament apply to Christians today? is asked frequently by those who are serious about studying the whole Bible. One hermeneutical approach concludes that there are universal laws applicable for all cultures and times, and that there are culture-bound laws applicable only to Israel. Thus, application for today only involves the universal laws. Culture-bound laws can be ignored. But this approach proves impossible, since there is no evidence in the text that the original authors ever intended a distinction between universal and culture-bound laws.

A different hermeneutical approach is needed. From what Jesus suggested in the Sermon on the Mount—that the Old Testament law is applicable in the New Covenant—it becomes evident that the commitment presupposed in the law for the Israelites is a much more serious matter for Christians than most realize. In fact, the very nature of law as a genre suggests this. For unlike other genres, law exemplifies commitment to a relationship. While the function of other genres is to advise, teach, acknowledge God's attributes, or call people to repentance, the function of the genre of law is to confirm and illustrate (both for self and for the world) the *value* of the relationship between God and his people.

The interaction of the New Testament with Old Testament law indicates that the law of the Mosaic covenant applies under the new covenant, though not in the same way. Believers today are not bound to follow the ceremonial law prohibiting the mixing of different kinds of cloth in garments, but they are bound to the significance of that prohibition: purity. For Old Testament saints, the prohibition was a physical reminder of their commitment. For New Testament saints, the prohibition is a spiritual reminder of their commitment that carries thorough implications for how they live personally and relationally in this world. The former was external (with internal significance); the latter is internal and motivational. To be pure on the inside is even more challenging than not mixing different kinds of cloth on the outside.

As spiritual descendants of Abraham, Christians are bound to study all of the Old Testament law, in particular the *reason* for the law. From that Old Testament law comes a wealth of imagery that underscores the values that affirm the Christian's relationship with God under the new covenant. Christians have communion and baptism as physical reminders of Christ's work, but they need to see the significance of the regulations of the Old Testament law as illustrations of true commitment in a covenant-relationship with God. Covenant is a bond—not a bond of glue or nails or rivets, but a *relational* bond. And a relational bond is strengthened by tangible expressions of that bond.[38]

Recommended Reading

Covenant

Baltzer, Klaus. *The Covenant Formulary in Old Testament, Jewish, and Early Christian Writings.* Translated from German by David E. Green. Philadelphia: Fortress, 1971. An often-referred-to classic study of the structure of biblical covenant texts and their relationship to ANE treaties.

Davidson, Robert. "Covenant Ideology in Ancient Israel." In *The World of Ancient Israel,* edited by R. E. Clements, 323–347. Cambridge: Cambridge University Press, 1989. An astute summary of the modern scholarly debate about covenants in the Bible in light of ANE analogues and inner-biblical patterns.

Kitchen, Kenneth A. "The Fall and Rise of Covenant, Law and Treaty." *TynBul* 40 (1989): 118–35. A conservative response by a well-known scholar to some recent trends among scholars to view covenant as a late development in Israel.

McCarthy, Dennis J. *Treaty and Covenant: A Study in Form in the Ancient Oriental Documents and in the Old Testament.* 2d ed. AnBib 21A. Rome: Biblical Institute Press, 1981. The most impor-

---

38. It is a pleasure to dedicate this chapter to my friend and colleague, Dr. Richard Patterson. Although we never taught together on the same faculty, his example of serious evangelical Old Testament scholarship and his displays of kindness and encouragement to me as a younger scholar have been a stimulus to my own scholarly endeavors and service to the LORD.

tant treatment of the relationship between ANE treaties and biblical covenants. Some of the texts not found in ANET are translated in the appendix of this book.

Tadmor, Hayim. "Treaty and Oath in the Ancient Near East." In *Humanizing America's Iconic Book,* edited by Gene M. Tucker and Douglas A. Knight. Chico, Calif.: Scholars Press, 1982. A very important article rethinking the comparisons between the OT covenants and ANE treaties based on careful analysis of terminology and the character of texts.

Weinfeld, Moshe. "The Covenant of Grant in the Old Testament and in the Ancient Near East." *JAOS* 90 (1970): 184–203. A heavily quoted article noted for distinguishing between ANE grants versus treaties and suggesting that certain Old Testament covenants follow the pattern of grants rather than treaties, especially the Abrahamic and Davidic covenants.

————. "The Loyalty Oath in the Ancient Near East." *UF* 8 (1976): 379–414. The authors attempt to push the discussion of biblical covenants in still another direction based on another set of ANE analogues.

Law

Jackson, B. S. "Ideas of Law and Legal Administration: A Semiotic Approach." In *The World of Ancient Israel,* edited by R. E. Clements, 185-202. Cambridge: Cambridge University Press, 1989. A very good discussion of the nature of the biblical law internally as well as in relation to ANE texts.

Mendenhall, George E. "Ancient Oriental and Biblical Law." In *Biblical Archaeology Reader,* 3-24. Vol. 3, 1954. Reprint, New York: Doubleday, 1970. A well-known study of the forms of biblical law and the relationship between Old Testament covenant and law.

Patrick, Dale. *Old Testament Law,* Atlanta: John Knox, 1985. The most readable overall summary of the modern scholarly treatment of the Old Testament law, written for students, not scholars.

Paul, Shalom. *Studies in the Book of the Covenant in the Light of Cuneiform and Biblical Law.* VTSup 18. Leiden: E. J. Brill, 1970. Now a classic in the field of the comparative study of the laws in the Book of the Covenant.

Sprinkle, Joe M. *"The Book of the Covenant": A Literary Approach.* JSOTSup 174; Sheffield: Sheffield Academic Press, 1994. A recent and very helpful discussion of Exodus 19–24 primarily from a literary rather than a legal point of view.

Weinfeld, Moshe. "The Decalogue: Its Significance, Uniqueness, and Place in Israel's Tradition," In *Religion and Law: Biblical-Judaic and Islamic Perspectives*, edited by Edwin B. Firmage, et al. 3-47. Winona Lake, Indiana: Eisenbrauns, 1990. A major article reviewing the importance of the Decalgue in biblical covenant and law.

Westbrook, Raymond. *Studies in Biblical and Cuneiform Law.* CahRB 26. Paris: J. Gabalda, 1988. An introduction and series of focused studies on the comparative relationship between biblical and cuneiform (i.e., ancient Mesopotamian) law by one of the major scholars in the field today.

Cult

Anderson, Gary A. *Sacrifices and Offerings in Ancient Israel: Studies in their Social and Political Importance.* HSM 41. Atlanta: Scholars Press, 1987. One of the many recent monographs on ancient Israelite sacrifice as it relates to its world.

Cohen, Mark E. *The Cultic Calendars of the Ancient Near East.* Bethesda, Md.: CDL Press, 1993. A very scholarly treatment of the different calendars of ritual activities and related festivals in the ANE from Mesopotamia to the Levant.

Haran, Menahem. *Temples and Temple-Service in Ancient Israel: An Inquiry into Biblical Cult Phenomena and the Historical Setting of the Priestly School.* Winona Lake, Ind.: Eisenbrauns, 1985.

A reprint with corrections of this highly regarded 1978 work covering temples, the priesthood, centralization of the cult, rituals, symbols, and festivals.

Toorn, K. van der. *Sin and Sanction in Israel and Mesopotamia: A Comparative Study.* The Netherlands: Van Gorcum, 1985. A treatment of major issues in the law and the cult from the comparative point of view in which the author concludes that the moral standards of the OT are not superior to those of the ancient Babylonians.

7

ORACLES OF SALVATION
Willem A. VanGemeren

The fabric of the Old and New Testaments is held together by a single thread: salvation. Without this common theme of promise, blessing, and salvation, the books of the Bible would never have been stitched together into the tapestry now recognized as God's revelation. God is sovereign and his gracious deliverance is expressed in many ways: forgiveness of sin, justification, sanctification, and deliverance from difficulties. All of these things can be summed up in the word *salvation*. Salvation is any act of God's goodness and care, of his justice and fairness, of his grace in answering the prayers of sinners.

One facet of salvation is *promise*,[1] a prominent concept especially in the Old Testament. Representative of God's promises is his pledge to the patriarchs:[2] "I will establish my covenant as an

---

1. For the progress of salvation from Eden to the New Jerusalem along redemptive-historical lines, see Willem A. VanGemeren, *The Progress of Redemption: The Story of Salvation from Creation to the New Jerusalem* (Grand Rapids: Zondervan, 1988).

2. For the emphasis on promise, see Walter C. Kaiser, Jr., *Toward an Old Testament Theology* (Grand Rapids: Zondervan, 1978); see also Claus Westermann, *The Promises to the Fathers: Studies on the Patriarchal Narratives*, trans. David E. Green (Philadelphia: Fortress, 1980).

everlasting covenant between me and you and your descendants after you for the generations to come, to be your God and the God of your descendants after you" (Gen. 17:7). Guaranteeing the promise with his presence, this pledge reassured the patriarchs in their sojournings and the Israelites during their oppression in Egypt. Promise is the assurance that the LORD will deliver his people and renew his blessing. The promise of God extends his goodness from generation to generation, as he said to Isaac, "I am the God of your father Abraham. Do not be afraid, for I am with you" (Gen. 26:24).

God is also the source of *blessing*. This facet of salvation assures his creatures of vitality and well-being. Blessing is a situation in which life is meaningful and in which people flourish. In this state they experience the fulfillment of their basic needs (food, drink, shelter, security), the enjoyment of life, a sense of accomplishment in employment, and a happy family life. Blessing is the assurance that the LORD will maintain the experience of well-being for his people. The theme of blessing is especially prominent in Genesis.[3] The book opens with God's blessing of all creatures, particularly humans (chap. 1), and ends with Jacob blessing his sons in Egypt (Gen. 49).

The full application of God's promises and the extension of his blessing is a hope of better things ahead in the future.[4] The saints in the Old Testament, as well as those since the coming of Jesus, have lived with the hope for a new age in which there will be no more pain and anguish and in which the goodness of God will embrace them forevermore. This expectation of a new state of harmonious and blessed existence is referred to as "the city of God" in the Book of Hebrews: "For he [Abraham] was looking forward to the city with foundations, whose architect and builder is God" (Heb. 11:10; cf. 13:14).

---

3. A. P. Ross, *Creation and Blessing: A Guide to the Study and Exposition of the Book of Genesis* (Grand Rapids: Baker, 1988); Claus Westermann, "The Blessing God and Creation," in *What Does the Old Testament Say About God?* ed. Friedemann W. Golka (Atlanta: John Knox, 1979), 39–52.

4. This theme is more fully developed in my work on the prophets: *Interpreting the Prophetic Word* (Grand Rapids: Zondervan, 1990), see especially 88–92.

The patriarchal narratives in Genesis reveal how God's chosen people lived with the reality of adversity even though God had promised blessing. In the absence of fulfillment, they struggled with God as they awaited the realization of his promise (Gen. 12:2–3). Yet they knew that God is faithful, even if the fulfillment of promise is interrupted by the vagaries of life. Facing adversities, such as childlessness, they received comfort by a word of deliverance, such as the encouragement given to Abraham, "Do not be afraid, Abram. I am your shield, your very great reward" (Gen. 15:1). This word was in the form of an *oracle of salvation.*

In the Book of Exodus the Israelites cried out in their pain and in the absence of God's blessing: "[They] groaned in their slavery and cried out, and their cry for help because of their slavery went up to God. God heard their groaning and he remembered his covenant with Abraham, with Isaac and with Jacob. So God looked on the Israelites and was concerned about them" (Exod. 2:23–25). God's answer came in the form of an oracle to Moses by the burning bush: "I will be with you. And this will be the sign to you that it is I who have sent you: When you have brought the people out of Egypt, you will worship God on this mountain" (Exod. 3:12).

Oracles—God's direct statements to his people—are common throughout the Old Testament. Oracles address individuals in a specific and present need, comfort them with a message of God's presence, and promise deliverance in the future. This is essential background for understanding the messages of the prophets.

What Makes Oracles of Salvation Unique

The prophetic oracles of salvation are continuous with God's earlier revelation to the patriarchs and to Moses. In the prophets, however, they are couched in a new context of the oracles of judgment. Unlike the earlier oracles of salvation, here the context is divine threatening, speaking about Israel's sin, breach of covenant, and the inevitable and imminent coming of the Day of the LORD.

Judgment was necessary. The malaise of each generation in Israel was the complacent belief that God was bound to his covenant, that he owed the people protection from their enemies, fulfillment of his promises, and an ultimate state of blessing. Although false prophets sought, by their own oracles of salvation, to advance a prosperity theology, true prophets continuously reminded the people that those who flaunted wickedness only deceived themselves if they expected deliverance (see Amos 5:18; Jer. 7:4, 10; 8:8–12). In the midst of these announcements of judgment are oracles of salvation.

At first glance, words of salvation are strangely out of place in the midst of such judgment. Yet it is precisely because of God's promises to the patriarchs and Moses that they are not out of place at all. Whereas they were previously part of the narratives of the struggles of the patriarchs or the bondage of Egypt, now they are set among announcements of judgment because of the people's breach of covenant. Since throughout the Old Testament God consistently sought to bring about salvation and blessing, the people's disobedience constitutes one more era in which this takes place. True prophets of God both afflict the comfortable and comfort the afflicted.

As part of the comfort, the prophets proclaimed an oracle of assurance that God had heard the prayers of his people. The prophetic words of salvation, whether in the historical narratives or in the prophetical writings, reveal two main parts:

- The *messenger formula*. The prophet authenticated his message by an appeal to the one who had sent him. Though the words were the human author's, they were God's in his power to fulfill the oracle. So it was common for the prophets to appeal to their position as messengers in stereotypical phrases, such as "for this is what the Lord, the God of Israel, says" or "thus says the Lord." Like oracles of salvation, announcements of judgment also begin with a messenger formula.

- A *word of salvation*. The word is an encouragement to the people not to be afraid by a reassurance of God's presence and of his intervention on their behalf. Announcements of judgment, on the other hand, follow the messenger formula with an accusation of wrongdoing followed by the consequences of such wrongdoing (judgment).

The function of oracles of salvation as a prophetic genre is to offer reassurance to the faithful that God hears and to affirm that God is committed to his promises. On the other hand, the function of announcements of judgment as a prophetic genre is either to proclaim judgment (in part so that people will know it comes from

God's sovereign hand) or to warn of judgment (to bring about repentance before judgment comes). As seen in Isaiah, Hosea, Zephaniah, and Habakkuk, prophets often include these two concerns side-by-side: justice together with mercy; judgment and the ending of the relationship together with ideas of cleansing, a remnant, and a new kingdom.

In addition to distinguishing between oracles of salvation and announcements of judgment, the oracles of salvation of the writing prophets need to be differentiated from those of the oral prophets (such as Elijah, who did not write a canonical book). In the historical books, the *oral* prophets address individuals during a time of crisis or threat (famine, political disturbance, war) and the narrative records the moment of fulfillment. Ahijah prophesied that the kingdom would be divided upon the death of Solomon. This happened when the northern tribes seceded, and Jeroboam, the recipient of the oracle, became king over these tribes. Its fulfillment is now a record of history and vindication of God's fidelity to his word. Similarly, in the story of Israel's conflict with the Arameans, an anonymous prophet encouraged the godless Ahab with an oracle of salvation: "This is what the LORD says: 'Do you see this vast army? I will give it into your hand today, and then you will know that I am the LORD'" (1 Kings 20:13). Ahab was victorious. On the other hand, the *writing* prophets usually address groups of people. They open up the eyes of faith to God's working out of his salvation in a more distant future as part of a series of interrelated events. Instead of a moment, there is a history of fulfillment.

Though oracles of salvation have distinctives that separate them from other kinds of prophecy, they are a composite of at least two subgenres, as borrowed and adapted by the prophets in composing oracles of salvation.[5] One subgenre, the *promise of salvation*, addresses the needs of the people by using the form of an oracle of assurance to an individual. Israel is thus treated as if it were a person. Such promises of salvation include: The reassurance of God's promise, the basis for the reassurance, and the future

---

5. See Claus Westermann, *Isaiah 40-66: A Commentary,* OTL trans. D. M. G. Stalker (Philadelphia: Westminster, 1969), 11–14; idem, *Prophetic Oracles of Salvation in the Old Testament,* trans. Keith Crim (Louisville: Westminster/Knox, 1991).

transformation from judgment to salvation or from sorrow to joy (though not necessarily in this order). For example:

Reassurance	"Do not be afraid, for I am with you;
Future transformation	I will bring your children from the east and gather you from the west. I will say to the north, 'Give them up!' and to the south, 'Do not hold them back.' Bring my sons from afar and my daughters from the ends of the earth—everyone who is called by my name,
Basis for reassurance	whom I created for my glory, whom I formed and made" (Isa. 43:5–7).

Another subgenre, the *proclamation of salvation*, responds to a communal lament and, in doing so, draws much of its language from lament. The proclamation reassures the people of God and gives them a basis of hope that God's future acts will relieve the present situation. Thus, the proclamation also has the three components of reassurance of God's promise, the basis for the reassurance, and the future transformation. In contrast to the assurance of salvation where the prophet comforts the people in their fear and calls them to look at God's past and present acts, the proclamation of salvation calls upon the people to look in faith to the *future* acts of salvation as the basis of comfort. For example:

Lament	"The poor and needy search for water, but there is none; their tongues are parched with thirst.
Reassurance	But I the LORD will answer them; I, the God of Israel, will not forsake them.
Future transformation	I will make rivers flow on barren heights, and springs within the valleys. I will turn the desert into pools of water, and the parched ground into springs. I will put in the desert the cedar and the acacia, the myrtle and the olive. I will set pines in the wasteland, the fir and the cypress together,
Reassurance	so that people may see and know, may consider and understand,

144

Basis for reassurance   that the hand of the LORD has done this, that the Holy One of Israel has created it" (Isa. 41:17–20).

The oracle of salvation is, in sum, a word from God that assures people of the validity of God's promise during a crisis and of his deliverance from an adverse situation. It is often introduced by a messenger formula like, "Thus says the LORD;" it offers reassurance to Israel by exhorting them not to be afraid (e.g., Isa. 41:14; Jer. 30:10); it affirms God's commitment to his promises; and it reiterates salvation as part of the promise. The salvation can be a victory from enemies, joy resulting from a new act of God, or a restoration of the chosen people to the promised land.

Where Oracles of Salvation Are Found

In the literature of the ancient Near East few formal parallels to oracles of salvation appear. The formula "fear not" is illustrated in an oracle concerning Esarhaddon, where the goddess Ishtar reassures him that the present problem will be alleviated:

> [Esarhad]don, king of the lands, fear not! That wind which blows against you—I need only say a word and I can bring it to an end. Your enemies . . . will flee even at your approach . . . I am Ishtar of Arbela! I shall lie in wait for your enemies. I shall give them to you. I, Ishtar of Arbela, will go before you and behind you. Fear not! . . . Fear not, Esarhaddon! I, the god Bel, am speaking to you . . . Sixty great gods are standing together with me and protect you . . . ranged for battle.[6]

A similar oracle is given to Ashurbanipal,

> The goddess Ishtar heard my anxious sighs and said, "Fear not!" and gave me confidence, (saying) . . . "Eat, drink wine, make merry, praise my divinity, while I go and accomplish that work to help you attain your heart's desire."[7]

Not only do Near Eastern oracles promise protection and victory, they also assure blessing. In a series of prophecies concerning rulers, the oracle promises that the people will experience adversity, but also blessing: "The temples of the gods [will be restored]

---

6. *ANET*3 605.
7. Ibid., 606.

. . . [There will be] (favorable) rain and light water in the land. The people who have experienced evil [will experience good]."[8]

The extra-biblical parallels differ from the prophetic oracles in the Bible, however. The prophets addressed the people at large, whereas the extra-biblical parallels pronounce oracles to individuals (kings).[9] Further, the oracles of salvation are a unique development in Israel in that the prophetic messages are not only grounded in a common heritage but are integrally related to each other. The individual oracles were collected and placed into a new context of a canonical writing, which in turn is a part of a prophetic corpus, and this corpus is related organically and canonically to the Law and to the Writings.

How to Interpret Oracles of Salvation

As is true for all of Scripture, the prophetic books reflect certain characteristics from the cultural, religious, and literary context in which they were written. For correct interpretation, the following principles will guide readers to an understanding of the content and context of the oracles of salvation.

Guidelines for Interpretation

1. *Be sensitive to the prophetic imagery.* Instead of giving a straightforward or analytical statement of salvation—as is often done by the oral prophets—oracles of salvation express God's word in images. These images challenge modern minds to connect text with text and image with image, and to discover a more holistic understanding of God's word. For example, Isaiah likens the exile to a wasteland or desert: "The fortress will be abandoned, the noisy city deserted; citadel and watchtower will become a wasteland forever" (Isa. 32:14; cf. 6:11; 27:10; 32:14). In contrast, restoration is likened to streams, a road, and to the renewal of the desert: "The desert and the parched land will be glad; the wilder-

---

8. Ibid., 607.

9. For a further discussion, see John H. Walton, *Ancient Israelite Literature in Its Cultural Context: A Survey of Parallels Between Biblical and Ancient Near Eastern Texts* (Grand Rapids: Zondervan, 1989) and Willem A. VanGemeren, *Interpreting the Prophetic Word* (Grand Rapids: Zondervan, 1990).

ness will rejoice and blossom. The burning sand will become a pool, the thirsty ground bubbling springs" (Isa. 35:1, 7a). This imagery vividly underscores the prophet's message of judgment and restoration.

2. *Relate the assurances of promises and blessing to God's previous commitments made with creation, Abraham, Moses, and David.* The background for interpretation must always be God's revelation of his promises. He assured Noah of his continued care for life, Abraham of his presence, protection, a faithful offspring, and a land; Moses of the consecration of an elect, holy, and royal people of God; and David of a dynasty and kingdom. Oracles are to be understood in relation to each other.

Oracles of salvation are not only based on God's previous commitments, they complement them. For instance, in the prophets God's promise of salvation is explained in the person of a Davidic ruler who will come in humility: "Rejoice greatly, O Daughter of Zion! Shout, Daughter of Jerusalem! See, your king comes to you, righteous and having salvation, gentle and riding on a donkey, on a colt, the foal of a donkey" (Zech. 9:9; cf. Isa. 42:1–4). And he will suffer vicariously (see Isa. 52:13–53:12). It is the prophets who reveal the inclusion of other nations in the promises and blessing of God. Though the prophets are ambivalent on the nature of that inclusion, they open the door to equal participation in the Davidic covenant (see Amos 9:12),[10] to prayer (see Isa. 56), to the worship of God (see Zeph. 2:11; Mal. 1:11), and to the kingdom of God (see Mic. 4:1–5; Zech. 8:20–23; 9:10).

Hence, the kingdom of God undergoes a universalization and the concept of the people of God an internalization. On the one hand, God's rule will be from shore to shore: "For the earth will be filled with the knowledge of the glory of the LORD" (Hab. 2:14; cf. Isa. 6:3). On the other hand, the subjects of his rule will undergo a spiritual transformation by which all whom the LORD has called have the Spirit of God in them, be they male or female, ex-

---

10. Walter C. Kaiser, Jr. speaks of the Davidic covenant as a "charter for humanity" in "The Blessing of David: The Charter for Humanity," in *F.S. Allis, The Law and the Prophets: Old Testament Studies Prepared in Honor of Oswald Thompson Allis,* John H. Skilton, ed. (Nutley NJ: Presbyterian and Reformed, 1974), 298–318.

alted or lowly, young or old, Jew or Gentile (see Joel 2:28–32). Consequently, the prophetic oracles anticipate the extension of the promises and of God's blessing beyond the promised land to a "new earth." The renewed state will be characterized by the Spirit of God and by true righteousness:

> . . . till the Spirit is poured upon us from on high,
>   and the desert becomes a fertile field,
>   and the fertile field seems like a forest.
> Justice will dwell in the desert
>   and righteousness live in the fertile field.
> The fruit of righteousness will be peace;
>   the effect of righteousness will be quietness and confidence for-
> ever.
> My people will live in peaceful dwelling places,
>   in secure homes,
>   in undisturbed places of rest.
> How blessed you will be. (Isa. 32:15–20; cf. 65:17–24)

The wicked, however, will not share in these visions and their fulfillment. The prophetic oracles open up deliverance for the meek and the humble, but close it off to the proud and the arrogant: "They will neither harm nor destroy on all my holy mountain says the LORD" (Isa. 65:25; cf. 11:9).

3. *Examine the dual background of the exile and restoration of the exiles to the land.* The prophets comforted people who cried out for God's deliverance in the context of judgment and affliction. Isaiah 40–55 forms a collection of oracles of salvation, introduced by the familiar words, "Comfort, comfort my people, says your God" (40:1). These words of consolation proclaim a grand future. The exile is not the end! Beyond the exile is an era of renewal and transformation.

When the LORD revoked Israel's privileges and removed his grace, the people of the covenant were disgraced and trampled by the nations: "The gates of Zion will lament and mourn; destitute, she will sit on the ground" (Isa. 3:26). The exile was an era of humiliation and an expression of the Day of the LORD in history (see Isa. 3:13–14).

The prophet's proclamation of salvation in Isaiah 4 is a reversal of disgrace and a window into the great and glorious future. Instead of disgrace and shame, the people will enjoy a renewed status of beauty and glory. Instead of being judged unworthy of his grace and outcasts of his city, the LORD will cleanse, forgive, and sanctify: "Those who are left in Zion, who remain in Jerusalem, will be called holy, all who are recorded among the living in Jerusalem. The LORD will wash away the filth of the women of Zion" (vv. 3–4). Instead of leaving his people without security, he assures them of his care and protection in the imagery of the cloud and the fire that comforted Israel in the wilderness: "It will be a shelter and shade from the heat of the day, and a refuge and hiding place from the storm and rain" (v. 6).

4. *Interpret the prophetic oracles from the perspective of transformation.* It is a transformation that extends to all areas: the people, leadership, and the earth. The people will once again be humble, faithful, and Spirit-filled. The reality of salvation will transform the exile ("former things") into a "new" era of divine activity: "See, the former things have taken place, and new things I declare; before they spring into being I announce them to you" (Isa. 42:9). In the imagery of a path through the wilderness, he invites his audience to see the salvation of the LORD: "See, I am doing a new thing! Now it springs up; do you not perceive it? I am making a way in the desert and streams in the wasteland" (Isa. 43:19).

The transformation extends to the leadership. The prophet points in the direction of a Child-King, a descendant of David. He will be a faithful and righteous King (see Isa. 11:3–4) and will extend and establish the kingdom of God: "Of the increase of his government and peace there will be no end. He will reign on David's throne and over his kingdom, establishing and upholding it with justice and righteousness from that time on and forever" (Isa. 9:7). This new era of salvation will bring with it an era of unparalleled blessing and glory: "In that day the Root of Jesse will stand as a banner for the peoples; the nations will rally to him, and his place of rest will be glorious" (Isa. 11:10). His kingdom will be global extending its benefits to Israel/Judah (vv. 12–16) and to the nations (v. 10). Life on earth will change radically.

5. *Understand fulfillment of oracles as a process.* The operation of God in redemptive history reveals an inner connection among his acts of deliverance. The connections are organic as well as progressive. Each act reveals more about the nature of the fulfillment.

In the progress of fulfillment, the meaning of the oracle becomes increasingly clear.

Unlike the oracle spoken to individuals, fulfillment is progressive in time, not bound to a specific moment in time. Thus, God spoke to Hezekiah during the siege of Jerusalem: "This year you will eat what grows by itself, and the second year what springs from that. But in the third year sow and reap, plant vineyards and eat their fruit" (2 Kings 19:29). God also said: "I will rejoice over Jerusalem and take delight in my people; the sound of weeping and of crying will be heard in it no more" (Isa. 65:19). The latter oracle of salvation assures the people of God of a transformation that began with the restoration from exile. The sorrow of the exile was transformed into sounds of joy when God restored the people (see Ps. 126).[11] The restoration from exile is a stage in the progress of redemption and is an integral part of the subsequent developments: the coming of Christ, the Church age, the establishment of the Kingdom of Christ, and the new heaven and earth. In each era, the godly have experienced a token of the reality of God's presence to which the prophet witnesses: "For they will be a people blessed by the LORD, they and their descendants with them. Before they call I will answer; while they are still speaking I will hear" (Isa. 65:23–24).

Thus, it is better to speak of fulfillment as a process, rather than a single moment of fulfillment, or even moments of fulfillment. Fulfillment has many stages, and each stage is related to the progress of redemption. It is like the flow of a river in its constancy of movement. But like a river it may reveal periods of sudden movement or periods of stagnancy. The history of redemption has many distinctive moments of divine activity in history: restoration from exile, Jesus' coming, the Holy Spirit, the Gentile mission, and the Church age.

6. *Ask what response the prophet was eliciting.* Oracles of salvation do not call for comparing newspapers with Bibles and getting lost in the details of the fulfillment. By trying to figure out how a particular prophecy fits within a chronological sequence, interpreters neglect the prophetic fusion of time with eternity. This fusion

---

11. Willem A. VanGemeren, "Psalms," in *The Expositor's Commentary on the Bible*, ed. F. E. Gaebelein (Grand Rapids: Zondervan, 1991), 789–92.

is resolved in the new heaven and earth when promise is fulfilled and when the state of blessing will be reality. However, any stage before the eternal state needs to be seen as a token of the reality. The "already" is an anticipation of the "not yet." The prophecy regarding the new heaven and earth is more than a chronological goal, or a prophecy pertaining to a particular era in redemptive history, or even a description of a millennial kingdom. It is eschatological; nevertheless, the language of God's presence is very realistic and applicable to all epochs of redemptive history: "Before they call I will answer; while they are still speaking I will hear" (Isa. 65:24).

Rather than providing a chronology of the future, the proclamation invites a response in the present. The salvation being provided is gracious and free, but people must respond to God's free offer. On the one hand, the sinner must repent by returning to God as the sole source of goodness and blessing, by turning away from his evil way of life, and by looking at his own "good" acts as corrupt. These two aspects are a part of Isaiah's proclamation: "Seek the LORD while he may be found; call on him while he is near. Let the wicked forsake his way and the evil man his thoughts. Let him turn to the LORD, and he will have mercy on him, and to our God, for he will freely pardon" (Isa. 55:6–5; cf. 64:6–7).

On the other hand, the message is to be proclaimed loudly and widely. All must hear that the LORD is just and that he cares for his own. The witnesses speak of God's involvement in the history of redemption, of his rule, and of his ultimate sovereignty over all nations: "Do not tremble, do not be afraid. Did I not proclaim this and foretell it long ago? You are my witnesses. Is there any God besides me? No, there is no other Rock; I know not one" (Isa. 44:8; cf. 43:9–12; 55:4).

7. *Look for the complete fulfillment of the oracles of salvation in the coming of Jesus.* The "gospel" of the Old Testament sets the stage for the gospel of the kingdom in the New Testament. Salvation is the subject of the Old Testament as God's people received assurances of such salvation and enjoyed the benefits of God's acts

151

of deliverance. The Old Testament is God's record of his fidelity. In the coming of Jesus, salvation is made more sure:

> Concerning this salvation, the prophets, who spoke of the grace that was to come to you, searched intently and with the greatest care, trying to find out the time and circumstances to which the Spirit of Christ in them was pointing when he predicted the sufferings of Christ and the glories that would follow. It was revealed to them that they were not serving themselves but you, when they spoke of the things that have now been told you by those who have preached the gospel to you by the Holy Spirit sent from heaven. Even angels long to look into these things. (1 Pet. 1:10–12)

The benefits of Christ's rule are already shared by all who are new creatures in Jesus Christ, but the fulfillment of their heritage awaits his coming in glory when he will establish his kingdom and renew all things. Then the blessings of God will overtake them. The promises will be theirs when their sorrow is forever exchanged for joy:

> On this mountain he will destroy
>   the shroud that enfolds all peoples,
> the sheet that covers all nations;
>   he will swallow up death forever.
> The Sovereign LORD will wipe away the tears
>   from all faces;
> he will remove the disgrace of his people
>   from all the earth. (Isa. 25:7–8)

Reading Jeremiah for More than Judgment

Jeremiah is often thought of as either the weeping prophet for his lamentations, or the prophet of doom and gloom for his many announcements of judgment. But words of hope in the form of oracles of salvation can be found in the midst of passages that speak of accusation and destruction. For instance, in the heart of the book, Jehoiachin (also called Jeconiah or Coniah) was given the severest of judgmental prophecies (see Jer. 22:24–30), false prophets were reprimanded (chap. 23), and captivity was determined (chaps. 25 and 27). Throughout these chapters, though, words of hope can be found, such as the prophecy of the righteous branch (23:5) and the letter of encouragement to those in exile (chap. 29).

Jeremiah 30, a collection of oracles bookended with the phrase "the days to come" (vv. 3, 24), continues to intertwine judgment and salvation. Though the chapter opens with a brief encouragement of ultimate restoration (v. 3), this restoration is accomplished only through acute pain (vv. 6–7). The idea of punishment resurfaces in verses 14–15, yet the focus of the chapter lies in oracles of salvation such as verses 10–11. It is as if the prophet is providing poetic images of the salvation promised in the letter in chapter 29.

> "So do not fear, O Jacob my servant;
>   do not be dismayed, O Israel,"declares the LORD.
> "I will surely save you out of a distant place,
>   your descendants from the land of their exile.
> Jacob will again have peace and security,
>   and no one will make him afraid.
> I am with you and will save you,"
>   declares the LORD (Jer. 30:10–11a).

This oracle evidences all of the major characteristics of oracles of salvation, including a *messenger formula* affirming its authenticity (the phrase "declares the LORD") and a *word of salvation* ("I will surely save you . . ."). The end of the oracle is marked by another messenger formula, introducing a new oracle.

Given to people in need, oracles include two elements of content: They comfort the people with a message of God's presence, and they promise deliverance. Comfort is given through the opening phrase of reassurance ("do not fear"), while promise is seen in an eschatological blessing: deliverance from bondage, return to the land of promise, and a state of blessing ("peace and security," with "no one to make afraid"). In terms of a more specific structure, this oracle is a *promise of salvation*. The form of this subgenre expresses its oracle to an individual, and indeed Israel is addressed here as Jacob, a servant. The elements of reassurance ("do not fear"), the basis of reassurance ("I am with you"), and future transformation are all present even in this brief text.

At least two literary conventions were utilized by Jeremiah. To bring the mind of the listener back to the patriarchs (and the promises made to them), the name *Jacob* is used twice. This repetition aids in relating the assurances of promises and blessings to God's prior commitments (made with creation, Abraham, Jacob, Moses, etc.). At the same time, another literary device emphasizes the promise of deliverance by beginning and ending the oracle with the same term (inclusion): "I will surely *save* you . . . I am with you and will *save* you."

In the context of all of Jeremiah 30, the dual background of exile and restoration is evident. Discipline is necessary for the people of God (vv. 11–17), yet restoration is promised (vv. 18–21). This transformation ("restoration" and "healing," v. 17) is a *process*, and the fulfillment of such promise should not be looked for in one moment of history. As tangible fulfillments of the promise grow, people engage in songs of thanksgiving, experience growth in numbers, and bear children who grow in a context of security and even prosperity (vv. 19–20). The process includes the rise of a new leader, whose origin is found within the community (v. 21). He is not an outsider who is thrust upon Israel.

Conclusion

The oracle of salvation has a long history. It spans the testaments with its wonderful message that God has not abandoned his people. The oracle is God's word that he is present, that he sees, that he cares, and that he will transform adversity into something good for his people. It lifts up the eye of faith to the one who has made the promise and has assured his blessing on all who have put their faith in him. In the coming of Jesus Christ, the promises of God find their confirmation "For no matter how many promises God has made, they are 'Yes' in Christ. And so through him the 'Amen' is spoken by us to the glory of God" (2 Cor. 1:20). In Jesus Christ we are richly blessed and have received the Holy Spirit as a guarantee of our inheritance: "And you also were included in Christ when you heard the word of truth, the gospel of your salvation. Having believed, you were marked in him with a seal, the promised Holy Spirit, who is a deposit guaranteeing our inheritance until the redemption of those who are God's possession—to the praise of his glory" (Eph. 1:13–14).

As long as we are waiting for the coming of the LORD Jesus, the oracles of salvation encourage us to persevere in faith, to endure in the hope of our glorious calling, and to persist in our love for God and our fellow-humans. Jesus is coming and when he comes he will usher in the fullness of our redemption, "an inheritance that can never perish, spoil or fade—kept in heaven for you, who through faith are shielded by God's power until the coming of the salvation that is ready to be revealed in the last time. In this you greatly rejoice, though now for a little while you may have had to suffer grief in all kinds of trials" (1 Pet. 1:3b–6).

Recommended Reading

Scott, R. B. Y. *The Relevance of the Prophets*. Rev. ed. New York: Macmillan, 1968. Though an older source, chapter 5 ("The Prophetic Word") is a good introduction to forms of prophetic oracles.

VanGemeren, Willem A. *Interpreting the Prophetic Word*. Grand Rapids: Zondervan, 1990. The author opens up the relevance of the prophets by developing a hermeneutic of progressive fulfillment, connecting the prophets to the New Testament and to the contemporary situation.

Westermann, Claus. *Prophetic Oracles of Salvation in the Old Testament*. Translated by Keith Crim. Louisville: Westminster/Knox, 1991. A helpful review and categorization of oracles along strict form-critical lines of investigation.

Since there are few books dealing with the genre of salvation oracles, interpreters should not neglect works on biblical theology that discuss salvation or journal articles that discuss terms or expressions found in oracles of salvation. Examples are:

Conrad, Edgar W. "The Fear Not Oracles in Second Isaiah." *VT* 34 (1984): 126–52.

VanGemeren, Willem A. *The Progress of Redemption: The Story of Salvation from Creation to the New Jerusalem*. Grand Rapids: Zondervan, 1988.

8

ANNOUNCEMENTS OF JUDGMENT
Trent C. Butler

God's prophets faced an impossible task: Make God's chosen people believe God would judge, discipline, and punish them. What alternative did the prophets have? God had spoken. He had established his covenant with Moses on Sinai and led a rebellious people through the wilderness. Then he watched a victorious people under Joshua become a people where each acted according to personal opinion rather than according to God's covenant demands. He set up a kingdom, made his people the richest and most powerful in the world, and then watched them perfect disobedience as a lifestyle. He used prophets like Nathan, Elijah, and Elisha to direct his people and win them back—to no avail. He divided one kingdom into two. Such discipline accomplished little in turning people back to him. Judgment seemed the only option left for God to offer. Thus, whether the audience liked what they heard or not, the prophets faithfully preached an impending judgment. God's parental love longed for a love relationship with his people; his righteousness demanded obedience so a people could fulfill his redemptive mission:

> When Israel was a youth I loved him,
> And out of Egypt I called My son.

157

The more they called them,
The more they went from them;
They kept sacrificing to the Baals
And burning incense to idols.
Yet it is I who taught Ephraim to walk,
I took them in My arms;
But they did not know that I healed them.
I led them with cords of a man, with bonds of love,
And I became to them as one who lifts the yoke from their jaws;
And I bent down and fed them.
They will not return to the land of Egypt;
But Assyria—he will be their king.
Because they refused to return to Me. (Hos. 11:1–5 NASB)

God-called messengers entered the marketplaces of Israel and Judah to proclaim God's message. But that message of impending judgment found no buyers. Ahaz turned a deaf ear to Isaiah's call for faith (see Isa. 7). Israel spurned the love Hosea proclaimed in personal life and in spoken word. Amaziah the priest threw Amos out of the temple at Bethel (see Amos 7). Judah ignored Micah's call for justice, mercy, and humility before God (see Mic. 6). Finally, Habakkuk questioned God about his justice in punishing evil and learned that the just must live by faith, a lifestyle Judah rejected (see Hab. 2). God had every reason to bring wicked Babylon to punish the unfaithful children he had chosen for his mission. Jeremiah cried before God to relieve him of his prophetic call even as he suffered persecution, rejection, and imprisonment from Judah's kings. Jeremiah saw no other recourse. Following God's word, he called the people to submit to the Babylonian enemy and endure the punishment God had proclaimed.

Such a message was not marketable. Rather the marketplace destroyed the vendors. The inspired New Testament writer summarized the destruction of the prophetic voice vividly: ". . . others experienced mockings and scourgings, yes, also chains and imprisonment. They were stoned, they were sawn in two, they were tempted, they were put to death with the sword; they went about in sheepskins, in goatskins, being destitute, afflicted, ill-treated (men of whom the world was not worthy), wandering in deserts and mountains and caves and holes in the ground" (Heb. 11:36–38, NASB).

How the Prophets
Proclaimed the Message from God

The prophets tried continually to warn the people, preaching sermon after sermon about the coming judgment. How? They listened to God. They took the message he gave, used creative poetry with its unforgettable imagery to catch the audience's attention, and announced to Israel and Judah what the Lord God said. They used powerful patterns of speech designed to transform the people's thinking.[1]

Why judgment? This question is central to the study of biblical prophecy. Only a thorough analysis of the prophets' warnings of judgment can provide an answer. Such an analysis and answer will lead away from easy misunderstandings of the prophets, their task, and message, as well as lead to an understanding of who the prophets were, what they sought to achieve, and how they achieved it. The analysis will center on the prophetic announcement of judgment, since this is the major speech instrument they chose.

Study of prophetic speeches has developed from one of two approaches. The prophets are seen as issuing threats and reproaches (Gunkel), or they are seen to issue announcements of judgment and reasons for it (Westermann). The first approach calls for a response to avert judgment. Repentance would be one such response.[2] The second approach apparently makes response useless, simply announcing and explaining the unavoidable judgment.[3] The two approaches show why understanding of prophetic

---

1. Gary V. Smith, *Prophets as Preachers: An Introduction to the Hebrew Prophets* (Nashville: Broadman & Holman, 1994), offers an analysis of the prophets in light of recent theory on how human thinking can be transformed.

2. Hermann Gunkel, "The Israelite Prophecy from the Time of Amos," in *Twentieth Century Theology in the Making*, ed. J. Pelikan, trans. R. A. Wilson (New York: Harper & Row, 1969), 48-75; originally published in *RGG*, 4:1866-86. Compare more recently Klaus Koch, *The Growth of the Biblical Tradition*, trans. S. M. Cupit (London: Adam and Charles Black, 1969), 191-94, 205-17.

3. Claus Westermann, *Basic Forms of Prophetic Speech*, trans. Hugh Clayton White (Philadelphia: Westminster, 1967).

genres is so important. Understanding the genre helps readers understand the type of response expected.

The same headline may appear on the front page of a newspaper, on the editorial page, or in an advertising section. People will respond to the same words in different ways. Why? The location of the headline and the type of material that follows it help people respond to the material. These indicators give readers the key to know the genre or literary type of the material. Their only key to the intention of the prophetic sermon may lie in knowing the prophetic genre and how it functions. Is the prophet teaching about the nature of God's judgment or about the nature of the judging God? That is, does the prophet want hearers to learn intellectual knowledge? Or does the prophet expect a change in attitude toward God, accepting God's right to bring judgment on people who can do nothing to avert that judgment? Or is God warning people so they can avoid that judgment by a change of attitude and action? The prophet's intention in using a specific genre helps them know their options before God. If they do not know the options the prophet presents, they may act wrongly through ignorance rather than through disobedience.

How Announcements of Judgment Function

How could the prophets convince Judah and Israel to take a product they did not want? They added to a prophetic tradition in which prophets entered the royal throne room to announce God's plans to God's kings. Samuel, Nathan, Elijah, and Elisha paved the way for the writing prophets. The writing prophets also took up roles Israel already understood from the throne room of the king and the court room of the judge.

The prophetic judgment speech may have represented a prophetic use of the political messenger's speech. A king sent his messenger or ambassador to a foreign court with a message. The message was delivered in the exact words of the king and then explained. The messenger's speech thus had two parts: an accusation and an announcement. A messenger formula, "Thus says the Lord," joined the two parts into one speech.

The messenger, especially in written reports, introduced his speech by reporting the commissioning of the messenger and issuing a summons to hear.

First Kings 21:18–19 and 2 Kings 1:3–4 become prime examples of the form, with Amos 7:16–17 an illustration from the prophetic books, where the commissioning of the messenger does not appear. First Kings 21:17–19, NRSV illustrate the parts of the messenger speech:

Commissioning:

Then the word of the LORD came to Elijah the Tishbite, saying:
Go down to meet King Ahab of Israel, who rules in Samaria; he is now in the vineyard of Naboth, where he has gone to take possession. You shall say to him,

Messenger Formula:

"Thus says the LORD:

Accusation:

Have you killed, and also taken possession?"

Announcement of Judgment (including a second messenger formula):

You shall say to him, "Thus says the LORD: In the place where dogs licked up the blood of Naboth, dogs will also lick up your blood."

2 Kings 1:3–4 shows another example:

Commissioning:

But the angel of the LORD said to Elijah the Tishbite, "Get up, go to meet the messengers of the king of Samaria, and say to them,

Accusation:

'Is it because there is no God in Israel that you are going to inquire of Baal-zebub, the god of Ekron?'

Messenger Formula:

Now therefore thus says the LORD,

Announcement of Judgment:

'You shall not leave the bed to which you have gone, but you shall surely die.'"

The judgment speech assumes the individual has violated the law on which the covenant between God and his people rested. It is God's way of carrying out normal judicial procedure against a king who seems to stand above such procedure and has no person to institute legal process against him.

The announcement itself consists of one sentence in personal address informing the addressee of a future catastrophe coming for the guilty party. The prophets often included reasons for the judgment. The reasons begin with a very generalized formulation of the accusation; this is then developed in more concrete detail with examples or a citation from the guilty party showing crimes committed. Whereas the announcement is often in second person, the reasons may switch to third person. Examples of the form appear in Amos 4:1–2; Hosea 2:5–7; Isaiah 8:6–8; 30:12–14; Micah 3:1–2,4; 2:1–4; 3:9–12; Jeremiah 5:10–14; and 7:16–18, 20.

Another perspective on the method of the prophets moves further from dependence on the legal sphere.[4] Koch talks of a *prophecy of disaster* with three parts: the indication of the situation (or diatribe), the prediction of disaster (or threat), and a concluding characterization that may characterize either the sender or recipient of the message. The first part often begins with *because (ya'an 'asher,* see Jer. 19:4) or an interrogative. The prediction of disaster unexpectedly uses an imperfect verb tense with the negative *lo'* instead of the expected prophetic perfect. A second sentence describes the consequences of God's intervention. The concluding characterization usually begins with *because* or *for (kî)* and is brief. The messenger formula may appear either before the first or second section. All prophets, true and false, used the same prophetic form.

God did not leave his messengers with a cupboard bare of genres. They incorporated genres from many elements of daily life into their one major genre. The list is virtually endless, complete only when every single narrative about prophets in the Bible is analyzed as well as every single prophetic sermon. We will look at a few of the main elements that prophets incorporated into their pronouncements of judgment.

---

4. Koch, *Growth of the Biblical Tradition, 191-94, 205-17.*

The *woe oracle* is a major element. It is "used in the prophetic literature to criticize particular actions or attitudes of people, and sometimes to announce punishment upon them."[5] The woe oracle has two parts: The first part is an exclamation of dismay introduced by *woe* or *alas* (the particle *hoy*); the second is a participle describing the wrongful action or a noun giving a negative characterization of the people. The oracle continues with several grammatical forms to show the results of the woeful behavior. Questions arise as to the setting that commenced the woe cries and thus the emotion the cry should evoke from the audience. Is it an educational device from wisdom schools contrasting blessed and cursed ways of action?[6] Or is it the grief cry at a funeral (see Jer. 22:18)?[7] The latter seems more likely, the prophet expressing grief over the action of God's people and conveying God's anger at such action. Woe oracles cluster in Isaiah 5; 10:1–11; 28:1–4; 29:1–4,15; 30:1–3; 31:1–4; Amos 5:18–6:7; Micah 2:1–4; and Habakkuk 2.

The *prophetic lawsuit (rib)* summons Israel to court to hear God's verdict. This has five parts:

1. an introduction calling the audience to hear and often appealing to heavens and earth as witnesses

2. questioning of witnesses and statement of the accusation

3. the prosecuting attorney's address to the court contrasting the people's sins with God's saving acts

4. description of the inability of cultic ritual to atone for such wrong acts

5. a warning and a call to turn back to God and obey him.

Such a format comes from the international treaty form, from Israel's covenant with God, and from the pattern of trials in the courtrooms of biblical times. The formula may reflect actual

---

5. Ronald M. Hals, *Ezekiel,* FOTL 19 (Grand Rapids: Eerdmans, 1989), 358.

6. Erhard Gerstenberger, "The Woe-Oracles of the Prophets," *JBL* 81 (1962), 249–63.

7. Waldemar Janzen, *Mourning Cry and Woe Oracle,* BZAW 125 (Berlin: Walter de Gruyter, 1989), 40–80.

happenings in Israel's worship life. It appears in Isaiah 1, Micah 6, and Jeremiah 2.[8]

The *summons to repentance* is a form often debated by scholars.[9] With it the prophet clearly calls the people to a change in lifestyle. To summon the people the prophet uses the following elements:

- an appeal using messenger formula, vocative, and admonition

- A motivation with promise, accusation, and threat

These appear in Isaiah 1:19–20; 55:6–7; Jeremiah 3:12–13; 4:1—4; Joel 2:12–13; and Amos 5:4–7, 14–15 as major elements and in other places in a more subordinate role.

One final subgenre must be mentioned, though discussion can lead more to confusion than to clarification. *Oracles against foreign nations*[10] form major sections of several prophetic books (Amos 1–2; Isa. 13–23; Jer. 46–51; Ezek. 25–32; Nahum; Obadiah). The addressee as nations other than Israel is the basic unifying element since these oracles do not share common structures or genres. Even the addressee can be debated since the oracles overtly address foreigners but seem most likely to have been delivered in an Israelite setting for the benefit of the Israelite audience. This means that overt announcements of judgment may function as indirect announcements of salvation for Israel. Such oracles may originally belong to a military setting pronouncing curses on ene-

---

8. See Eugene March, "Prophecy," in *Old Testament Form Criticism,* ed. John H. Hayes (San Antonio: Trinity University Press, 1974), 166-68.

9. Thomas M. Raitt, "The Prophetic Summons to Repentance," *ZAW* 83 (1971): 30-49; see the discussion by Gene Tucker, "Prophecy and Prophetic Literature," in *The Hebrew Bible and Its Modern Interpreters,* ed. Douglas A. Knight and Gene M. Tucker (Philadelphia: Fortress, 1985), 339.

10. See Duane L. Christensen, *Transformation of the War Oracle in Old Testament Prophecy: Studies in the Oracles Against the Nations,* HDR 3. (Missoula, Mont.: Scholars Press, 1975). Compare the discussions of Hals, *Ezekiel* 178-229, 351; Tucker, "Prophecy and Prophetic Literature," 340; Gary V. Smith, *Amos: A Commentary* (Grand Rapids: Zondervan, 1989), 29-96; Lamar Eugene Cooper, Sr., *Ezekiel,* New American Commentary 17 (Nashville: Broadman & Holman Publishers, 1994), 241-89; F. B. Huey, Jr. *Jeremiah, Lamentations,* New American Commentary 16 (Nashville: Broadman & Holman Publishers, 1993), 373-431.

my armies before battle and may have been taken up into worship settings for the whole nation to participate in preparation for military action. As they stand in prophetic books, they represent a literary collection designed for specific literary purposes in each collection.

Where Announcements of Judgment Are Found

Israel held no monopoly on prophets. The biblical literature itself repeatedly mentions foreign prophets and their activities (e.g., 1 Kings 18; 2 Kings 10). Recent study has revealed prophetic activity in northern Syria, Ugarit, Phoenicia, southern Syria, Ammon, Anatolia, Uruk, Mari, Ischali, and Assyria.[11] Most attention focuses on Mari, where about fifty texts dating from about 1800 B.C. mention at least eighteen prophets related to a dozen gods. Many of the prophecies relate directly to the royal house, are related to sacrifices in the temple, and deal with times of crisis. The prophetic messenger formula, "Thus says the god," is used. The texts do include warnings to the king, especially if the king neglects the god's demands, but nothing in available literature notes any form resembling Israel's warnings of national destruction nor genres related to the announcements of judgment in Israel. Indeed, the Mari materials are preserved in letters which report secondhand the prophetic oracles.

> The content is generally an assurance to the king or a warning to the king of dangers (and an assurance of divine assistance); but a number of messages deviate from this pattern. . . . More serious charges come from Addu of Aleppo and Addu of Kallassu: the king, who owes his throne to the deity, has been inattentive in offerings and in recognition of the deity's claims—what Addu has given, Addu can take away. Moreover, the deity does not speak in terms of self-interest, for the king has a fundamental obligation to deal justly in his realm with all who appeal to him. An obedient king will be richly rewarded.[12]

---

11. H. B. Huffmon, "Prophecy (ANE)," *ABD* (New York: Doubleday, 1992), 5:477-78.

12. Ibid., 5:479. Compare Tucker, "Prophecy and Prophetic Literature," 345-47; S. B. Parker, "Official Attitudes Toward Prophecy at Mari and in Israel," *VT* 43 (1993): 50-68.

Additional study on recently published texts should shed further light on the nature and message of prophecy in ancient Israel's environment and thus on Israelite prophecy.[13]

Guidelines for Interpretation

Guilt plays a major role in religion because guilt forms a major part of human personality. Despite attempts in the postmodern church to accentuate the positive, God continues to call the church to guide people through the guilt trips they face daily. Obviously, the prophets offer one model in dealing with guilt. The modern preacher who ignores this model does disservice to self and congregation. Learning from the prophetic model of expounding congregational guilt is itself a path fraught with danger. Too easily the preacher seeks to assume the prophetic role and heap guilt upon a congregation seeking good news. To understand the prophetic form and function of announcing judgment, the modern preacher must go beyond mere form-critical analysis to understand the rhetorical and canonical issues of prophetic preaching. Certain signposts to guide the interpretation of announcements of judgment can be noticed.

1. *Announcement of judgment came in a specific historical situation based on a specific word from God.* No preacher is free to preach absolute judgment to a people without a similar experience with God. God's judgment on sin is absolute. God's judgment on a specific congregation comes in his timing at his bidding.

2. *Announcement of judgment rested on firm historical evidence that God's people had developed a lifestyle that ignored God and broke the people's covenant commitments.* God brings judgment only after a long history of sin and discipline.

3. *Announcement of judgment resulted in widely differing responses.* Nineveh surprised Jonah in repenting (see Jon. 3). King Jehoiakim surprised in the other direction. He burned the scroll announcing judgment (see Jer. 36), when he should have reverently and fearfully called the nation to mourning (Jer. 36:24).

---

13. Recent texts are published in French by J.M. Durand, *Archives epistolaires de Mari I/1,* ARM 26 (Paris, 1988). See citations by Huffmon and Parker.

4. *Announcement of judgment does not try to get something out of the people to benefit the preacher or congregation.* Announcement of judgment informs the people of God's intended actions based on past performance. It does not represent an attempt to bribe the people.

5. *Announcement of judgment "in itself brings the hearers (or a third party) under judgment.* It initiates an objective state of condemnation."[14] No announcement of judgment plays games with the audience, claiming to bring judgment when its real purpose is to avoid judgment. To announce God's judgment is to face an audience with certain punishment. To announce judgment is to paint one part of God's reality with a rebellious world—a part that cannot be ignored.

6. *Announcement of judgment does not entrap God.* The God of the Bible rejects Jonah's self-pitying response and self-serving delight in the projected destruction of the enemy. Even Isaiah's word of hardening left room for a holy seed, a remnant to return (Isa. 6–8). Amos's summons to meet God maintained a faint "perhaps" of divine grace (Amos 4–5). God always maintains the freedom not to punish. The announcement of judgment reveals God's intention to a people and must be taken seriously (number 5 above), but the announcement does not tie God's hands. He remains in a free love relationship with his people and can respond to them as they respond to him. The one who announces God's judgment can fully expect that judgment to come. The messenger is not the king. Only the king decides if and when to bring the announced judgment.

7. *Announcement of judgment is only a part of the prophetic message, and, indeed, the introductory part.* The inspired people God used to collect prophetic words into prophetic canon intentionally formed a canon moving from—or perhaps better through—judgment of the nation to judgment of the enemy to restoration of the nation and final salvation. Judgment forms God's prelude, not his closing finale. The canonical message paints the picture of God's loving salvation. Judgment is an unde-

---

14. Walter Houston, "What Did the Prophets Think They Were Doing? Speech Acts and Prophetic Discourse in the Old Testament," *Biblical Interpretation* 1 (1993), 180.

sirable alternative. The congregation needs always to see God's choice for his people, not only the alternative the people seem at present to choose. A sinful people chooses judgment. A loving God holds out hope for repentance and salvation until judgment comes.

A Prophecy of Jeremiah Against Backsliders
Jeremiah 8:4–13

Introduction:

Commission:

You shall say to them,

Messenger Speech:

Thus Yahweh spoke:

Body

Indication of the Situation (introduced by interrogative):

"Do they fall and not stand?
If they turn, do they not return?
Why has this people turned?
Jerusalem eternally turning?

Development of the Situation:

They grasp deceit.
They refuse to return.
I paid attention and heard:
Untruth they spoke.
Nobody regrets their evil,

(Citation):

Saying, 'What have I done?'
Everyone returns to their own life's run
As a horse storming into battle.
Even a heron in the heavens knows its season,
And a turtledove, swift, and thrush obey the time of their coming.
But my people do not know
The judgment of Yahweh.
How *('eykah)* can you say,

(Citation):

'Wise are we,
And the Torah of Yahweh is with us?'

When in reality *('aken, hineh)* into a lie it has transformed it—
The lying pen of the scribes.
Shameful are the wise ones.

Sentence:

They will be shattered and captured.
Because the word of Yahweh they have rejected.
And wisdom, what is it to them?

Prediction of Disaster:

Therefore *(laken)*

Intervention of God:

I will give their wives to others
And their fields to conquerors,

Concluding Characterization:

Because *(ki)* from the least to the greatest everyone wants a cut.
From the prophet to the priest
Everyone acts out a lie.
They heal the fracture of the daughter of my people
Superficially saying, 'Shalom, Shalom.'
But there is no Shalom.
They are shamed because they created abomination.
Even shame does not make ashamed;
Disgrace they do not know.

Prediction of Disaster:

Therefore *(laken)*
They will fall among the falling ones.
At the time of mustering, they shall stumble,
Yahweh said.

Intervention of God:

I will reap their reapings.

(Prophetic Utterance Formula)

Oracle of Yahweh

Concluding Characterization:

There will be no grapes on the grape vine
And no figs on the fig tree.
The leaf has withered,
And I have given them . . .

They will pass away from them.
(author's translation)

Jeremiah faced the impossible task: Pronounce God's judgment on the religious leaders of God's people. How could he accomplish the task? He had only the tools of human speech, tools in which the religious leaders were trained and skilled. God sent him with a devastating announcement of disaster: The religious leaders would fall. Jeremiah took the traditional prophetic way of announcing judgment and transformed it to meet his specific needs. He explicitly reported the commission God gave him (8:4a) and moved the messenger formula from the prediction of disaster to the opening statement of his speech. The audience needed to know from the outset that this was God's doings and God's words, not Jeremiah's strategy and Jeremiah's composition.

A direct challenge accusing the people might shut off the audience before he could make his announcement. Therefore, Jeremiah introduced a feature—rhetorical questions—to gain their attention and let the audience establish the mood of guilt. He continued to leave the accusation up in the air, turning repeatedly to forms of the Hebrew *shuv* with its various meanings of turn, return, turn away, turn back, repent. Finally, he identified the audience—Jerusalem, this people—and made the accusation clear—deceit, lying. He highlighted the problem with the stark contrast of God's actions: God pays attention and hears. The people simply speak—all lies and with no regrets. God listens so well he can cite what they say—their bewildered question, "What have I done?"

Thus, Jeremiah's audience quickly knows the situation at hand. It is their word against God's word, their bewildered question against God's rhetorical questions. How can Jeremiah convince them?

He turns to the realm of nature. They have a run they love to take. So do horses, but their's leads to battle. So do birds as they migrate. One problem—the run of the people should be the run God set out. But "my people"—using the first person possessive to indicate God's identity with and possession of the people—"my people" remain ignorant. They do not know the judgment *(mishpat)* about the run their life should take and the judgment about the laws they should obey and the judgment awaiting them if they remain on their own run and refuse to turn back to God's justice (*mishpat*).

Before he loses the audience, the prophet injects another citation, something these religious leaders proudly proclaim: "Wise are we." We have God's Torah. He cleverly introduces the citation with a word familiar to an audience suffering from enemy armies, the word *how ('eykah)*, that marked the beginning of laments. The audience could hear the sorrowful pain in the prophet's voice as he addressed them in grief over their proud claims. To respond to their claim, the prophet joined two particles. The first, *when ('aken)*, closely resembled the marker of lament but marked instead a turn to reality. The second particle *(hineh)* marked off the following as immediate and urgent. Transposed sentence order then emphasized the double use of "lies, falsehood" to mark off the type of action and the type of actors. Scribes dedicated to copying and teaching God's word with total accuracy did just the opposite. The Torah with them was certainly not God's; it was a false torah. If they were wise scribes, they were shamefully wise.

Unexpectedly, the prophet breaks with the announcement of disaster form. He does not let the audience hear the familiar *therefore (laken)* introducing the second major part: the prediction of disaster. Rather he strikes quickly, pronouncing the sentence of the heavenly court. They will be shattered and captured, expressed in military terms but not for an army. The sheltered scribes in their copying tent face military punishment. Why? Because they are inadequate soldiers? No! Because they reject the very word they claim to copy and teach! Because they have no use for the wisdom about which they brag and by which they gain their position as wise men and scribes.

Now Jeremiah is ready for the normal approach to announcing disaster. He shouts forth the dreaded word *laken* and with it shares God's prediction of disaster with the audience of esteemed religious leaders. The first-person divine speech in imperfect[15] states the prediction tersely: They will lose what they most cherish:—family and fields. Why? The concluding characterization,

---

15. The Hebrew verb system most often uses two forms to indicate the aspect of action: prefixed or imperfect verbs and suffixed or perfect verbs. Incomplete action appears in the imperfect form.

with its normal introduction with *because* (the particle *kî*) shows the reason.

Everyone wants a cut of the action. Wise scribes are not the only ones included. Prophet and priest must line up for disaster, too. Lying is their business as much as it is the scribes. The scribes injure God's word. Prophets and priests use their treasured homiletical skills to injure a people already fractured. The persons responsible for intercession for a wounded people have only superficial promises: Shalom, Shalom—Wholeness, Wholeness. That is not the reality Jeremiah proclaims. Reality is shame, but these leaders know no shame nor disgrace.

Jeremiah repeats the form, proclaiming yet another *therefore (laken)* and its prediction of disaster. The concluding characterization has been made to serve a double purpose. It becomes the indication of situation for this second prediction of disaster. Thus, Jeremiah makes it clear. Prophet and priest must face disaster just as the scribes must. Again the prophet grasps a military image. Prophet and priest must face army muster. As they answer the call to battle, they will stumble and fall. This places them among the deserters or fallen ones, not among the soldiers ready for battle— thus, the dreaded first-person intervention of God surrounded by authorizing formulas of the divine word. God will reap the harvest, not human harvesters. This sets the stage for the final concluding characterization. No grapes. No figs. Withered trees. God still gives. But everything passes away.

This passage then represents a complex combination of elements to form a repeated announcement of judgment. Too much deliberation has centered on which elements belong and which are secondary. Careful genre analysis may point the way to seeing this as an artistic unit in which the prophet masterfully manipulates a traditional genre to gain the audience's attention and to ensure that they hear and understand the situation their evil has placed them in before God. They are condemned. Judgment rushes in.

How should they react? Is the announcement to scribes, prophets, and priests a call to repentance or a simple announcement of judgment? Perhaps Walter Houston has opened the door a bit: "The question whether the intention of judgment prophecy is to condemn absolutely or to awaken repentance is transcended. Both possibilities exist within the single form of the judgement oracle and within reported responses to it, though as we have noted, only one theme may be dominant."[16] For Jeremiah, the theme that certainly dominated was judgment.

Conclusion

Genre study introduces the fascinating variety of ways in which prophets performed the unenviable tasks of persuading God's people that he was angry with them and would punish them. It shows the necessity for standard forms to provide continuity and establish the prophetic authority as God's messenger with God's message. It also shows the need for variety to create the emotional atmosphere needed to do more than inform the people, but also to transform their thinking and actions.

What have we learned about how prophets could thunder down judgment upon the people of God? They portrayed themselves as God's messengers bringing the divine king's word to his subjects. They utilized a basic form the audience would immediately recognize as prophetic speech. They listed the wrongs in God's accusation against his people, thus providing concrete evidence. They compressed the actual announcement of judgment into one sentence the audience could not misunderstand. No audience could fail to be impressed. They could deny the accusation; they could question whether the God they served was of such a nature as to carry out the punishment; they might claim the punishment did not fit the crime; but they could not claim lack of information. God provided his messengers a form that made clear his intention among a guilty people.

The announcement of judgment sought to do more than make the message plain. Prophets also sought to create an emotional setting wherein the people would see God and his justice at work in judgment. To do this prophets did not just monotonously repeat the same message in the same stale format each time God informed them of his intent to punish. Most often the prophets clothed the prophecy of disaster in poetry with all its attendant images. This endowed the audience with more than a piece of

---

16. Houston, "What Did the Prophets Think They Were Doing?" 187.

information. The prophets placed their audience squarely before the divine king and relayed his message. Images danced into their heads that would not cease. Pictures of their wrongdoings, images of the irate deity coming to discipline his people, and indelible presentations of the suffering they faced lingered menacingly in their minds long after the prophet shut his mouth. Poetry painted God and his judgment on the canvas of his people's minds.

Recommended Reading

Bullock, C. Hassell. *An Introduction to the Old Testament Prophetic Books.* Chicago: Moody Press, 1986. A recent evangelical introduction to prophetic books with brief review of genre categories. Basic bibliography given.

Brueggemann, Walter. "The Prophetic Word of God and History," *Int.* 48 (1994): 239–251. A creative attempt to restore the church's right to discuss history with the contemporary world in terms of God's freeing acts bringing healing and hope.

Clements, Ronald E. "Woe," *ABD,* New York: Doubleday, 1992. 6:945–46. The best recent summary of the woe oracle with search for distinction between lament and woe, grief and anger. Succinct bibliography.

Exum, J. Cheryl. "Of Broken Pots, Fluttering Birds, and Visions in the Night: Extended Simile and Poetic Technique in Isaiah." In *Beyond Form Criticism. Essays in Old Testament Literary Criticism.* Sources for Biblical and Theological Study 2, ed. Paul R. House, Winona Lake, Ind.: Eisenbrauns, 1992, 349–72. A recent example of rhetorical study emphasizing poetic metaphor and literary patterns and their significance in the prophets—a necessary step in conjunction with genre analysis.

Hals, Ronald M. *Ezekiel.* FOTL 19 Grand Rapids: Eerdmans, 1989. The major commentary centered on genre analysis, providing a detailed examination of the genres at each level of composition from entire book to major sections to the smallest formula. Provides glossary with definitions of major prophetic genre elements that appear in Ezekiel, making it an indispensable tool for the student of prophetic genres.

Houston, Walter. "What Did the Prophets Think They Were Doing? Speech Acts and Prophetic Discourse in the Old Testament."

Biblical Interpretation 1 (1993): 167–88. An attempt to use the theory of "speech acts" developed by J. L. Austin and J. R. Searle to show the nature of prophetic speaking as illustrated in oracles of judgment, resulting in claim that intention of speech act to establish a person in state of judgment does not automatically eliminate possibility of repentance.

Huffmon, H. B. "Prophecy (ANE)." *ABD*, 5:477–82. The most recent discussion of prophecy within Israel's extended environment with particular attention to Mari. Latest bibliography, especially pointing to new materials from Mari.

Koch, Klaus. *The Growth of the Biblical Tradition,* 183–220. 1964 German. Reprint, London: Adam and Charles Black, 1969. A summary of methodological approaches to biblical literature encompassing genre study within the larger framework of other literary methodologies employed at time of publication. Revises Westermann's analysis and establishes vocabulary used in much, if not most, prophetic genre analysis today. Index of literary forms in Old Testament study.

Lindblom, J. *Prophecy in Ancient Israel.* Philadelphia: Fortress Press, 1962. A classic study of prophecy without mention of genre analysis.

Parker, Simon B. "Official Attitudes Toward Prophecy at Mari and in Israel." *VT* 43 (1993). 50–68. Uses the latest materials from Mari to examine how materials were transmitted from prophet to royal official to king, how the process affected the materials, and how the officials and kings regarded the materials. Footnotes provide some recent bibliographical materials.

Smith, Gary V. *The Prophets as Preachers: An Introduction to the Hebrew Prophets.* Nashville: Broadman & Holman Publishers, 1994. The latest evangelical introduction to prophecy and the prophetic books based on a sociological understanding of communication and transformation theory showing how prophets worked to transform thinking of their audiences. Good bibliography.

VanGemeren, Willem A. *Interpreting the Prophetic Word.* Grand Rapids: Zondervan, 1990. An extensive evangelical introduction to prophecy and the prophetic books with a cautious and brief introduction to genre study. Up-to-date bibliography.

Westermann, Claus. *Basic Forms of Prophetic Speech*. Translated by Hugh Clayton White. Philadelphia: The Westminster Press, 1967. The pioneering work in summarizing and critiquing work on prophetic speech forms and in providing a form-critical analysis of biblical judgment speeches. Needs to be read in conversation with Klaus Koch above.

9

APOCALYPTIC
D. Brent Sandy and Martin G. Abegg, Jr.

Of the genres in the Old Testament, apocalyptic is probably the most unusual if not the most misunderstood. Even its name may seem strange. Yet like cliffs for the climber or caviar for the connoisseur, apocalyptic can provide special delight for those who learn to appreciate it. Once properly understood, the apocalyptic portions of Scripture become uplifting and comforting.

Apocalyptic deserves notice as remarkably good literature. If a literary text makes something come alive through narrative, rather than stating it by proposition; and engages readers in something to be experienced and lived, rather than to be analyzed; and uses images to impact the brain's right hemisphere, rather than to transmit data into the left hemisphere; then apocalyptic is intensely literary. Like music, apocalyptic appeals to emotions. It is powerfully affective communication. Like the imaginary stories of children's literature, apocalyptic creates compelling images that shape values, which in turn impact behavior. Like poetry, apocalyptic is aesthetically crafted. Like visual media, apocalyptic graphically portrays scenes of high drama.

Figures of speech and special literary techniques abound in apocalyptic. Metaphor, simile, metonymy, synecdoche, hyperbole, apostrophe, allusion, personification, paradox, pun, irony, parallelism, repetition, rhythm, and rhetorical devices appear with a high level of frequency. Add to these literary features apocalyptic's special subject matter focusing on future events, and this genre offers readers a universe of literary artistry and fascinating reading.

What Makes Apocalyptic Unique?

In simple terms apocalyptic is prophecy—but of a specialized kind. The Book of Revelation has been the most recognized example of the apocalyptic genre, even giving the genre its name (the first word of John's Revelation is *apokalypsis*). As with the Book of Revelation, apocalyptic is prophecy but with a special focus and in a striking format. While the lines that divide apocalyptic from prophecy are often blurred, the following characteristics are common—though not rigid—distinctions between prophecy and apocalyptic:[1]

Prophecy	Apocalyptic
Prophecy laments the sinfulness on the earth and urges people to repent.	Apocalyptic considers the ever-present wickedness beyond hope. The only solution is total destruction: The earth is going to melt with fervent heat.
Prophecy reveals God's displeasure with the irreverent attitudes and conduct of his chosen people.	Apocalyptic assumes that the readers are themselves displeased with the evil around them and are anxious for God to provide a solution.

---

1. For more complete discussion of prophecy, see chapters 7 and 8 above, and Richard Patterson, "Old Testament Prophecy," in *A Complete Literary Guide to the Bible*, ed. Leland Ryken and Tremper Longman III (Grand Rapids: Zondervan, 1993), 296–309.

Prophecy	Apocalyptic
Prophecy calls the people of God back to obedience to God.	Apocalyptic calls for the few remaining faithful to persevere until the end: In the face of difficult odds they are to keep their robes pure.
Prophecy announces that God is going to judge sin and offer salvation, usually to be accomplished through natural means or human agents.	Apocalyptic announces that God himself is going to intervene and judge the world through supernatural means: he will ride out of heaven on a white horse and rule the nations.
Prophecy presents its message as direct speech from God: "Thus says the LORD."	Apocalyptic presents its message in graphic images, visions, and symbols. The message of apocalyptic is sometimes shrouded in mystery: This title was written on her forehead: "Mystery, Babylon the great, the mother of prostitutes and of the abominations of the earth" (Rev. 17:5).
Prophecy predicts both immediate and distant aspects of God's judgment and salvation.	Apocalyptic focuses primarily on final solutions. The situation is too serious for short-term answers. The only hope is for God to bring the history of man's sinfulness to conclusion and to establish a solution that will last for eternity: There will be no more night, and they will reign forever and ever.

Though apocalyptic's basic message is not difficult to grasp, its striking format leaves many readers bewildered. In some senses an apocalyptic author is like a political cartoonist, sketching the course of world events and the prominent leaders of the world in figurative, graphic, and even bizarre ways. As a result, the reader is often left puzzled by what is encountered:

- jaw-dropping scenes of animals, rivers, mountains, and stars that jump off the page with movie-like special effects (see Dan. 8:2–14; Zech 6:1–7)

- natural catastrophes producing cosmic chaos throughout the universe, ushering in the dreadful day of judgment (see Ezek. 38:19–22; Isa. 24:18–20)

- harmful and disruptive evil contributing to constant crises and producing a seemingly hopeless pessimism with the course of current events (see Dan. 7:19–25; Isa. 57:3–13)

- an underlying determinism resting in the unquestioned conviction that somehow God is maintaining sovereign control (see Isa. 25:1; 26:1–4)

- ecstatic expectation that God will soon intervene and suppress all evil forces working against his predetermined plan (see Zech. 14:3–9; Mal 3:1–5)

- ethical teaching aimed at giving courage and comfort to the faithful and confirming them in righteous living (see Zech. 7:9–10; 8:16–17; Isa. 56:1–2)

- visions of celestial scenes and beings with an other-worldly perspective (see Dan. 10:4–19; Zech. 3:1–10)

- heavenly interpreters explaining the scenes in language that may also be figurative (see Ezek. 40:3–4, Dan. 8:15–17)

- a dualistic perspective that categorizes things into contrasting elements such as good and evil, this age and the age to come (see Zech. 1:14–15; Dan. 12:2)

- a very stylized structure of how the visions are presented, with events and time organized around numerical patterns and repetition of similar sets (see Dan. 9:24–27, Ezek. 38–39)

- and foundational to all the above, God's promise to act in the last days to restore his people and establish a new and glorious order (see Isa. 27:12–13; Zech. 8:1–8).[2]

---

2. In this list of characteristics of apocalyptic, there is one notable omission. Most apocalypses in the ancient world were pseudonymous. However, in the Bible the only apocalyptic text seriously claimed to be pseudonymous is Daniel. For example, John J. Collins, *Daniel,* Hermeneia (Minneapolis: Fortress, 1994), 56–58. For arguments in favor of Daniel as the author, see Joyce G. Baldwin, *Daniel: An Introduction and Commentary,* TOTC (Downers Grove: InterVarsity, 1978), 13–59.

These characteristics of apocalyptic take readers on a fascinating journey that invites "us to enter a whole world of imagination and to live in that world before we move beyond it."[3] Unless interpreters understand the unique characteristics of apocalyptic, they are likely to make major mistakes in their study of this genre in Scripture.[4]

Where Apocalyptic Is Found

Extra-Biblical Writings

Apocalyptic appears in many forms and in many places, both within the canon of Scripture and in extra-biblical writings. In some cases, however, it is difficult to decide what qualifies as apocalyptic, because there is uncertainty about how many characteristics of apocalyptic are required to consider a text apocalyptic.[5] While a partial consensus is forming among scholars of how apocalyptic should be defined, it must be remembered that genres as literary classifications are largely modern concepts. A genre is not a fixed collection of texts with clear boundaries dividing it from another collection of texts, for some pieces of literature inevitably fall somewhere between the commonly accepted categories. The apocalyptic genre can have as many as twenty-eight distinguishing characteristics, but no single text contains all of those characteristics, and some texts not considered formally a part of the apocalyptic genre have some of those characteristics.[6]

---

3. Leland Ryken, *Words of Life: A Literary Introduction to the New Testament* (Grand Rapids: Baker, 1987), 23. Though Ryken's statement is referring to biblical literature in general, it is especially fitting for apocalyptic.

4. There are many discussions of the characteristics of apocalyptic. For example: see M. E. Stone, "Apocalyptic Literature," in *Jewish Writings of the Second Temple Period,* CRINT, ed M. E. Stone (Philadelphia: Fortress, 1984), 392–94; and Grant Osborne, *The Hermeneutical Spiral: A Comprehensive Introduction to Biblical Interpretation* (Downers Grove: InterVarsity 1991), 221–27.

5. Much has been written on the definition of the apocalyptic genre. For a helpful review, see Dave Mathewson, "Revelation in Recent Genre Criticism: Some Implications for Interpretation," *TJ, n.s.* 13, no. 2 (Fall 1992): 193–204.

6. John J. Collins, "Introduction: Towards the Morphology of a Genre," in *Apocalypse: The Morphology of a Genre,* Semeia 14 (1979): 5–8.

Apocalyptic apparently grew out of a diverse matrix of Hebrew prophecy, Israelite wisdom, and Babylonian, Persian, and Hellenistic materials. During the Babylonian exile and after, the crises faced by the Jews brought them to their knees in despair under the weight of the seeming hopelessness of the world's condition. It became increasingly clear to some that the only hope was for a radical divine intervention. Describing that intervention in vivid visionary forms and motifs was natural, given the apocalypticism that was common in the ancient Near East.[7]

Though fully developed apocalyptic is not extant until the Persian period, there are striking predictions of the future preserved in Akkadian literature, dated as early as 1000 B.C. Among the Babylonians, mysterious signs and symbols and overtones of determinism are apparent in the mantic wisdom. Dream visions are also attested. The Persian material, though plagued with uncertain dating, has the clearest evidence of apocalyptic thought in the ancient Near East, including a historical apocalypse that describes a divine being who interprets a revelation, and an apocalypse involving a heavenly journey.[8]

While some evidence of apocalyptic expression is found in the ancient Near East, apocalyptic as a genre was a Jewish phenomenon, though subsequently adopted by Christians. The most commonly recognized extra-biblical apocalypses are 1 Enoch, 2 Enoch, 4 Ezra, Apocalypse of Abraham, 2 and 3 Apocalypse of Baruch, and Apocalypse of Peter. Most of these are a part of the corpus of Jewish literature now known as the Pseudepigrapha, written after the time of the Hebrew Scriptures.[9]

Of these extra-biblical examples of apocalyptic literature, 1 Enoch has the clearest parallels to Old Testament apocalyptic, especially Daniel.[10] The biblical character of Enoch, whose signifi-

---

7. "The roots of the apocalypse should be sought in biblical literature, first and foremost in prophecy" (Stone, "Apocalyptic Literature," 384).

8. John J. Collins, "Persian Apocalypses," in *Apocalypse: The Morphology of a Genre*, Semeia 14 (1979): 207–17.

9. For English translations of apocalyptic texts in the pseudepigrapha related to the OT, see James H. Charlesworth, ed., *The Old Testament Pseudepigrapha*, vol. 1, *Apocalyptic Literature and Testaments* (Garden City, N.Y.: Doubleday, 1983).

10. Collins, *Daniel*, 59–60.

cance was heightened by his most singular disappearance (see Gen. 5:24), had become associated with special divine knowledge centuries before Christ. The book which bears his name is actually a collection of five books, each with its own title and purpose. The first part, the *Book of the Watchers*, explains the origin of sin on the basis of Genesis 6 rather than Genesis 3. The second, the *Similitudes*, echoes Daniel 7 in its expectation of a savior, the Son of Man or Elect One. The third part, the *Book of the Luminaries*, discusses the moral implications of a perfect 364-day solar calendar. Part four, the *Dream Visions*, is made up of a "prophetic account" of the coming flood and then "foretells" history down to the second century B.C. Finally, book five, the *Epistle of Enoch*, contains ethical teaching with an emphasis on righteous living in the last days.

Though examples of apocalyptic written by the early Christians include the *Shepherd of Hermas, Apocalypse of James, Apocalypse of Paul, Apocalypse of Thomas,* and the *Ascension of Isaiah,* the *Apocalypse of Peter* is probably the earliest and most influential of extra-biblical Christian apocalyptic.[11] Written within fifty years after the Revelation of John, the *Apocalypse of Peter* records an expanded and embellished version of Jesus' transfiguration and Olivet Discourse on the end times. Peter is shown a vision reflecting in particular the wrath of God against all evildoers and the rewards for the righteous, and Jesus describes a beautiful garden, which is the eternal abode for the saints.

Examples of apocalyptic literature also exist among the Dead Sea Scrolls found in the caves at Qumran.[12] This collection, most likely the library of a group of sectarian Jews who were in many ways more closely related to early Christianity than the more well-known Pharisees and Sadducees, includes only the book of 1 Enoch from the list of previously known extra-biblical apocalypses. Portions of four of the five 'books' of 1 Enoch were found at Qumran. Missing is the *Similitudes* with its important messianic

---

11. For English translations of early Christian apocalyptic, see J. K. Elliott, *The Apocryphal New Testament: A Collection of Apocryphal Christian Literature in an English Translation* (Oxford, 1993).

12. For English translations of the Scrolls, see Geza Vermes, *The Dead Sea Scrolls in English,* 2d ed. (New York: Penguin, 1975).

implications. However, the remaining composite survived in a grand total of twenty copies! 1 Enoch is thus in a tie with fourth-place Genesis on the Dead Sea best-seller list—eclipsed only by the Psalms, Deuteronomy, and Isaiah. It must be remembered that a few lines from the first book of 1 Enoch are quoted in the New Testament by Jude (vv. 14–15), underlining the fact that this work was important not only among early Jews but Jewish Christians as well.

In addition to 1 Enoch, there are two previously unknown works found at Qumran that might best be labeled apocalyptic. 1) There are ten scrolls which contain sections describing a gigantic messianic temple (the New Jerusalem), works clearly patterned after Ezekiel 40–48. Also to be included in this group of temple apocalypses is Revelation 21:10–27. The other new work is found in some nine copies and known by the title *War Scroll*. To some degree the sectarian equivalent to the Book of Revelation, this text describes the final battles between the Sons of Darkness and the Sons of Light. In a sectarian foreshadowing of baseball's World Series, the scoreboard shows a tie of 3 to 3 after six contests. In the final confrontation the Messiah, bearing the title the Prince of the Congregation, comes forth to lead the Sons of Light to a total and eternal victory over evil, ushering in the Messianic Age. The message is clear: Although God's work may now seem to be opposed by an equally determined and pernicious evil, in the end he will intervene in power and suppress all wicked forces working against his predetermined plan.

Old Testament Writings

In the Old Testament canon the most obvious apocalyptic portion is Daniel 7–12, usually considered full-blown apocalyptic. Daniel has multiple visions full of symbolism and mystery, including a progression of strange beasts that succeed one another. When the last one is destroyed, the "Son of Man" comes to earth to rule a kingdom that will never be destroyed (see 7:13–14). Before that happens, however, Daniel is shown how terrible the trials will be for God's chosen as the end draws near. War will be waged in and around the "Beautiful Land," leaving destruction at every turn (see 8:9–13). Fortunately, Daniel learns that there is a time limit for the wickedness of this world, for God is in control and has decreed the end of transgression (see 9:24–27). The righteous will finally be delivered and will shine like the stars forever and ever (12:3).

There are parts of other books in the Old Testament that have some of the characteristics of apocalyptic, though not everyone agrees that they should be called apocalyptic. Isaiah 24–27, sometimes called the Isaiah Apocalypse, is one of the earliest examples of apocalyptic content and technique. According to the prophet, the earth's condition is wretched and, apart from outside intervention, seemingly hopeless. But God is going to rise up and destroy wickedness from the earth and inaugurate a new order. Isaiah 56–66, another passage with apocalyptic characteristics, pictures a sharp contrast between the righteous who are helplessly suffering under the present world order and God's radical solution when he will violently destroy the wicked and create a new heaven and new earth.

In Ezekiel 38–39 the pouring out of God's judgment on the earth is described in graphic terms, followed by the cleansing of the land and the restoration of the faithful to a place of security. It is a dreadful day for the earth's inhabitants in Joel 2:28–3:21 when God vents his anger against sin and restores the good life to the pardoned. In Zechariah 1–6 and 12–14 the prophet sees numerous visions showing God's intervention to remove evil and to establish a new era of blessing. The prophet Malachi is concerned about the unfaithfulness of the chosen and announces that a day of reckoning is coming when God will purge those who do evil, followed by the creation of a new society.

This selection of passages suggests that a shift from prophetic to apocalyptic eschatology was a trend at the end of the Old Testament period. The office of prophet begins to be replaced by that of the seer led by his angelic guide. To explain this shift in genre, researchers have suggested various factors—from political turmoil to foreign influence. Although a completely satisfying explanation may not be possible, certain clear parallels can be seen in our own world. One need only compare the possible modes and styles of communication available before the advent of television to those which are currently popular. We have traveled from the filmstrip and flannel board to "virtual-reality" in less than a half-century! Cultural shifts have produced an equally shocking change in the genre of the message as well. Likewise, the rapidly changing world both before and after the Jewish exile to Babylon produced comparable shifts in the delivery of God's message. Thus, the disconcerting and often confusing images of apocalyptic literature require some explanation for those of us still more comfortable with the "good old days" of the prophet!

How Apocalyptic Functions

Apocalyptic addresses a serious crisis of faith. If God is truly in control, why has he allowed things to get so bad here on this earth? In reply, apocalyptic proclaims that God has not turned his back on the world but will radically and unexpectedly intervene and introduce a universal solution that will solve all problems.

When faced with severe adversity such as the Jews experienced at the hands of the Assyrians or Babylonians or Syrians (or the Nazis), the response of many was to call on God for salvation. When relief failed to come, patience became thin and doubts about God's control and mercy arose. People understandably lost sight of the bigger picture of how God might be at work in the affairs of this world and became preoccupied with the immediacy of their own misfortunes.

Largely in response to this kind of crisis, apocalyptic literature gives its readers a roller-coaster ride through the heavens and into the future. There are thrills as those faced with crisis get a glimpse beyond the problems of the present. The heavenly journeys and descriptions of activities and creatures in the domain of heaven—all so unlike anything known on this earth—help the persecuted put their own misfortunes in perspective: What they are going through is relatively insignificant in the bigger picture of things. But the roller coaster also takes the riders down in the valleys of gloom and despair. The crisis of the present is only going to get worse, for the wickedness so prevalent will increase until it reaches a level unknown in human existence. Through all of this the stage is being set for God's sudden intervention. He is still in control and will win the fight once and for all; he will introduce an eternal solution, which will provide peace on earth. The feeling at the end of the roller-coaster ride is everlasting exhilaration.

The effect of the language of apocalyptic on those who heard was dramatic. It was uplifting as the faithful were reminded of how great God is: Apocalyptic is a call to stand in awe and to worship the sovereign LORD of the universe. It was comforting as the faithful were given new hope that this evil world would eventually come to an end: Apocalyptic is a promise of a new age when God will have his way on this earth as he does in heaven. The spell-binding scenes of heaven, often revealing the cosmic battle between good and evil, assured the faithful that what they were experiencing was simply a part of a larger conflict between God and Satan. It increased the saints' resolve: If the persecution became so intense that it resulted in death, they would be so much better off, given what they had to look forward to. The graphic descriptions of God's personal visit to the earth to correct all the wrongs, to punish all the wicked, and to create a radically new world encouraged the saints to be patient: The Lamb will once again stand on Mount Zion, and every knee will bow in adoration. All of this was a challenge to ethical purity, for the things of this world are temporal and tainted by sin. Those who remain faithful will eventually be honored with the glory of the new heaven and earth.

How to Interpret Apocalyptic Literature

The apocalyptic genre has been subjected to some of the most fallacious interpretations imaginable, largely because Christians are often not careful to understand it as intended and as originally heard. Any portion of Scripture divorced from its primary culture and the intent of the author is a homeless child wandering the streets, vulnerable to violent abuses.

Contrary to the practice of some interpreters, the meaning of a text hinges on what it meant when it was written (not on what it may at first glance seem to mean today). Until we become students of the biblical world and the mind-set of that era, we will err in our understanding of what the Bible intends to reveal. This does not revoke, however, the Bible's relevance for today. It simply indicates that the present significance of a text grows out of what it meant originally. There are essential principles of interpretation to guide contemporary readers through the special characteristics of the apocalyptic genre.[13]

Guidelines for Interpretation

1. *Study biblical apocalyptic in the light of apocalyptic ways of thinking in the ancient world.* Apocalyptic is a unique genre with specific codes and ways of communicating, but it was not a genre unique to the Bible. Apocalyptic ways of envisioning things were very common in the biblical world near the end of the Old Testament and through the time of the New Testament. Thus, understanding the biblical examples of apocalyptic within the scope of non-biblical examples is essential.

2. *Read apocalyptic in view of a context of crisis.* People frustrated to the point of despair were the expected hearers of apocalyptic, and authors sought ways to communicate encouragement for them to withstand the torrent of tribulation and to stand tall in the faith.

3. *Do not look for something in apocalyptic that it does not intend to disclose.* The function of an apocalyptic text is the key to understanding it. Though apocalyptic authors do have something important to communicate, it is more hope for the future than information about the future. Since the meaning of a passage is closely tied to the impact that the passage is designed to have on the readers, apocalyptic is generally not a chronological account of the future but a literary shock treatment of bold and graphic images to take our attention away from the problems we currently face and give us hope that God will win a resounding victory over all evil.

4. *Expect apocalyptic to be full of metaphorical language.* Because the apocalyptic genre is intensely literary—with an abundance of figures of speech such as metaphor, hyperbole, and

---

13. For other helpful discussions of hermeneutical principles for apocalyptic, see D. S. Russell, *Prophecy and the Apocalyptic Dream: Protest and Promise* (Peabody, Mass.: Hendrickson, 1994): 94–121; Gordon D. Fee and Douglas Stuart, *How to Read the Bible for All Its Worth: A Guide to Understanding the Bible,* 2d ed. (Grand Rapids: Zondervan, 1993), 231–45; William W. Klein, Craig L. Blomberg, and Robert L. Hubbard, Jr., *Introduction to Biblical Interpretation* (Dallas: Word, 1993), 311–12; and Osborne, *The Hermeneutical Spiral,* 221–32.

irony—readers must look carefully at the literary techniques of the authors. The compelling scenes and images are intended to draw readers into the story so that they can experience it like a child enraptured in a fairy tale. Apocalyptic is intentionally vivid in how it describes things.

5. *Do not attempt to identify the significance of every detail in apocalyptic.* The metaphorical language of apocalyptic often cannot be deciphered, partially because its language is so unique that other uses in Scripture of similar motifs may be of little value for understanding apocalyptic. Furthermore, the images within a single apocalypse may be fluid, such that the meaning of a motif varies within the same piece of literature. This may leave the significance of some portions of an apocalypse a mystery. And that is the way it should be: If we could solve all the puzzles of apocalyptic, it would defraud the genre of the mystery that is intended to surround it.

6. *Keep all options open for how apocalyptic predictions will be fulfilled.* The subject matter of apocalyptic is heaven and the future, both areas unknown in human experience. Because of the inherent limitations of human language to describe something that humans have never experienced, the descriptions of creatures, scenes, and people of heaven or of the future may not be the same in reality as they are in the visionary literature of apocalyptic.

7. *Seek to understand the main point of an apocalyptic unit.* Apocalyptic tends to be impressionistic, more like an abstract painting which communicates an overall impression. If you stand too close to the painting trying to examine the detail of the artist's work, you fail to grasp what the picture is intended to present. Likewise, correct interpretation of apocalyptic seeks to understand the big picture—the meaning of the whole rather than the meaning of the parts. Sometimes the details in apocalyptic are for dramatic effect; there may be no significance other than how the imagery of the scene is enhanced by the details. The details in apocalyptic must not be seen as allegorical in the sense that each detail has a corresponding reality.

8. *Appreciate the full and rich symbolism of apocalyptic.* Once apocalyptic is correctly understood, readers will be freed to enjoy the beautiful imagery used to describe heaven and the future.

Though the terminology of apocalyptic often denotes something different from what those same words may mean in their normal sense—the description may be more symbolic than literal—nevertheless, every detail in apocalyptic is significant in portraying God's perspective on things to come.

The Judgment of Gog

Ezekiel 38–39, a prophecy concerning Gog, provides an example for applying the principles of interpretation for "drawing out the meaning" of biblical apocalyptic.[14] In the broad sense, Ezekiel 38–39 is prophetic literature, though with clear apocalyptic characteristics. This illustrates the most likely beginning of all apocalyptic literature, originating in prophecy. Some students of apocalyptic classify this pericope as an example of transitional apocalyptic—standing midway in the development from prophecy to full-blown apocalyptic.[15]

Metaphorical symbolism is not so highly developed in these two chapters of Ezekiel as in Daniel, or in later apocalyptic literature, yet there are a number of clear metaphorical images. The character of Gog, the seven-year burning of his weapons (39:9), the seven-month search for bones (39:15), and the gathering of beasts and birds to eat the flesh and drink the blood of the fallen enemy and his horses (39:17–20) are examples of expressions which have an element of mystery. The repetition of similar sets or cycles of prophecies obviated by such expressions as "prophesy and say" (Ezek. 38:2, 14; 39:1), "son of man" (Ezek. 38:2,14; 39:1,17, NASB), and "thus says the LORD God" (Ezek. 38:3, 10, 14, 17; 39:1, 17, 25, NASB) are also evidences of apocalyptic genre.

Contextually, Ezekiel 38–39 forms the future and final judgment on the heathen nations, in the guise of Gog, for the purpose of establishing a restored Israel safely in the land (see Ezek. 37). Having

---

14. Dr. Patterson regularly assigned a paper in his Major Prophets class to be entitled: "Apocalypticism and the Prophet Ezekiel." When I took this class in the spring of 1981, I instead prepared a study on the New Covenant in Ezekiel—a paper which he graciously received. I am thankful for this opportunity to fulfill his course requirement even if it is somewhat late! (MGA)

15. Stone, "Apocalyptic Literature," 385–87.

been thus established, the prophet relates final details pertaining to the eschatological temple, worship of God, and final division of the Holy Land (see Ezek. 40–48).

The controlling purpose or "big idea" of the passage is the hope of security for those God has "resurrected" or restored (see Ezek. 37). Despite all the hardships that life might bring, with true apocalyptic character, God demonstrates his sovereign control (38:4), suppresses all evil forces working against his predetermined plan (38:22), comforts his people with a knowledge of himself (39:22), and promises that he will never abandon his redeemed people (39:29).

As noted above, these two chapters are clearly constructed around the repetition of similar sets or cycles of prophecies. God's command to Ezekiel (son of man) to prophesy forms the major divisions, while the formula "thus says the LORD God" introduces subordinate discussions or scenes.

The Word of the Lord to Ezekiel Concerning the Future Foe (38–39)

Prophecy #1:	The Foe moves against God's people/Two perspectives (38:2–13)
Scene a:	I (God) will bring you against my people (38:3–9)
Scene b:	You (Gog) have devised this evil against my people (38:10–13)
Prophecy #2:	The Foe is judged/God is made known in judgment (38:14–23)
Scene a:	You (Gog) will attack in the "last days" (38:14–16)
Scene b:	I (God) have announced judgment in the "former days" (38:17–23)
Prophecy #3:	The Foe is destroyed/Trial brings blessing (39:1–16)
Scene a:	I (God) will judge as I have spoken (39:1–8)
Scene b:	God's people are blessed in the aftermath of trial (39:9–16)
Prophecy #4:	The Foe is sacrificed/God does not forsake his people (39:17–29)
Scene a:	God's people are satiated with God's supply (39:17–24)
Scene b:	I (God) will never hide from those who are truly mine (39:25–29)

This four-part structure reveals a literary masterpiece whose conception clearly rivals the most ingenious of present-day writers. In the first scene of prophecy #1, Ezekiel examines God's initiation of Gog's unprovoked attack (see 38:3–9). The second scene probes the same incident from the point of view of Gog himself, as he devises "an evil plan" against an "unprotected" people (38:10–13). Ezekiel would have us ponder the paradox of events in our lives; none of them are to be separated from either God's design or from human responsibility.

Prophecy #2 reviews the attack upon God's people from Gog's perspective, an event now revealed to be reserved for the "last days" (38:14–16). Plowing new ground, the second scene of prophecy #2 reveals that indeed God had spoken in "former days" through his prophets concerning Gog's attack on Israel. God is not caught unaware. Indeed he has already given notice of the attack which is yet to occur.

Verse 17 also makes it clear that, for Ezekiel, Gog is a metaphor for "enemy." We miss the point in searching for the present geographical descendant of this mysterious character. The message declares that these enemies of God's people will be judged (see 38:17–23). Natural catastrophes form the apocalyptic agents of his judgment (see 38:19–22) for the now clear purpose that the nations "will know that I am the LORD" (38:23).

Prophecy #3 again reviews the judgment of God on Gog (see 39:1–8) and underlines the purpose stated in the previous scene (39:6–7). In the latter part of prophecy #3—here introduced by "then"—an astounding fact is revealed: The trials of God's people bring incredible blessing in their wake (39:9–16). Instead of dying under implements of war, they are now sustained by them. Instead of becoming spoil, God's people take spoil. In an ironic twist (especially evident in the Hebrew), Gog is given a place in Israel (39:11)—a place of burial! God is a master of transforming our trials into blessing.

In a now familiar pattern, prophecy #4 returns to emphasize the second scene of prophecy #3 as God's people have their needs satisfied by the spoils of war (see 39:17–24). The metaphorical imagery is constructed of components unique to the biblical text. God is pictured as sacrificing the foe to his people, filling them with the fat and blood—elements which are elsewhere reserved for God alone (see Lev. 3:17; 17:6). In the second scene, Ezekiel closes the pericope with a pointed play on words. Having gathered his exiled people to their land, God promises that "I will leave (*'otîr*) none of them [in exile] any longer. And I will not hide (*'astîr*) My face from them any longer, for I shall have poured out My Spirit on the house of Israel" (39:28b–29, NASB). God will never abandon his regenerate people.

The principles of interpretation suggested above have rescued the message of this passage from a number of unhelpful rabbit trails (Does Gog stand for Russia?) and troubling questions (Can modern weapons be burned as fuel?). The expectation of metaphor in apocalyptic literature underlines the graphic nature of these elements. The rich irony (or otherwise biblical impossibility!) presented in the picture of God's sacrificing the enemy to Israel and feeding his people forbidden fat—and quenching their thirst with banned blood—presents a shocking portrait speaking of both great judgment upon the godless and miraculous supply for the elect. These bold images draw the reader into the composition in a way that a simple statement of encouragement could never do. Characteristic of apocalyptic, Ezekiel gives his prophecy in a way that captivates the imagination.

Ezekiel's message, proclaimed to a people still ensnared in the bonds of Babylonian captivity, is one of hope. Although clearly declaring that the future of God's people included additional trials, the passage emphasizes that God is in total control and will bring ultimate judgment upon his enemies and glorious blessing upon his people.

Conclusion

The unique and often mystifying characteristics of apocalyptic literature can lead interpreters to two equally problematic conclusions. On the one hand, it would appear at first glance that the crucial task is the interpretation of symbols and the application of passages to current events—all this in a well-meant attempt to prove the Bible to be as up-to-date as this evening's newscast. Changes in the political arena, such as in the Middle-East and the former Soviet Union, have spawned dozens of books and broadcasts explaining how prophecy is being fulfilled and that the end of the world is near. Similarly in decades past, the war to end all wars, the atrocities of Nazi Germany and policies of the Catholic Church fueled a similar industry. On the other hand, some students of the Word simply throw up hands in despair of understanding such outlandish passages of apocalyptic and move on to texts which on the surface appear to be more applicable to "where we live." Obviously either approach should be described as shrinking "from declaring . . . the whole purpose of God" (Acts 20:27, NASB).

The genius of apocalyptic literature is the message of hope. In the face of perverse evil God's people are being exhorted to persevere to the end. For although the game may seem lost—or for the more optimistic, tied up—we are assured that God is preparing to intervene and judge evil by supernatural means. Biblical apocalyptic is a wake-up call to a most refreshing eternal perspective: God will bring a permanent solution to sin's evil effects, and we will be there to enjoy it!

Recommended Reading

Collins, John J., ed. *Apocalypse: Towards the Morphology of a Genre.* Semeia 14. 1979. This collection of articles deals with the questions of definition and description of apocalyptic literature in the canon and various Near Eastern sources.

————. *The Apocalyptic Imagination: An Introduction to the Jewish Matrix of Christianity.* New York: Crossroad, 1984. This volume is an indispensable analysis of the full range of apocalyptic literature composed by the Jews. Form, authorship, date, and content of each apocalypse are discussed in detail.

————. "Apocalyptic Literature." In *Early Judaism and Its Modern Interpreters,* edited by R. A. Kraft and G. W. E. Nickelsburg. Philadelphia: Fortress, 1986. This chapter is a review of research on Jewish apocalyptic and an assessment of the present status of scholarship. It includes a very helpful bibliography.

Collins, John J. and James H. Charlesworth, eds. *Mysteries and Revelations: Apocalyptic Studies Since the Uppsala Colloquium.* Sheffield: JSOT Press, 1991. This collection of eight essays by leading scholars in the field of Jewish apocalypticism reflects the current status of research on apocalyptic in the biblical world.

Hanson, Paul D. "Apocalyptic Literature." In *The Hebrew Bible and Its Modern Interpreters*, edited by Douglas A. Knight and Gene M. Tucker. Chico, Ca.: Scholars Press, 1985. This chapter summarizes the problems of definition, time of origin, and sources of apocalyptic, with specific focus on apocalyptic texts in the Old Testament. Helpful bibliography is included.

————. *Old Testament Apocalyptic*. Interpreting Biblical Texts. Nashville: Abingdon, 1987. This overview of Old Testament apocalyptic is written for a general audience of serious Bible interpreters. Special attention is given to the significance of apocalyptic for today, with specific examples of apocalyptic passages and their relevance.

Hellholm, David, ed. *Apocalypticism in the Mediterranean World and the Near East: Proceedings of the International Colloquium on Apocalypticism, Uppsala, August 12–17, 1979*. Tübingen: J.C.B. Mohr, 1983. The wide-ranging papers collected here were presented at a conference that has become a watershed in the study of apocalyptic. Many of these papers are still very important.

Hewitt, C. M. Kempton. "Guidelines to the Interpretation of Daniel and Revelation." In *A Guide to Biblical Prophecy*, edited by C. E. Armerding and W. W. Gasque, 101–16. Peabody, Mass: Hendrickson, 1989. Written from an evangelical viewpoint, this chapter is a balanced discussion of how to interpret Daniel and Revelation since they are apocalyptic. Other chapters in this book are also valuable.

Morris, Leon. *Apocalyptic*. Grand Rapids: Eerdmans, 1972. This brief but classic introduction to apocalyptic surveys the characteristics of the genre and the importance of the genre for biblical studies.

Reddish, Mitchell G., ed. *Apocalyptic Literature: A Reader*. Nashville: Abingdon, 1990. This anthology of apocalyptic literature—intended as a reader to introduce students to the genre—is a very handy collection of the principal forms of apocalyptic, including the Dead Sea Scrolls and Christian apocalypses.

Rowland, Christopher. *The Open Heaven: A Study of Apocalyptic in Judaism and Early Christianity.* New York: Crossroad, 1982. This thorough analysis of apocalypticism—with special attention to rabbinic and early Christian apocalyptic—focuses on apocalyptic revelation of the mysteries of the four realms of the universe.

Russell, D. S. *Divine Disclosure: An Introduction to Jewish Apocalyptic.* Minneapolis: Fortress, 1992. This solid introduction to apocalyptic summarizes most of the important questions about apocalyptic. The discussion of the various ways to define apocalyptic is especially helpful.

———. *Prophecy and the Apocalyptic Dream: Protest and Promise.* Peabody, Mass.: Hendrickson, 1994. This popular introduction to apocalyptic is written for Christians who are perplexed by Daniel and Revelation and the many confusing explanations of future events. It includes a helpful discussion of principles of interpretation.

Stone, M. E. "Apocalyptic Literature." In *Jewish Writings of the Second Temple Period.* CRINT 2 edited by M. E. Stone, 383–441. Philadelphia: Fortress, 1984. This survey of the apocalyptic genre is a thorough discussion of common features in apocalyptic and the relationship of apocalyptic to wisdom and prophecy.

10

LAMENT

Tremper Longman III

Lament and joy are opposites. They constitute the north pole and the south pole in the world of emotions. While joy reacts to the world with happiness and praise, lament reacts with disappointment and grief.

Most people think of Christianity as a religion of joy rather than lament. After all, the fruit of the Spirit includes "love, joy, peace, patience, kindness, goodness, faithfulness, gentleness and self-control" (Gal. 5:22–23). That makes lament seem closer in kind to the traits listed under the "sinful nature" (Gal. 5:19–20). Closer inspection of Scripture, however, reveals that lament plays a vital role in biblical religion. The Bible informs us right from the start (see Gen. 3) that the world is plunged into the darkness of sin and suffering, from which it will not be released until the end of time (see Rom. 8:18–25). The psalmist in particular showcases the role of lament in the practice of our faith. It is something many Christians have overlooked, and many interpreters of the Bible have misunderstood.

What Is a Lament?

The Psalms may be grouped into three major categories: psalms of orientation, disorientation, and reorientation.[1] The first group refers to psalms of pure praise to Yahweh. No obstacles stand in the way of the psalmist's relationship to God. The second group is composed of psalms of lament. Something has happened to disturb the divine-human relationship. The psalmist may feel that God has abandoned him, or perhaps, he may be experiencing God's hostility. Reorientation, the third group, describes those psalms where the lament has been heard and the relationship healed. The psalmist gives God thanks for hearing his prayers.

The lament is a prayer of disorientation. It is distinguished primarily by its content and mood and secondarily by its structure. In the case of a lament, content and mood are intertwined. A lament may be recognized quickly by expressions of grief, sorrow, fear, anger, contempt, shame, guilt, and other dark emotions. Laments often involve some kind of turn toward God and hope in the form of statements of confidence or hymns of joy (for an exception to this pattern, see Ps. 88).

Since the work of two pioneers in the form criticism of the Psalter (Gunkel and Begrich), two categories of lament have been identified: individual and communal laments. The two can be easily separated, for the former concerns the complaints of a single individual and the latter voices the concerns of the community. However, in practice it is often hard to decide whether a psalm is personal or corporate, since the "I" of the psalm could reflect a representative of the community. Along with this, some laments are clearly placed in the mouth of the king, who may represent the entire community. For this reason, royal lament should be added as a third category.[2]

Stylistically, lament is a poetic genre and demonstrates the traits which differentiate prose from poetry. No single trait or cluster of traits defines poetry in the Bible, but a heightened use of parallel-

---

1. W. Brueggemann, *The Message of the Psalms* (Minneapolis: Augsburg, 1984).
2. E. Gerstenberger, "Psalms," in *Old Testament Form Criticism* (San Antonio: Trinity University Press, 1977), 198–207.

ism, imagery, and other figurative language signal its presence. Perhaps more than anything, the consistent use of individual clauses that are joined to form parallel lines (cola), which combine to form verses, which in turn lead to stanzas, distinguishes poetry from prose (which contains sentences forming paragraphs). Terse expression—saying a lot with a few words—is the norm of poetry and explains why the margins are larger in English translations of the poetic portions of the Bible.

As a poetic form of speech, lament has at least one distinctive poetic trait associated with it: a special meter (called *qînâ*). In general, this term describes poetry in which the first colon of a parallel line is longer than the second. According to an older way of describing meter, the first colon has three beats, while the second has two. This metrical description has been associated with a kind of "limping dance," which mourners supposedly affected while following a corpse in a funeral procession.[3] While the long-short pattern holds valid for some lament literature, it does not seem strictly consistent; in any case, it is problematic to call this pattern metrical, since great doubt has been cast on the presence of meter in Hebrew poetry in general.

How the Psalmist Expresses Lament

Besides content, tone, and style, lament also has a distinctive structure. While some structural elements have a consistent place in a lament (for instance, if a "hymn of praise" occurs in the lament, it will be at the end), there is flexibility in terms of the order in which the elements appear and the frequency in which they occur (e.g., in Ps. 69 the "complaint" appears three times). Nonetheless, the following seven elements occur with some consistency in laments:

1. invocation
2. plea to God for help
3. complaints
4. confession of sin or an assertion of innocence
5. curse of enemies (imprecation)

---

3. See W. R. Garr, "The Qinah: A Study of Poetic Meter, Syntax, and Style," *ZAW* 95 (1983): 54–75.

6. confidence in God's response
7. hymn or blessing

The poet often begins with an invocation combined with a plea to God for help. There is no one the poet can turn to but God himself:

Help, LORD, for the godly are no more;
the faithful have vanished from among men (12:1).

Hear, O LORD, my righteous plea;
listen to my cry (17:1).

The *invocation* is simply the crying out of God's name in the vocative. The *plea* or petition is the request, usually expressed with the imperative mood.

The *complaint* is a focal point in the lament because it is here that we learn what has motivated the lamenter to prayer.

But I am a worm and not a man,
scorned by men and despised by the people.
All who see me mock me;
they hurl insults, shaking their heads (22:6–7).

Though the mood of the lament is generally melancholic, there are one or two moments when the lamenter makes clear his basic trust in God. This is true of the section in which he expresses his confidence:

Surely God is my help;
the LORD is the one who sustains me (54:4).

Since a lament predominantly reflects a downcast mood, it is surprising to note that almost all laments include some expression of trust in God.

The *curse on the enemies* (imprecation) is perhaps the most difficult part to reconcile with our feelings about God. A particularly hard-hitting imprecation is found in Psalm 109:

May his days be few;
may another take his place of leadership.
May his children be fatherless
and his wife a widow (109:8–9).

Laments may be further divided on the basis of whether the poet *confesses his sin* in the context of his suffering or, the opposite, *protests his innocence*.

You know my folly, O God;
  my guilt is not hidden from you (69:5).
Though you probe my heart and examine me at night,
  though you test me, you will find nothing;
  I have resolved that my mouth will not sin (17:3).

As Christians, we resonate with the confession but find the lamenter's assertion of innocence almost presumptuous. We may be offended by the latter because we think of Paul's strong statements on the total sinfulness of men and women (see Rom. 3:9–20). But we must remember that there are occasions when people are persecuted or harassed in situations or for reasons for which they are totally innocent. Assertions of innocence do have a proper place in the context of prayer.

Last, hymns of praise are common toward the conclusion of a lament. As the lamenter realizes what God can and will do for him, it leads him to the opposite of lament: praise.

My feet stand on level ground;
  in the great assembly I will praise the LORD (26:12).

The transition from complaint to praise is often so abrupt that many scholars feel that the laments presuppose the presence of a priest.[4] As the primary setting of the Psalms is in the formal worship service, the priest would hear the complaint and then respond with an assurance of pardon and God's help. This assurance would allow the psalmist to respond with joy. The priest's statements, so the argument runs, were not recorded in the psalm, though similar oracles are found elsewhere (see Jer. 30:10–11; Isa. 41:8–13; 43:1–7). This reconstruction, while not provable, seems reasonable, though the important point to notice is that sorrow turns to joy in most laments.

To Whom the Psalmist Expresses Lament

The complaints of a lament go in three directions. They are directed toward either the unspecified enemy of the lamenter, the lamenter himself, or—most unsettling of all—toward God. In the

---

4. This was first recognized by J. Begrich, "Das priesterliche Heilsorakel," *ZAW* 52 (1934): 81–92, cited and discussed in Brueggemann, *The Message of the Psalms*, 57–58.

first case, the enemy is the other person, the outside force, who persecutes, threatens, and undermines the speaker or the group that he represents. The enemy is usually anonymous in a lament. This is certainly the case with the Psalter. After all, the Psalter is a liturgical book. The psalms, though they may have been written with a specific historical event in mind,[5] have left that event unnamed in the body of the poem so the psalm could be reused and reapplied to similar, though not identical, later events. One person's enemy is not another person's, but the psalm can serve both. Even in a book like Lamentations, which clearly addresses the historical destruction of Jerusalem by the Babylonians, the enemy is described in general, not specific terms.

Second, the lamenter may direct his complaints toward himself. He recognizes that he, too, is a source of his problems. In Psalms 42–43, an original unity as indicated by the common refrain, the psalmist three times expresses the distress that he feels toward himself:

> Why are you so downcast, O my soul?
>   Why so disturbed within me?
> Put your hope in God,
>   for I will yet praise him,
>   my Savior and my God (42:5,11; 43:5).

Third, the lament may be directed toward God, because he has abandoned, brutalized, or undermined the lamenter. Divine abandonment or hostility evokes the greatest sense of terror or anger in the psalmist. This attitude may be observed in the opening stanza of Psalm 60:

> You have rejected us, O God, and burst forth upon us;
>   you have been angry—now restore us!
> You have shaken the land and torn it open;
>   mend its fractures, for it is quaking.
> You have shown your people desperate times;
>   you have given us wine that makes us stagger (60:1–3).

Thus, the complaints of the lament are directed toward three culprits—the enemy, the lamenter himself, or God. Of course, a single poem may address all three (Pss. 42–43 are a good example).

---

5. T. Longman III, *How to Read the Psalms* (Downers Grove: InterVarsity, 1988): xx.

Where Laments Are Found

Lament in the Old Testament

The widespread use of the lament in the Psalter deserves first mention. Because these laments have traditionally been used to define the genre, all other uses are compared to the Psalter laments. Lament is the predominant genre of the Psalter, with as many as fifty examples of individual laments and twenty examples of corporate laments.

Interestingly, however, the Psalter is not a depressing book. Two reasons account for this. First, the laments are concentrated in the first part of the book. Thus, by the time the reader comes to the end of the book, joy has overcome grief. The last five psalms form a climactic doxology, appropriately concluding a book known as "Praises" (*Tehillim*) in Jewish tradition. Second, as already noted, the laments themselves are not unrelieved poems of darkness. Almost always there is a turn to God and joy at the end. The presence of such a large number of personal and corporate laments in the Psalms, the worship book of the Old Testament, allowed the people of God to articulate their heartfelt needs and pain before their God.

The second major exemplar of the genre is the Book of Lamentations. Though Gunkel argued that Lamentations is a combination of several different types of literature—with chapters 1, 2, and 4 as funeral songs, chapter 3 an individual lament, and chapter 5 a communal lament[6]—recent studies have tended to view the book more holistically.

Lamentations is a communal lament, similar to the corporate laments found within the Psalter. A communal lament is, "a composition whose verbal content indicates that it was composed to be used by and/or on behalf of a community to express both complaint, and sorrow and grief over some perceived calamity, physical or cultural, which had befallen or was about to befall them and to appeal to God for deliverance."[7] The tone, content, and structure of the work all support its identification as a corporate

---

6. H. Gunkel, "Klagelieder Jeremiae," in *RGG* (2d ed., vol. 3) col. 1049–52.

7. P. W. Ferris, Jr., *The Communal Lament in the Bible and the Ancient Near East* (Atlanta: Scholars Press, 1992), 10.

lament. Indeed, the various titles given to the book—whether by the rabbis, or in the Greek Old Testament, or in the Vulgate—all mean laments, leading to the title given to the book in English translations.

Debate has surrounded the question whether the poem is consistently corporate, especially in the light of 3:1–21. This unit begins "I am the man who has seen affliction" and is often understood as the expression of a single individual. Much effort has been spent in an attempt to identify the speaker behind the "I." A sample of suggestions include Jehoiachin, a defeated soldier, and Jeremiah himself. More likely is the interpretation that the speaker is Jerusalem personified, but even if it is an individual, that individual gives utterance to the suffering and pain of the whole community. Thus, though there is variety of expression, the book as a whole is still correctly identified as a corporate lament.

Ferris provocatively discusses the possibility that Solomon's dedicatory prayer in 1 Kings 8 provides the setting for the corporate laments like Lamentations.[8] The king describes seven situations which evoke prayer in the temple, four of them are national disasters: (1) defeat in battle (8:33–34), (2) drought (8:35–36), (3) other natural disasters or disease (8:37–40), and (4) captivity (8:46–50). Of course, it is the first which motivates the lament prayer of Lamentations.

A third major locus of lament literature is found in the Book of Jeremiah. As is well recognized, Jeremiah as a person comes to the fore of his prophecy more than any other prophet.[9] In chapters 11–20[10] the prophet offers a series of plaintive, and occasionally angry, laments before God. Smith[11] well describes the function of these laments in the book:

---

8. Ferris, *The Communal Lament.*

9. Though many scholars, such as M. S. Smith, *The Laments of Jeremiah and Their Contexts* (SBLMS; Atlanta: Scholars Press, 1990), would argue that this is a fiction, not the historical Jeremiah.

10. Specifically, Jeremiah 11:18–23; 12:1–6; 15:15–21; 17:14–18; 18:18–23; 20:7–13.

11. Smith, *The Laments of Jeremiah*, xx.

The laments in context partake of three additional purposes beyond the laments' original function of defending the legitimacy of Jeremiah's prophetic vocation in the face of resistance. The laments in context function to announce Yahweh's judgement against Israel, to show the people's fault and the impact of that sin on Yahweh as the spurned partner to the covenant, and finally, to present Jeremiah's special identification with Yahweh as sign and symbol of Israel's relationship with Yahweh. In sum, the laments in context are designed primarily to present the guilt of the people and the necessity of judgement.[12]

The laments of the psalmist, Jeremiah, and the Book of Lamentations are perhaps the most notable, but the lament, as a cry to God out of desperation—whether angry or pitiable—occurs throughout the Torah, the Prophets, and the Writings.[13] We find the skeleton of the lament as early as the patriarchal period. After years of waiting for a child, Abram invokes the LORD and presents his complaint before him: "O Sovereign LORD, what can you give me since I remain childless and the one who will inherit my estate is Eliezer of Damascus?. . . You have given me no children; so a servant in my household will be my heir" (Gen. 15:2, 3). Other early examples include Genesis 25:22; Judges 15:18; 21:2–3.

Lament in the Ancient Near East

Lament is also attested in Near Eastern literature outside the Bible. God chose to address his people Israel in a language and with literary forms that they understood. Thus, it is not surprising to find many examples of the lament from the ancient Near East, particularly from Mesopotamia. Furthermore, all human beings experience pain and suffering in this world, both as individuals and as communities. It is natural for human beings who acknowledge a divine realm to turn to their gods, if not for help, at least for answers to the questions which their experience evoke.

Mesopotamian texts have played an important role in the discussion of an ancient Near Eastern background to the biblical lament

---

12. W. F. Lanahan, "The Speaking Voice in the Book of Lamentations," *JBL* 93 (1974): 41–49.

13. Besides the Book of Lamentations in the Writings, the lament is an important feature of the book of Job (see especially chap. 3 and the analysis of C. Westermann, *The Structure of the Book of Job* [Philadelphia: Fortress, 1981]).

genre. While one has to exercise considerable methodological caution in comparing biblical literature with that of its surrounding cultures,[14] it is still important to observe that there are analogues to both individual and corporate laments.

Mesopotamian literature attests a number of corporate laments, which traditionally are grouped in three subgenres:[15] (1) the city lament, (2) the *balag,* and (3) the *eršemma*.

There are six Sumerian city laments that narrate and theologically interpret the destruction of the city of Ur at the end of the third millennium B.C. They are the "Lament over the Destruction of Ur," the "Lament over the Destruction of Sumer and Ur," the "Nippur Lament," the "Eridu Lament," the "Uruk Lament," and the "Ekimar Lament."[16]

The *balag* and *eršemma* texts come later, written in Akkadian and appearing from the beginning of the second millennium B.C. down to the Seleucid period in the second half of the first millennium B.C. These texts also bewail the destruction of cities.

A comparison of lament in the biblical text with ancient Near Eastern examples leads to the difficult question of dependence. Some scholars advocate that Lamentations, for example, was influenced by Sumerian precursors.[17] Others draw attention to the large time and culture gap between the Sumerians and the biblical texts.[18] It is important to note that the similarities and differences may be found in a common cultural and literary tradition. Perhaps

---

14. See chapter 2 on the comparative method in T. Longman III, *Fictional Akkadian Autobiography* (Winona Lake, Ind.: Eisenbrauns, 1991).

15. The most recent description of the Mesopotamian genre and its relationship to biblical laments is found in F. W. Dobbs–Allsopp, *Weep, O Daughter of Zion: A Study of the City-Lament Genre in the Hebrew Bible* (Rome: Editrice Pontificio Istituto Biblico, 1993).

16. Easy access to English translations of the first two may be found in J. B. Pritchard, ed., *The Ancient Near East Texts Relating to the Old Testament* (Princeton: Princeton University Press, 1969), 455–63 and 611–19.

17. Originally proposed by S. N. Kramer, "Sumerian Literature and the Bible," in AnBib 12, Studia Biblica et Orientalia 3 (1959): 198–225; idem, 9 "Lamentation over the Destruction of Nippur: A Preliminary Report," *EI* 9 (1969): 85–115, supported more recently by W. C. Gwaltney, Jr. "The Biblical Book of Lamentations in the Context of Near Eastern Lament Literature," in *Scripture in Context II,* ed. W. W. Hallo, J. C. Moyer, and L. G. Perdue (Winona Lake, Ind.: Eisenbrauns, 1983).

18. And thus criticize Kramer and his supporters. See T. F. McDaniel, "Alleged Sumerian Influence on Lamentations," *VT* 18 (1968): 198–209 and Ferris, *The Communal Lament,* 174–75.

the best solution is that, while there are definite connections with the Mesopotamian lament genre, Israel also developed its own distinctive genre early on, thus accounting for similarities and dissimilarities between the biblical and Near Eastern texts.[19] Regardless of influence and borrowing, the presence of a corporate lament genre in Mesopotamia is important for the understanding of the biblical genre.

Lament in the New Testament

Nothing quite like a lament occurs in the New Testament. Of course, Old Testament laments are cited and are important to the theology of the New Testament, but no original laments are found in the New Testament. Indeed, there is very little poetic material in the New Testament, and those which occur are hymns of praise (see Luke 1:46–55, 68–79; Phil. 2:6–11). Nonetheless, lament makes its impact on the New Testament and should shape contemporary Christian piety as well.

Old Testament laments are key to the presentation of the gospel. Jesus and the early church expressed the depths of the Savior's anguish and pain through the laments, particularly Psalms 22 and 69. Most notably, Jesus took the words of Psalm 22:1 on his lips as he hung on the cross: "My God, my God, why have you forsaken me?" (Mark 15:34). We also learn of Christ's struggle with his approaching end in the Garden of Gethsemane. Jesus there invokes his divine Father and brings his complaints before him ("take this cup from me") before submitting to his Father's will (see Mark 14:32–42).

Jesus laments because he suffers. Indeed, he is the ultimate innocent sufferer. Though he suffers for the sins of the world, he himself has not sinned. Westermann disputes those who argue that Jesus' suffering has led to the eradication of lament as a legitimate expression of Christian theology. He notes how in the West confession of sin has replaced lament over suffering.[20] This move, however, is biblically unjustified. Note, for instance, the evidence of the "Lord's Prayer," a prayer which has rightly been taken as

---

19. F. W. Dobbs-Allsopp, *Weep, O Daughter of Zion*, 157–63.
20. C. Westermann, "The Role of the Lament in the Theology of the Old Testament," *Int* 28 (1974): 22.

paradigmatic for the Christian. Examination of that prayer indicates that lament combines with hymn, especially in the latter part when the petitions are addressed to God. The petitions recognize present distress, which the prayer asks God to alleviate.

Like the ancient Israelites who first uttered the Old Testament laments, Christians suffer in countless different ways. Close relatives and friends get sick and die; people are abused; women raped; children abandoned—the list is endless. We, too, are left wondering where is God in this fallen, painful world. The proper response is not repression but rather turning to God in order to honestly express our doubts and complaints. Only in this way can God turn our cries of sorrow into hymns of praise. The psalms and other laments can help us find words to address God in our pain.[21]

How to Interpret Lament

The following are guidelines that can help the reader interpret a lament with confidence. They are not ironclad rules that will be relevant with every lament text, nor are they all exclusive to the lament. They are principles that are generally helpful to interpreters who attempt to bridge the gap between the ancient author and their modern situation.

Guidelines for Interpretation

1. *Read the lament in its literary and historical context.* No text of the Bible is an isolated entity. It comes from a specific historical context and is embedded in a larger text. We cannot always be sure of the exact historical context, as with many of the lament psalms,[22] but sometimes the historical background makes an imprint on the text. This information is generally available within the historical books of the Bible itself (cf. Lamentations' relationship

---

21. See D. Allender and T. Longman III, *Cry of the Soul: How Our Emotions Reveal Our Deepest Questions About God* (Colorado Springs: Nav-Press, 1994) for a contemporary Christian use of the laments of the Old Testament.

22. However, attention should be given to those lament psalms which have historical titles (cf. Ps. 3). The titles are part of the Hebrew text of Psalms and should thus be considered canonical, even if they were not original to the psalm.

to the destruction of Jerusalem in 587/586 B.C.). But further historical studies in the ancient Near East can enrich our understanding of some texts. More critical is the literary context, which in the first place is the context within the book, but ultimately includes the Bible as a whole.

2. *Apply the conventions of ancient Semitic poetry to lament.* As has been observed, laments are poetical texts, with parallelism and imagery as the two most important poetical devices. These traits are powerful literary tools to compress thought. "Poetry says a lot using a few words," thus, for serious reading of a poem of lament, the interpreter must slow down and meditate, unpacking the rich thought of the poet.[23]

3. *Try to discover the reason for the lament.* This is often expressed by the presence of a *kî*-clause in Hebrew. The *kî* is usually translated as *for* or *because* and marks a complaint section in the psalm. The first of three complaint sections in Psalm 69 begins with the phrase, "for the waters have come up to my neck" (v. 1). By studying these clauses and the complaint sections we can see what led the lamenter to place his petition before the LORD. For example, there are laments of sickness, false accusation, defeat in battle, and persecution by enemies.

4. *Explore the theological teaching of the lament.* What is the lament teaching about God and our relationship with him? Often this teaching is presented through the imagery of the psalm. God may be pictured as a warrior, a king, a rock, or an enemy. Looking at the meaning behind the image teaches more about the nature of God. As Christians, though, we cannot restrict our theological explorations to the Old Testament. Jesus himself said that the whole Old Testament anticipated his coming suffering and glorification

---

23. Space does not permit a detailed explanation of parallelism and imagery. For more information, please consult T. Longman III, *Literary Approaches to Biblical Interpretation* (Grand Rapids: Zondervan, 1987); idem, *How to Read the Psalms* (Downers Grove: InterVarsity, 1988); and idem, "Poetry," in *A Complete Literary Guide to the Bible,* ed. L. Ryken and T. Longman III (Grand Rapids: Zondervan, 1993).

(see Luke 24:27, 44). Reflect on the lament as a prayer to Jesus and a prayer of Jesus.[24]

5. *Reflect on the lament's appeal to our emotions and our will.* Does it help us articulate what we are feeling? The lament psalms were written with this purpose in mind. They are not simply historical records; they are prayers written for the use of the people of God. They intend to help later worshipers who share similar though not necessarily identical feelings to express their emotions before God and the congregation. They encourage brutal honesty in prayer life before God. Calvin rightly called the Psalms a mirror of our souls,[25] and this applies to the laments as well.

But even further, psalms of lament direct our emotions and our will toward God. The transition from lament to praise which characterizes the majority of laments turns the attention of sufferers away from their pain and toward the joy of worship.[26]

A Midnight Struggle with God

Psalm 77 provides a good example of a lament, not because it illustrates every characteristic of a lament, but because it shows how flexible the genre is. The tone and content of the psalm allow us to identify the text as a lament the moment we begin reading. The composer identifies his actions as a cry to God for help:

> I cried out to God for help;
> I cried out to God to hear me.
> When I was in distress, I sought the LORD;
> at night I stretched out untiring hands
> and my soul refused to be comforted (vv. 1–2).

The psalmist, as is typical, does not name the specific trouble that induced his depression, but it was intense enough to deprive him of sleep. Rather than trying to fight off his troubled thoughts

---

24. See the study by E. P. Clowney, "The Singing Savior," *Moody Monthly* 79 (1978): 40–43.

25. John Calvin, *Psalms* (1571 reprint, Grand Rapids: Baker, 1981), xxxvii.

26. This dynamic is explored in relationship to anger, fear, jealousy, despair, contempt, and shame in D. Allender and T. Longman III, *Cry of the Soul.*

and seek the temporary forgetfulness of sleep, he spent his time praying. He turned toward his struggle instead of away from it, laying out his torment before God in what we would recognize as a more typical invocation and complaint section:

> I remembered you, O God, and I groaned;
>   I mused, and my spirit grew faint.
> You kept my eyes from closing;
>   I was too troubled to speak.
> I thought about the former days,
>   the years of long ago;
> I remembered my songs in the night.
>   My heart mused and my spirit inquired:
>   "Will the LORD reject forever?
>   Will he never show his favor again?
> Has his unfailing love vanished forever?
>   Has his promises failed for all time?
> Has God forgotten to be merciful?
>   Has he in anger withheld his compassion?" (vv. 3–9).

This is a lament directed most pointedly toward God. As the psalmist remembers God, he groans. It is as if God kept him from sleeping, was tormenting him, and had abandoned him and left him to twist and turn in agony at night. Long ago, God had promised to be with his people in a covenant relationship. That meant he would protect them and watch over them. He had promised to show them "favor," "unfailing love," to be "merciful," and keep his "promise." Now the psalmist confronts God and demands to know whether he is a liar. In the midst of his pain, he looks at his situation and wonders if God has reneged on his promises.

Note that this psalm illustrates the difficulty of differentiating individual from corporate laments. In one sense, the language seems clearly to point to a single individual doing the lamenting. However, the complaint language indicates an issue which has corporate implications: God's apparent refusal to honor his covenant agreements. Typical of laments, Psalm 77 also records a turn from lament to hope. As the psalmist recounts his midnight battle against his fears and against God, he experiences a remarkable change. This inversion takes him from the pit of his own private hell to the heights of joy. He leaves no doubt about the reason for his change of mind:

Then I thought, "To this I will appeal:
  the years of the right hand of the Most High."
I will remember the deeds of the LORD;
  yes, I will remember your miracles of long ago.
I will meditate on all your works
  and consider all your mighty deeds (vv. 10–12).

His thoughts turn from his troubles toward God to God's past acts of deliverance. In particular, the psalmist remembers what is perhaps the greatest salvation event in the Old Testament, the exodus from Egypt:

The waters saw you, O God,
  the waters saw you and writhed;
  the very depths were convulsed.
The clouds poured down water,
  the skies resounded with thunder;
  your arrows flashed back and forth.
Your thunder was heard in the whirlwind,
  your lightning lit up the world;
  the earth trembled and quaked.
Your path led through the sea,
  your way through the mighty waters,
  though your footprints were not seen.
You led your people like a flock
  by the hand of Moses and Aaron (vv. 16–20).

By the time this psalm was composed, the exodus was already an event of the distant past. It was ancient history to the psalmist, just as it is to us. But his memory of the exodus becomes a bulwark against his present troubles. If God could deliver his people from such dire troubles and deep fears in the past, he can certainly handle any present troubles.

Conclusion

A lament is the sad song of the soul (individual or corporate) in the midst of a fallen world. Though the lament is defined by its complaints and identified by its initial melancholic mood, it rarely ends on this note, especially in the Psalter. The Book of Lamentations—though it contains a hopeful section in the middle (3:11–42), which many consider climactic—does end with sadness, as does Job's lament. But in the Psalter, there is always a turn to joy and confidence. In this way, the psalm does more than give the worshiper a vent for negative emotions; it also turns him or her toward God. It is a mistake to take the abrupt turn as some kind of magical transformation that took place, a conversion on the spot, so to speak. The psalm compresses a long experience, a process, not just a single event. But the point of the psalm is to help the worshiper articulate heartfelt emotions, as dark as they might be, and then turn the worshiper toward God.

The presence of lament throughout the Bible encourages us to express our dark emotions—anger, fear, shame, contempt, jealousy—before God. However, we must open ourselves to God in this way only in the context of our confidence that he is able to help us. Otherwise, we will find ourselves in the unenviable position of the Israelites in the wilderness. They complained—or more accurately—grumbled against the LORD to Moses and Aaron (Num. 20:1–13) with the result that God punished them.

An honest turning to God in times of disappointment and grief—even in anger and confusion—turns sadness into singing (see Ps. 126:6). With a recognition of what God has done and can do, the opposite poles in the world of emotions are reversed. Joy replaces lament.

Recommended Reading

Allender, D. B. and T. Longman III. *Cry of the Soul: How Our Emotions Reveal Our Deepest Questions about God.* Colorado Springs: NavPress, 1994. This study concentrates on the laments of the Psalms and shows how they may be appropriated into contemporary Christian theology.

Boyce, R. N. *The Cry to God in the Old Testament.* SBLDS 103. Atlanta: Scholars Press, 1988. This study concentrates on the words s^cq/z^cq to study the turn to God for help in the Old Testament.

Brueggemann, W. *The Message of the Psalms.* Minneapolis: Augsburg, 1984. A wonderful theological introduction to the Psalms for layperson or scholar. Brueggemann treats psalms in three major categories: orientation, disorientation, and reorientation. The middle category is the lament (including penitential) psalm. These are psalms which are sung when things are not right in our relationship with God.

Dobbs-Allsopp, F. W. *Weep, O Daughter of Zion: A Study of the City-Lament Genre in the Hebrew Bible*. Rome: Editrice Pontificio Istituto Biblico, 1993. The most recent contender in the debate over the connection between the city laments, particularly Lamentations, in the Bible and from Mesopotamia. The author provides the most sophisticated analysis and concludes that we must account for some connection with Mesopotamia, while also acknowledging an older native genre of Hebrew city lament, discovered in the oracle against the nations.

Ferris, P. W., Jr. *The Genre of Communal Lament in the Bible and the Ancient Near East*. SBLDS 127. Atlanta: Scholars Press, 1992. An excellently researched and reasoned study of the communal lament in the Bible in the light of ancient Near Eastern parallels. Notable among the author's conclusions is the connection between communal lament in the Bible and Solomon's dedicatory prayer (1 Kings 8). Besides twenty psalms which he identifies as communal laments, Ferris also extensively treats the book of Lamentations.

Gerstenberger, E. "Psalms." In *Old Testament Form Criticism*, 179–223. San Antonio: Trinity University Press, 1974. A helpful and informative reprise of form critical work on the psalms since Gunkel-Begrich. Gerstenberger summarizes, evaluates, and presents his own views on different aspects of psalm research. Relevant to this study are his sections on individual, royal, and communal laments.

Longman, T. III. *How to Read the Psalms*. Downers Grove: InterVarsity, 1988. A historical, literary, and theological reading of the Book of Psalms. The lament is treated, using Psalm 69 as an extended example.

Smith, M. S. *The Laments of Jeremiah and Their Contexts*. Atlanta: Scholars Press, 1990. A form-critical and diachronic study of the laments of Jeremiah. Smith also discusses the laments in both their immediate context of chapters 11–20, as well as their broader context in the Book of Jeremiah.

Westermann, C. *Praise and Lament in the Psalms*. Atlanta: John Knox, 1965. A classic study on both the praise and lament forms in the Psalter. While Westermann's most notable contribution is the distinction between declarative and descriptive praise, his study of the lament is an excellent starting point to investigate the form criticism of the Psalms. Also notable is his chapter on "The 'Re-Presentation' of History in the Psalms."

————. "The Role of the Lament in the Theology of the Old Testament." *Int* 28 (1974): 20–38. An excellently written and stimulating study of the place of lament not only in the theology of the Old Testament, but also its significance for the New Testament, particularly in reference to Jesus, the lamenting Messiah.

Wevers, J. W. "A Study in the Form Criticism of Individual Complaint Psalms." *VT* 6 (1956): 80–96. A rather dated study of the genre. In his review of the structure of the genre, Wevers attempts to find a solution to the issue of the transition from complaint to joy in a "theology of the name" of God. He also divides the individual complaint psalm into three subtypes based on presumed settings in life: judicial psalms, psalms dealing with sorcerers, and psalms of sickness.

11

PRAISE

Kenneth L. Barker

"It is good to praise the LORD." So declared the psalmist in Psalm 92:1. But how should God's people praise him? David and the other psalmists answer: by recalling God's marvelous attributes; by reporting how he manifests and expresses those attributes through his mighty and redemptive acts for his people.

This understanding of the nature and quality of praise in the Psalms differs from the past. Psalms used to be divided into somewhat artificial and sometimes arbitrary categories based on the subject or theme of each psalm. It was a topical approach based on contents. Thus, individual psalms were labeled as instruction, trust, praise, distress and sorrow, thanksgiving, aspiration, penitence, history, imprecation, meditation, intercession, prophecy, and so on.

A German scholar, Hermann Gunkel (1862–1932)—a true pioneer in Psalms studies—changed all that.[1] He marked a new point of departure by focusing on types of psalms (*Gattungen*), grouped according to their function, form (or structure), and life-setting (*Sitz im Leben*), which refers to the situation that produced each

---

1. Hermann Gunkel, *The Psalms: A Form-Critical Introduction,* trans. Thomas M. Horner (Philadelphia: Fortress, 1967).

psalm or for which each was composed. This was a revolutionary approach and has influenced all studies in the Psalms since. It could be said that the progress in the study of the Psalter since World War I is largely due to the influence of one man.[2] It is not an overstatement to say that there has been no worthwhile commentary on the Psalms since Gunkel's that has not built on the approach he developed.[3]

How the Psalmist Expresses Praise

Praise is primarily a reciting of the *attributes* of God and of the *acts* of God, and then praising God for both. The first is descriptive praise, the second declarative praise. The worshiper rejoices because God is the kind of God he is and because he does the things he does. This, in turn, promotes greater trust in God, as well as a thankful heart. The Song of Miriam and the Song of Deborah show clearly that the life-setting of the hymn of praise is the experience of God's intervention in history. God has acted. He has helped his people. Now praise must be sung to him.[4]

Praising God for Who He Is
(Descriptive Praise).

Originally, psalms of descriptive praise were intended to be used either as a choral response or perhaps as a solo in the normal round of public or national worship. Because the psalmist

---

2. A. R. Johnson, "The Psalms," in *The Old Testament and Modern Study,* ed. H. H. Rowley (Oxford: Clarendon, 1951), 162.

3. John Bright, "Modern Study of Old Testament Literature," in *The Bible and the Ancient Near East,* ed. G. Ernest Wright (Garden City, N.Y.: Doubleday, 1961), 26–27. Also influential in the study of the Psalms is Mowinckel, a Norwegian scholar, who stresses the cultic character of the Psalms even more than Gunkel; Sigmund Mowinckel, *The Psalms in Israel's Worship,* trans. D. R. Ap-Thomas (Nashville: Abingdon, 1962). Mowinckel also makes much of psalms containing references to the so-called enthronement of Yahweh as King. He connects this with an alleged Jewish festival of the New Year, analogous to that in Babylon honoring the god Marduk. For cogent arguments against Mowinckel's view, see K. A. Kitchen, *Ancient Orient and Old Testament* (Chicago: InterVarsity, 1966), 102–6.

4. Claus Westermann, *Praise and Lament in the Psalms,* trans. Keith R. Crim and Richard N. Soulen (Atlanta: John Knox, 1981), 22.

was praising God primarily by describing his character, with a focus on the attributes of God—who he is and what he is like—these psalms are frequently called hymns of praise or descriptive psalms. The most common Hebrew verb used for this kind of praise is *hillel*. English readers are familiar with it in its imperative form: *Hallelu-Yah,* "Praise Yah!" (Yah is short for Yahweh, the LORD). There are five principal subcategories of this type of praise:

1. Hymns (e.g., Ps. 24; 29; 33; 100; 103; 105; 111; 113–14; 117; 135–36; 145–50)

> Praise the LORD, all you nations;
>> extol him, all you peoples.

> For great is his love toward us,
>> and the faithfulness of the LORD endures forever.

> Praise the LORD (Ps. 117).

2. Enthronement psalms (e.g., Ps. 47; 93; 95–99)

> The LORD reigns, let the nations tremble;
>> he sits enthroned between the cherubim, let the earth shake.

> Great is the LORD in Zion;
>> he is exalted over all the nations (Psalm 99:1–2).

3. Songs of Zion, including pilgrim psalms (e.g., Ps. 48; 84; 87; 120–34).

> I rejoiced with those who said to me,
>> "Let us go to the house of the LORD."

> Our feet are standing in your gates, O Jerusalem (Psalm 122:1–2).

4. Royal psalms (e.g., Ps. 2; 20–21; 45; 72; 89; 101; 110; 132; 144)

> My heart is stirred by a noble theme as I recite verses for the king;
>> my tongue is the pen of a skillful writer.

> You are the most excellent of men
>> and your lips have been anointed with grace,
>> since God has blessed you forever (Psalm 45:1–2).

5. Creation psalms (e.g., Ps. 8; 19:1–6; 104)

> He set the earth on its foundations;
>> it can never be moved.

> You covered it with the deep as with a garment;
>> the waters stood above the mountains (Psalm 104:5–6).

The expression "the LORD reigns" or "will reign" is characteristic of enthronement psalms. Because they are psalms that celebrate the LORD's universal and eternal rule, they may best be labeled theocratic psalms. All passages that speak of a future coming of the LORD to his people or to the earth, or that speak of a future rule of the LORD over Israel or over the whole earth, are enthronement psalms and may ultimately be messianic—indirectly or by extension—for to be fully realized, they require a future, Messianic Kingdom on the earth.[5]

Of the Songs of Zion, Psalms 120–34 are noteworthy, for they are also known as Songs of Ascent. Such psalms were probably sung by the pilgrims on their way to Jerusalem (and on their arrival there) to celebrate the three annual festivals (see Deut. 16:16): "Let us go to his dwelling place; let us worship at his footstool—arise, O LORD, and come to your resting place, you and the ark of your might" (Ps. 132:7–8).

In royal psalms praise is given to the heavenly King from an earthly king. In the period of the monarchy, the reigning king was considered to be in close relationship with the LORD and thus played a leading role in Israel's worship. Outstanding events in the life of a king are possible settings for psalms clearly concerned with a royal figure, events such as the anniversary of the founding of the Davidic dynasty or of the construction of the royal sanctuary on Mount Zion in Jerusalem, a king's enthronement or the anniversary of his enthronement, a royal wedding, the period just before the king departed for battle, or the celebration of his victorious return.

Royal psalms may be messianic psalms. Messianic prophecy can be direct, typical (or typological), and typical-prophetic. Many evangelical scholars would classify Psalm 110 as directly messianic, while many of the other royal psalms would be classified as typically messianic, in the sense that most (if not all) of the historical kings in the Davidic dynasty may function as types of the ultimate Son of David. A few other psalms could be classified as typically-prophetically messianic, such as Psalm 2. Here the language at

---

5. Kenneth L. Barker, "Zechariah," in *The Expositor's Bible Commentary,* ed. Frank E. Gaebelein, 12 vols. (Grand Rapids: Zondervan, 1985), 7:619.

times so transcends the experience of the psalmist that it becomes more directly prophetic of the Messiah.

Descriptive psalms have three main parts:[6]

- Introduction: a call to praise, or sometimes a reflection on praise
- Main section: the cause for praise, often introduced by "for"
- Recapitulation: the conclusion to praise, or frequently a renewed call to praise

Psalm 33 demonstrates beautifully the structure of descriptive praise: call to praise (vv. 1–3); cause for praise (vv. 4–19; note the "for" at the beginning of vv. 4 and 9); and conclusion to praise (vv. 20–22).

Call to praise

Sing joyfully to the LORD, you righteous;
  it is fitting for the upright to praise him.

Cause for praise

For the word of the LORD is right and true;
  he is faithful in all he does.
For he spoke, and it came to be;
  he commanded, and it stood firm.

Conclusion to praise

In him our hearts rejoice,
  for we trust in his holy name (Ps. 33:1, 4, 9, 21).

Praising God for What He Has Done (Declarative Praise)

When the psalmist had experienced dire need and had prayed to God for deliverance, and God had intervened by granting the psalmist an answer—a specific act of deliverance—the psalmist broke forth in praise. In front of the entire assembly, thanksgiving was voiced to God by declaring what God had done, usually accompanied by a public thank offering to God.

---

6. See Bernhard W. Anderson, *Out of the Depths* (Philadelphia: Westminster, 1974), 100–101; cf. Westermann, *Praise and Lament*, 122 ff. and chart on 156–57.

These psalms are called songs of thanksgiving or declarative psalms, because the psalmist was praising God by publicly declaring his mighty deeds. The emphasis was on the acts of God—what he had done or given or provided. The most frequently used Hebrew verb for this kind of praise is *hôdah*. Some English readers may be familiar with it in the form *tôdah*, a modern Hebrew way of saying "Thank you." Occasionally, descriptive praise and declarative praise are found in the same psalm, suggesting that praise can be *both* descriptive *and* declarative. There are two subcategories of declarative praise, depending on whether the thanksgiving is by an individual or the whole community:

1. Psalms of individual thanksgiving (e.g., Ps. 18 [= 2 Sam. 22]; 30; 34; 40:1–10 [mixed type]; 66:13–20 [mixed type]; 92; 116; 118; 121; 138; Jonah 2)

   This poor man called, and the LORD heard him;
     he saved him out of all his troubles (Ps. 34:6).

   In my distress I called to the LORD;
     I called out to my God.

   From his temple he heard my voice;
     my cry came to his ears (2 Sam 22:7).

2. Psalms of community thanksgiving (e.g., Ps. 46; 65; 66:1–12 [mixed type]; 67; 107; 124)

   For you, O God, tested us;
     you refined us like silver.

   You brought us into prison
     and laid burdens on our back.

   You let men ride over our heads;
     we went through fire and water,
     but you brought us to a place of abundance (Ps. 66:10–12).

Like psalms of descriptive praise, psalms of declarative praise have three main parts:[7]

- Introduction: Here the worshiper announces his intention to give thanks to God, or he simply announces what God has done.

---

7. See Anderson, *Out of the Depths*, 84–86; cf. Westermann, *Praise and Lament*, charts on 85–86, 103–4.

- Main section: Here the psalmist tells of the distress he was in, his cry to God for help, and his deliverance.
- Conclusion: The worshiper again testifies to the LORD's gracious act of deliverance. A prayer for future help, or a confession that the LORD is gracious, or some other formulation may be added.

When a psalm of declarative praise follows the same pattern as a psalm of descriptive praise, one must decide whether it is descriptive praise or declarative praise by the emphasis of the contents. Is the psalm more general, stressing the attributes of God? Then it is descriptive. Is it more specific, focusing on the acts of God? Then it is declarative.

Where Praise Is Found in the Ancient Near East

In Babylonian literature the psalms in praise of deity are mostly descriptive rather than declarative. The Babylonian psalms primarily praise "the god who exists in his world of gods. In Israel [the psalms or hymns] primarily praise the God who acts marvelously by intervening in the history of his people and in the history of the individual member of his people."[8] In Egypt the situation is similar: Declarative praise occurs very sporadically in the Egyptian psalms or hymns.

A sample of descriptive praise outside the Bible is this part of a Babylonian hymn of praise to the sun-god, Shamash, originally written in Akkadian:

Your splendor covers the vast mountains,
Your fierce light fills the lands to their limits.
You climb to the mountains surveying the earth,
You suspend from the heavens the circle of the lands.
You care for all the peoples of the lands,
And everything that Ea, king of the counselors,
had created is entrusted to you.
Whatever has breath you shepherd without exception,
You are their keeper in upper and lower regions.
Regularly and without cease you traverse the heavens,
Every day you pass over the broad earth.[9]

---

8. Westermann, *Praise and Lament*, 42.

9. W. G. Lambert, *Babylonian Wisdom Literature* (Oxford: Clarendon, 1960), 127, lines 17–28.

A sample of descriptive praise in Egyptian literature is this translation of part of Pharaoh Akhenaten's hymn of praise to the Aten (the sun disk as the source of life):

When thou settest in the western horizon,
The land is in darkness, in the manner of death.
They sleep in a room, with heads wrapped up,
Nor sees one eye the other. . . .
At daybreak, when thou arisest on the horizon,
When thou shinest as the Aton by day,
Thou drivest away the darkness and givest thy rays. . . .
How manifold it is, what thou hast made!
They are hidden from the face (of man).
O sole god, like whom there is no other!
Thou didst create the world according to thy desire.[10]

While scholars have demonstrated that there is much to learn from the study of parallels between biblical and ancient Near Eastern literature, one must not conclude too hastily that one depended on or borrowed from the other. So it is with the study of the praise literature in the Bible and the ancient Near Eastern world. While there are undeniable similarities between these hymns and the psalms of descriptive praise in the Old Testament, there are even more remarkable differences. Numerous instructive parallels may be evident—though more in form than in content—but there are even more significant differences. For example, why is declarative praise in the ancient Near East limited to war chronicles where the help of the god(s) is acknowledged? Those immersed in mythology, polytheism, and idolatry apparently could not attribute in their hymnic literature very many divine interventions to their gods. They had few mighty acts to celebrate, particularly in their hymns of praise. The reason for inaction by the other so-called gods is suggested in Scripture:

I, even I, am the LORD,
  and apart from me there is no savior.
I have revealed and saved and proclaimed—
  I, and not some foreign god among you (Isa. 43:11–12).
Do any of the worthless idols of the nations bring rain?

---

10. John A. Wilson, "Egyptian Hymns and Prayers," in *Ancient Near Eastern Texts Relating to the Old Testament,* ed. James B. Pritchard (Princeton: Princeton University Press, 1955), 370.

Do the skies themselves send down showers?
No, it is you, O LORD our God.
  Therefore our hope is in you,
  for you are the one who does all this (Jer. 14:22).
No other god can save in this way (Dan. 3:29).

Isaiah repeatedly mentions the worthlessness and impotence of
the pagan idols that represented false gods (e.g., Isa. 30:6–7; 44:10;
45:20; 46:7; see also Ps. 115:4–8). All such passages obviously function as polemics against competing religious beliefs.[11] Not only was
Israel's religion different from the religions of other people in Pal-
estine, it was unique in the ancient Near East. One thing is clear:
The Israelites believed that Yahweh, their God, had defeated Pharaoh and Egypt's gods through the plagues and the exodus (cf. Exod. 12:12; 14:17–18, 30–31; 15:11). So there is polemical value in
comparative studies.

How to Interpret Praise

In addition to the usual principles of interpretation for the study
of Scripture, special interpretive principles must be applied in analyzing praise literature.[12]

Guidelines for Interpretation

1. *Examine the parallelism that is typical of Hebrew poetry*. Parallelism, an especially important poetic feature, may be defined as
thoughts (or grammatical elements) arranged in a certain formal
relationship to each other. The three most common kinds of
parallelism are synonymous, antithetical, and synthetical. In synonymous parallelism one or more poetic lines not only repeat the
basic idea of the first line in different words but also stress, inten-
sify, or refine the thought in some way.

---

11. For further development of such a polemic purpose in many parts of
the Old Testament, see my article, "The Value of Ugaritic for Old Testament Studies," *BSac* 133 (April–June 1976): 120–23; cf. now Robert B. Chisholm, Jr., "The Polemic Against Baalism in Israel's Early History and
Literature," *BSac* 150 (July-Sept. 1994): 267–83.
12. See William W. Klein, Craig L. Blomberg, and Robert L. Hubbard, Jr.,
Introduction to Biblical Interpretation (Dallas: Word, 1993). Altogether,
they list eight principles for interpreting poetry (pp. 290–91).

The heavens declare the glory of God;
    the skies proclaim the work of his hands (Ps. 19:1).

Both lines mean essentially the same thing. The heavens *and* skies bring glory to God in that they are the work of his hands. When the lines of a psalm are synonymous, the emphasis is on the similarity of meaning though expressed in different words. In antithetical parallelism one thought is contrasted with another.

The LORD watches over the way of the righteous,
    but the way of the wicked will perish (Ps. 1:6).

In synthetical parallelism the thought is further extended, developed, supplemented, complemented, or completed.

To the LORD I cry aloud,
    and he answers me from his holy hill (Ps. 3:4).

While the understanding of synonymous, antithetical, and synthetical parallelism is continually being refined, an awareness of how parallelism functions is indispensable to interpreting the Psalms.[13] Paying attention to parallelism can prevent readers from certain mistakes in interpretation. For example, in Psalm 30:3 the synonymously parallel line, "you spared me from going down into the pit," gives insight into the first line, "O LORD, you brought me up from the grave." The point is not that David had actually died and been buried in the grave. Rather, "grave" (Hebrew, *Sheol*) simply depicts forcefully a near-death experience. We might put it: "I was as good as dead." David is thanking God for keeping him out of the grave.

2. *Allow for figurative language in Hebrew poetry.* Another common characteristic of the Psalms is figurative language that should not be understood literally.[14] Note the figures of speech that are common in praise literature:

---

13. See John H. Stek, "When the Spirit Was Poetic," in *The NIV: The Making of a Contemporary Translation,* ed. Kenneth L. Barker (Grand Rapids: Zondervan, 1986), 72–87, 158–61; cf. also Stek's introduction to the Psalms in *The NIV Study Bible,* ed. Kenneth L. Barker (Grand Rapids: Zondervan, 1985), particularly 783–84.
14. Cf. Herbert M. Wolf, "When 'Literal' Is Not Accurate," in *The NIV: The Making,* especially 134–36; C. B. Caird, *The Language and Imagery of the Bible* (Philadelphia: Westminster, 1980).

Simile:	"He is like a tree" (Ps. 1:3)
Metaphor:	"For the LORD God is a sun and shield" (Ps. 84:11)
Metonymy:	"You have laid your hand [= power and/or control] upon me" (Ps. 139:5)
Synecdoche:	"You . . . lift up my head [= me]" (Ps. 3:3)
Hyperbole:	"I beat [my enemies] as fine as the dust of the earth" (2 Sam. 22:43)
Personification:	"The waters saw you, O God" (Ps. 77:16)

Any reading of poetry must take into account the poetic license to express ideas in figurative and graphic ways. Metaphors such as king, shepherd, light, fortress, and rock are used in praise of God, and they are to be understood in the sense of what they symbolize.

3. *Try to discover the historical occasion for the psalm being studied.* The specific circumstances in the life of the individual or of the people that produced the psalm, or the situation for which the psalm was written, provide helpful insight into the meaning of the psalm. To discover such a historical context, study the form (or structure) and contents of the psalm. Where they exist, the psalm titles or superscriptions are often helpful for reconstructing the historical background. Unfortunately, most psalms have no historical notation (only three of the praise psalms have such superscriptions, namely, 18, 30, and 34). And the content of many psalms is frequently too general to use in determining the occasion. So it is better to admit ignorance of the specific historical setting than to arbitrarily assign a particular historical life-setting when there is not adequate evidence to justify such a reconstruction.

4. *Determine the type of psalm,* whether it features descriptive praise or declarative praise and whether the praise is by an individual or the people as a whole. For example, Psalm 33 is classified as a psalm of descriptive praise by the people, not as a psalm of declarative praise by an individual. This means that it is a psalm for public worship. So it should be expounded in view of that. Here it must be remembered that "I" in certain psalms can be collective, representing the people instead of an individual.

5. *Identify timeless spiritual principles that are valid and applicable to all people in the same or similar circumstances.* Descrip-

tive praise of God is generally timeless and can be used by any true worshiper. Declarative praise can be used by those in the psalmist's situation or in a similar situation.

Because God's mighty acts, such as his redemptive acts through Christ, call for new songs of thanksgiving, it is not surprising to find such declarative praise in the New Testament (e.g., Mary's song, the "Magnificat" in Luke 1:46–55, and Zechariah's song, the "Benedictus" in Luke 1:68–75). All Christians are encouraged to continue the practice of praise and thanksgiving (see Eph. 5:19–20 and Col. 3:15–17). New psalms of thanksgiving (declarative praise) modeled after the Psalms can be composed by those who experience divine deliverance and their own answers to prayer.

What bearing should all this have on church hymnology today? Putting the psalms of the Old Testament to music, praising God for all that he is (descriptive praise), and thanking him for all that he does and provides (declarative praise) are especially appropriate expressions of worship. The hymns and worship choruses of thanksgiving should focus on what the LORD has done and on the fact that he has done it.

Jonah's Psalm of Praise

Jonah 2:2–9 is an excellent example of declarative praise, and it is appropriate here as a reminder that there are psalms of praise outside the Psalter, and to correct a popular misconception that understands Jonah 2 as a prayer for deliverance from the great fish. The very structure and contents show that this is a song of thanksgiving or psalm of declarative praise for deliverance already experienced, not a psalm of lament and/or prayer for deliverance. Jonah utters his declarative praise from inside the fish (v. 1), and he thanks God for delivering him from drowning in the Mediterranean Sea by rescuing him with the fish. That is why the verb tenses are past (except in v. 9). The fish, then, is an instrument of grace and deliverance, not of punishment and judgment.[15]

---

15. Edward J. Young pointed this out as early as 1960 in *An Introduction to the Old Testament* (Grand Rapids: Eerdmans, 1960), 281–82. Keil pointed it out even earlier in the 1949 reprint of Carl Friedrich Keil, *The Twelve Minor Prophets*, 2 vols., *Biblical Commentary on the Old Testament* by C. F. Keil and F. Delitzsch, trans. James Martin (Grand Rapids: Eerdmans, 1949), 1:398–99.

This does not mean that Jonah 2 cannot be a prayer as stated in 2:1. There is no conflict between a song of thanksgiving and the statement that Jonah prayed, for thanksgiving is the very essence of prayer. This, then, is a prayer, not of petition for deliverance, but of thanksgiving for deliverance already experienced.

Some have maintained that the text of the Book of Jonah reads smoothly without this psalm, if 2:10 is placed immediately after 2:1. So it is concluded that the psalm was probably not part of the book originally. If 2:2–9 is removed, however, the symmetry of the book is damaged, for the book falls into two halves (chaps.1–2, and 3–4). Jonah 2:2 and 4:2 correspond in that both mention Jonah's praying. In one case there is a song of thanksgiving, in the other a complaint. The psalm, therefore, is to be regarded as in its proper place.

The events recorded in Jonah 1:1–2:1 provide the historical setting for the psalm in 2:2–9. The form or structure of declarative praise may be applied to Jonah's prayer or song of thanksgiving as follows:

- Introduction: summary of Jonah's testimony (v. 2)
- Main section: narration of Jonah's experience (vv. 3–7)
- Conclusion: acknowledgment of God's gracious act and a promise to present a thank-offering (vv. 8–9)

In the introduction (v. 2) Jonah's distress refers to drowning in the Mediterranean Sea (cf. 1:15), and the grave is a hyperbole for his brink-of-death experience (as in Ps. 18:5; 30:3). While still in the fish, Jonah states that God had already answered him. In the main section of Jonah's psalm, he begins with a portrayal of his affliction (2:3–6a), looking back at his time of need. The synonymous parallelism of terms for the stormy sea (deep, seas, currents, waves, breakers, engulfing waters, and seaweed) all depict drowning in the sea, not in the fish's stomach. Jonah's petition for help (v. 7) was voiced when he was about to drown in the sea. Jonah also gives thanks for the deliverance already experienced (v. 6b). In the conclusion to Jonah's psalm he is looking forward. He anticipates the completion of his deliverance (v. 10). Truly "Salvation [or deliverance] comes from the LORD" (v. 9), and with a polemical twist he says that it does not come from "worthless idols"

(v. 8; cf. 1:5–6, 14–16). The principle involved in Jonah's deliverance, "Salvation comes from the LORD," is still valid for us today.

Conclusion

The genre of praise has important lessons to teach. God is to be praised by recalling and meditating on his marvelous attributes (such as love, grace, faithfulness, holiness, righteousness, omniscience, omnipresence, omnipotence). That is descriptive praise for who he is and what he is like. God is also to be praised by reporting divine interventions and answers to prayer through his specific acts of deliverance. That is declarative praise for what he has done and provided.

Unfortunately, the genre of praise is sometimes misunderstood by those who overlook important principles for interpretation. Failing to recognize the various types of praise psalms, failing to study the settings of the psalms, overlooking the significance of parallelism between the lines of psalms, and misconstruing the figurative language in the psalms lead to incorrect interpretations and applications of this genre. Just as unfortunate is the failure to meditate on the words of praise in the psalms. "I will meditate on all your works and consider all your mighty deeds" (Ps. 77:12). "My eyes stay open through the watches of the night, that I may meditate on your promises" (Ps. 119:148). The songs of praise composed by David and the other psalmists are timeless expressions of the true worshiper's heart for God. "It is good to praise the LORD."[16]

Recommended Reading

Allen, Ronald B. *Praise! A Matter of Life and Breath*. Nashville: Thomas Nelson, 1980. The most useful practical introduction to the Psalms.

---

16. I take great pleasure in contributing a chapter to this volume in honor of my dear friend and former colleague, Dick Patterson. When I was general editor of the short-lived *Wycliffe Exegetical Commentary* (Moody), Dick was one of my valued Old Testament editors. His own commentary (*Nahum, Habakkuk, Zephaniah*) is one of the finest in that series.

Anderson, Bernhard W. *Out of the Depths*. Philadelphia: Westminster, 1974. A somewhat simpler introduction to psalm-types and their forms than Westermann's.

Bullinger, E. W. *Figures of Speech Used in the Bible*. 1898. Reprint, Grand Rapids: Baker, 1968. A comprehensive treatment of figurative language used in Scripture.

Bullock, C. Hassell. *An Introduction to the Poetic Books of the Old Testament*. Chicago: Moody, 1979. Probably the best conservative-evangelical introduction to the books of poetry, including psalm-types.

Geller, Stephen A. *Parallelism in Early Biblical Poetry*. Missoula, Mont.: Scholars Press, 1979. Represents some of the new thinking with respect to poetic parallelism.

Gray, George B. *The Forms of Hebrew Poetry*. New York: KTAV, 1972. Still worth consulting, though somewhat dated. David Noel Freedman's prolegomenon updates it.

Gunkel, Hermann. *The Psalms: A Form-Critical Introduction*. Translated by Thomas M. Horner. Philadelphia: Fortress, 1967. A concise presentation of Gunkel's pioneering efforts.

Longman, Tremper III. *How to Read the Psalms*. Downers Grove, Ill.: InterVarsity, 1988. Another good introduction to the study of the Psalms, along with those by Allen, Anderson, and Westermann.

Mowinckel, Sigmund. *The Psalms in Israel's Worship*. Translated by D.R. Ap-Thomas. Nashville: Abingdon, 1962. Mowinckel's attempt to find a cultic background for every psalm helped to generate an extremist school known as "Myth and Ritual."

Sabourin, Leopold. *The Psalms: Their Origin and Meaning*. New York: Alba House, 1974. A helpful summary of recent research on the Psalms.

Stek, John H. "When the Spirit Was Poetic." In *The NIV: The Making of a Contemporary Translation*, edited by Kenneth L. Barker, 72–87, 158–61. Grand Rapids: Zondervan, 1986. An excellent discussion of the problems encountered in translating Hebrew poetry in general and the Psalms in particular. See also Stek's introduction to the Psalms and the study notes on Psalms in *The NIV Study Bible*.

Westermann, Claus. *Praise and Lament in the Psalms*. Translated by Keith R. Crim and Richard N. Soulen. Atlanta: John Knox, 1981. The best introduction to the study of psalm-types and their forms or structures, though somewhat technical.

12

PROVERB

Ted A. Hildebrandt

The proverbial genre is paradoxical. Proverbs are simple, concrete, and mundane, and at the same time profound, abstract, and transcendent. Their meanings are singular and particular, yet multifaceted and universal. Proverbs are widespread among the common folk, yet they are collected and utilized by the royal court. They are given as instruction for the young and savored by the aged as well. They present themselves as ancient wisdom, yet are amazingly contemporary. They appear to be closed, fixed, cliché-like, and authoritative, yet they are open to transformation, exception, and situational variation.

Proverbs are like popcorn. They are tight little kernels that seem to be difficult to crack. Yet by applying the correct type of hermeneutical heat, the meaning-packed kernels pop open with delightful insights. The proverbial form is easily recognized even though those who collect and study proverbs (called paremiologists) have not been able to give this genre a comprehensive definition. "Short sentences drawn from long experience," and "The wisdom of many, the wit of one" are definitions that capture much of the essence of the proverbial genre.[1]

---

1. These definitions are attributed to Cervantes and Lord Russell. For discussion of what a proverb is, see R. Finnegan, "Proverbs in Africa," in *The Wisdom of Many: Essays on the Proverb*, ed. W. Mieder and A. Dundes (New York: Garland, 1981) 10–42; W. Mieder and B. Mieder, "Tradition and Innovation: Proverbs in Advertising," in *The Wisdom of Many*, 309–21; A. Taylor, *The Proverb* (Cambridge: Harvard University Press, 1931).

Though proverbs do not contribute as much to the culture of the Western world as they did to the world of the Bible, they are not strange to our ears. Modern advertising agencies realize the potency of proverbs. A computer graphics company, for example, used the proverb "A picture is worth a thousand words" in an attempt to capture the market. Proverbs are powerful tools of communication. They move with an air of trustworthiness, presenting traditional wisdom that has been tried and found true.

For many contemporary readers of the Bible, the genre of proverbs is problematic. Since the Bible is the revelation of divine truth, how should we respond when experience casts doubt on the truthfulness of a saying? How should the proverb "A good man leaves an inheritance for his children's children" (Prov. 13:22) be applied to a man who is rapidly losing the inheritance that he had saved for his children, because of legal fees to defend himself in a lawsuit for which he is innocent? Should the proverb be spiritualized or projected into the distant future? What is the intended meaning of the proverb? How should we understand and apply proverbs to our own circumstances?

What Is a Proverb?

A proverb is usually a short, salty, concrete, fixed, paradigmatic, poetically-crafted saying. Each of these features plays a part in giving the proverb its punch.

Proverbs are *short*. Often they are compressed into a single line: "From evildoers come evil deeds" (1 Sam. 24:13). The compactness of proverbs distills a wide variety of observations into a broad generalization stated in a few well-chosen words, such as "Look before you leap." In Hebrew poetry, proverbs are often formulated as a balanced pair of antithetical lines (see Prov. 10:1ff.).

Proverbs are *salty*. They are wise sayings drawn from the particulars of everyday life. They offer counsel on issues of ultimate concern (life/death, love/hate, righteousness/wickedness, wisdom/folly). They also give advice on the simple concerns of life (prosperity/poverty, friends/enemies, sexual intimacy/conflict, family/work, and speech/actions).

Often proverbs are built around *concrete* graphic images, such as "Don't count your chickens before they hatch." Metaphors, similes, and vivid imagery abound in the proverbial literature. "In vain the net is baited while the bird is watching" (Prov. 1:17).

A proverb often appears to be a *fixed* formula, a stagnant cliché, commonly known and accepted by many. Often a familiar, seemingly over-used saying is played on as a user seeks to give the proverb a new twist or to fit it more closely to a particular situation. Thus, its root form is open to countless variations, transformations, and applications. Variations of the proverb "Like father, like son" are "The son of a duck is a quacker," "As the baker, so the buns" and in Ezekiel 16:44, "Like mother, like daughter." The proverb, "A woman's place is in the home," has on some occasions been changed, substituting "home" for "house," in order to fit a woman's election to the house of representatives.

Proverbs present life in the form of *paradigms*, patterns, and stereotypical generalizations. The sages did not see the order of the world as mechanistic or deterministic but rather as proof that God's mysterious reign penetrates and permeates everything (see Prov. 16:9; 21:30). The fear of the LORD is where the sages' worldview began and ended (see Prov. 1:8; 31:30). They carefully instructed the young to learn their limits in light of the predictability and unpredictability of life.

Proverbs are *poetically crafted*. Israel's sages artistically arranged their sayings using standard Hebrew poetic techniques. They are marked by one or more literary features:

- Variation in word order: For example, rather than a standard word order, such as "mighty oaks grow from little acorns," the proverb is "Mighty oaks from little acorns grow" (cf. Prov. 10:5).
- Phonetic repetition: For example, "Many men, many minds" (cf. Prov. 10:18).
- Semantic balance: For example, "Different strokes for different folks" (cf. Prov. 10:1).
- Rhetorical enhancement: For example, "A bird in the hand is worth two in the bush" (cf. Prov. 30:18–31).
- Parallelism of four types, that appear commonly throughout Hebrew poetry:

1. synonymous parallelism:

"Pride goes before destruction,
a haughty spirit before a fall" (Prov. 16:18);

2. antithetic parallelism:

"Hatred stirs up strife,
but love covers all offenses" (Prov. 10:12, NRSV);

3. emblematic parallelism:

"Like clouds and wind without rain is one who boasts of
a gift never given" (Prov. 25:14, NRSV);

4. synthetic couplet (related but not parallel lines):

"The lazy person does not plow in season;
harvest comes, and there is nothing to be found" (Prov.
20:4, NRSV).

A frequent mistake when interpreting proverbial poetry is to seek a difference in meaning between two words that are being used as synonyms. Interpreters should note that some forms of parallelism emphasize how each of the elements are similar in meaning between the poetic lines.

One approach that provides a useful tool for uncovering the patterns of meaning in proverbs is the "topic/comment" method.[2] For example, the proverb "Diligent hands bring wealth" (Prov. 10:4) establishes a topic and then makes a comment on the topic. In this case, a character trait (diligence) produces a consequence (wealth). Thus, it is a character–consequence type saying. An analysis of Proverbs 10–15 has revealed the following categories of proverbial thought:

character	⟶	consequence	(10:1, 4, 6)
character	⟶	act	(10:12, 23, 32)
character	⟶	evaluation	(10:11a, 20)
act	⟶	evaluation	(10:5; 29:5)
act	⟶	consequence	(10:9a, 17)
item	⟶	evaluation	(10:2a, 15)

---

2. A. Taylor, "The Wisdom of Many and the Wit of One," in *The Wisdom of Many*, 3–9; A. Dundes, "On the Structure of the Proverbs," in *The Wisdom of Many*, 43–64; R. Van Leeuwen, *Context and Meaning in Proverbs 25–27* (Atlanta: Scholars Press, 1988).

For interpreting proverbs it is helpful to note the core movement of the proverb. Is character, a particular action, or an item the main topic of the proverb? Is the comment made on that main topic an evaluation, motivation, or a consequence? How exactly are the topic and comment connected in the proverb?

Where Proverbs Are Found

The cultural context from which a proverb arises and in which it is used affects how a proverb should be understood. For example, in Scotland the proverb "A rolling stone gathers no moss" means "Keep abreast of modern ideas so you will not become antiquated and useless (like moss)." In Scotland moss is considered undesirable. But in England "A rolling stone gathers no moss" means "If things are continually in a state of flux, desirable features (like moss) will not have time to develop."[3] In England moss is valued as a sign of stability. Note that this proverb has exactly the same words both for the English and the Scottish yet very different meanings in each culture. Thus, it is critical that the reader examine the cultural context of proverbs.

The Proverbial Genre in the Ancient Near East

Proverbs originated and were used in four principal cultural settings: family, royal court, schools, and scribal circles.

Family. The family is the most explicit proverbial setting. From the Sumerian "Instructions of Suruppak," to the Babylonian "Counsels of Wisdom," and to the Ugaritic "Counsel of Shubeawilum," ancient fathers instructed their sons using the literary forms of wisdom.[4] In Egypt, Ptah-hotep and Ka-gem-ni were aged masters who gathered their children to give them instruction.[5] In Israel the instructions repeatedly use the formula "Listen, my son." While the term *father* may be a technical term for teacher, the father was the

---

3. B. Kirshenblatt-Gimblett, "Toward a Theory of Proverb Meaning," *Proverbium* 22 (1973): 821–27.
4. B. Alster, *The Instructions of Suruppak: A Sumerian Proverb Collection* (Copenhagen: Akademisk Forlag, 1974); W. Lambert, *Babylonian Wisdom Literature* (Oxford: Clarendon Press, 1960).
5. J. Pritchard, ed., *Ancient Near Eastern Texts Relating to the Old Testament* (Princeton: Princeton University Press, 1969); M. Lichtheim, *Ancient Egyptian Literature* (Los Angeles: University of California Press, 1980).

one who taught children his trade, his faith, and his wisdom. The mother was also frequently involved in teaching. King Lemuel tells of wisdom that "his mother taught him" (Prov. 31:1–3). Madame Wisdom herself may echo an original authoritative feminine source of instruction (see Prov. 1:20ff.; 8:1ff.; 9:1ff.).[6] The topics of many of the proverbs also confirm an original familial setting.

Royal Court. The royal court was one of the central places for collecting and propagating wisdom in Egypt, Mesopotamia, and Israel (see 1 Kings 4:30–34; Prov. 25:1; 31:1). King Solomon was the great patron of wisdom in Israel, and King Hezekiah's men edited Solomon's sayings, while King Lemuel authored his own. Furthermore, many of the proverbs contain advice to the king as well as counsel about deportment before a king.

Schools. Learning how to write was a major objective in schools, and copying wisdom texts provided a large portion of the curriculum. Debate has centered on when schools began in Israel and whether they were a source of Israelite wisdom. Since the first explicit reference to schools in Israel is not until the time of Ben Sirach (ca. 180 B.C.; Sirach 51:23), the presence of Israelite schools in Solomonic times (ca. 960 B.C.) is a matter of speculation based more on analogies with Egypt, Mesopotamia and Ugarit than on solid Israelite evidence.

Scribes. The government, temple, and international economic system, as well as the difficulty of writing Akkadian cuneiform, created a need for scribes in Mesopotamia.[7] In Egypt, the scribes collected instructional wisdom for millennia; in the Old Testament, Israelite scribes are mentioned (see 2 Kings 18:18). This scribal setting may explain why so many of the proverbs reflect aristocratic urban concerns. Thus, many proverbial sayings that originated in the family or clan were collected by the royal court and copied by the schools and scribes.

---

6. C. V. Camp, *Wisdom and the Feminine in the Book of Proverbs* (Sheffield: Almond, JSOT, 1985); idem, "The Female Sage in Ancient Israel and in the Biblical Wisdom Literature," in *The Sage in Israel and the Ancient Near East,* ed. J. Gammie and L. Perdue (Winona Lake, Ind.: Eisenbrauns, 1990): 185–204; C. Fontaine "The Sage in Family and Tribe," in *The Sage in Israel,* 155–64.

7. J. G. Gammie and L. G. Perdue, eds., *The Sage in Israel* (Winona Lake, Ind.: Eisenbrauns, 1990).

The Proverbial Genre in
the Literature of the Hebrews

Though proverbs are salted throughout the Scriptures—in the historical narratives (Judg. 8:2, 21), Psalms (Ps. 34:11–14), prophets (Jer. 13:12–14), gospels (Mark 10:25, 31), and the epistles (James 4:6; 1 Pet. 4:8)—the major collection of proverbial wisdom is the Book of Proverbs, while Job and Ecclesiastes are liberally sprinkled with proverbial sayings. In the apocryphal book of Sirach, wisdom and law are much more explicitly connected than in Proverbs, where the law is almost never mentioned.

A notable omission from the Book of Proverbs is reference to significant aspects of the faith of the Hebrews: sacrifices, prayer, temple worship, and Israel's salvation history (deliverance from Egypt, the wilderness wanderings, the covenant, and the promised land). But this is not grounds for seeing a tension between cult and wisdom, or for concluding that wisdom reflects a purely secular stance among the Jews.[8] Nor is it grounds for taking major theological themes from other genres such as covenant and forcing those themes onto wisdom passages. Such leveling tendencies should be resisted. The uniquenesses and emphases of each genre should be honored.

How Proverbs Are Stated

A wide variety of proverbial forms were used to express wisdom, but they may be grouped into two major forms: instructions and sayings. The instructions are longer didactic discourses often given by a father in personal address to his son: "Listen, my son" (Prov. 1–9; 22:17–24:22, 31:1–9). They usually begin with a call for the son to hear his father's instruction, followed by several admonitions. The second proverbial form is the sentence proverb or saying. The sayings are found largely in Proverbs 10:1–22:16 and 25–29. They are usually short sentences which make a general third-person observation about life. They lack the second person direct address, "My son," which characterizes the instructions.

---

8. Perdue has conclusively demonstrated that this modern tension between the cult and wisdom is without grounds in ancient Mesopotamia, Egypt, and Israel. L. Perdue, *Wisdom and Cult*, SBLD 30 (Missoula, Mont.: Scholars Press, 1977).

Eleven types of proverbs need to be examined, for some of these specific forms require different methods of analysis.

Form	Example	Reference
1. Instruction	Listen my son	Prov. 4:1
2. Admonition	Guard your heart	Prov. 4:23
3. Numerical Saying	Three things . . . four	Prov. 30:18–19
4. "Better-than" Saying	Better wisdom than gold	Prov. 16:16
5. Comparative Saying	For as churning milk	Prov. 30:33
6. Abomination Saying	The LORD detests	Prov. 15:8
7. Beatitude	Blessed is he who	Prov. 14:21
8. Paradoxical Saying	A gentle tongue breaks	Prov. 25:15b
9. Acrostic	Virtuous woman poem	Prov. 31:10ff
10. Popular/folk Saying	As a man is, so his	Judg. 8:21
11. Pairs	Do this/do not do that	Prov. 26:4–5

Instruction

Listen, my sons, to a father's instruction;
pay attention and gain understanding (Prov. 4:1).

The instruction form, a "call to hear," was common in the ancient world, occurring as early as the Sumerian "Instructions of Suruppak" (ca. 2500 B.C.). Similarities between the Egyptian "Instructions of Amenemope" and Prov. 22:17ff have led to debate about the nature and direction of borrowing between the two.[9] Solomon (ca. 960 B.C.) used this form extensively in Proverbs 1–9.

An instruction gives general advice and warnings about life. Several cautions should control the interpretation of instructions. First, the "father" and "son" should not be understood exclusively in a family context, for the terms may refer to teacher and student. Second, the reader must understand that wisdom and folly are personified as two women vying for the young man's allegiances. Third, when authors use multiple terms for wisdom (see Prov. 1:2–7), the point at which the meaning of the terms intersect should be emphasized, rather than the differences between the terms. Fourth, the sexually explicit instructions (see Prov. 5, 7) should not

9. G. Bryce, *A Legacy of Wisdom: An Egyptian Contribution to the Wisdom of Israel* (London: Associated University Presses, 1979); J. Ruffle, "The Teaching of Amenemope and Its Connection with the Book of Proverbs," *TynBul* 28 (1977): 29–68.

be spiritualized or taken as figurative. Rather, they suggest a model of biblical sex education.

Admonition

> Above all else, guard your heart,
> for it is the wellspring of life (Prov. 4:23).

Within the longer sections of instruction, admonitions are the most frequent proverbial form. They usually consist of a command followed by a motive clause. The command element is often marked by the use of an imperative (do this or do not do that). The motive clause adds motivational support by giving an explanation or a reason for obeying the command. In Proverbs 4:23 the wise father anticipated his son's "Why should I?" question and used reason in conjunction with authoritative assertion to motivate.

For admonitions, readers should observe what is being commanded and how the sage is attempting to motivate the student. The connections between the command and the motivation are important clues to the point of admonitions.

Numerical Saying

> There are three things that are too amazing for me,
>> four that I do not understand:
>> the way of an eagle in the sky,
>> the way of a snake on a rock,
>> the way of a ship on the high seas,
> and the way of a man with a maiden (Prov. 30:18–19).

The numerical saying usually contains a number and a list. The number allows the sage to coordinate similar phenomena, thereby heightening the reader's interest in discovering the common link among what initially appear to be divergent items. Numbering formats also aid the student's memory. This form is used extensively in Proverbs 30 and may be used in relation to sexual topics (even Confucius used it in that regard).[10] To interpret numerical sayings, it is important to discover the element that bonds the list together

---

10. Crenshaw, "Wisdom," in *Old Testament Form Criticism*, ed. John Hayes (San Antonio: Trinity University Press, 1974), 238.

and how the point of the saying is emphasized by that bonding element.

Better-than Saying

> Better a poor man whose walk is blameless
> than a rich man whose ways are perverse (Prov. 28:6).

This proverbial form explains that one thing is to be valued over something else. It seeks to present the student with a set of clear values and priorities. "Better-than" sayings appear frequently in Egyptian instructions. Ankhsheshonq, for example, gives this evaluation: "Better dumbness than a hasty tongue."[11] The sages used this form extensively in the Book of Ecclesiastes and the apocryphal Sirach (e.g., Eccl. 4:3; Sir. 16:3).

Some interpreters incorrectly perceive "better-than" sayings to suggest the sages' movement to a more relativistic stance of preference rather than a dichotomous right and wrong mind-set. It is more correct to understand better-than proverbs as exclusive proverbs that eliminate one element and affirm another. Thus, the reader should ask what is being affirmed and what is being eliminated. It is also important to explore how these two values are related and how they compete for a person's allegiance.

Comparative Saying

> For as churning the milk produces butter,
> and as twisting the nose produces blood,
> so stirring up anger produces strife (Prov. 30:33).

A comparative proverb uses a metaphor or simile to heighten the impact of the message. "The metaphorical proverb allows its users to move easily from message to application, and provides its user with protection from those who might disagree by means of the 'indirection' of its language."[12] The rapid juxtaposition of images in the proverbial genre is like a strobe light quickly highlighting images before the reader. This form is well suited to modern

---

11. Lichtheim, *Ancient Egyptian Literature*, 3:171.
12. C. Fontaine, *Traditional Sayings in the Old Testament: A Contextual Study*, Bible and Literature Series, ed. D. M. Gunn (Sheffield: Almond, 1982), 80.

settings where the rapid transition between electronic worlds is made by the click of a remote control.

For understanding proverbial figures of speech, it is essential to note the image used, the topic being discussed, and the point of contact between the image and topic. For example, the images in Proverbs 30:33 are churning milk producing butter and a twisting nose producing blood. The topic is stirring up anger. And the point of contact between the images and the topic is that a certain behavior will produce a sure set of results (butter and blood and strife). Thus, the buttery milk and the bloody nose similes vividly emphasize the certainty that stirring up anger will indeed produce strife.

Abomination Saying

> The LORD detests the sacrifice of the wicked,
>   but the prayer of the upright pleases him (Prov. 15:8),

Abomination sayings fit the format "X is an abomination to the LORD." Often what the LORD detests is in antithesis to those things that delight the LORD (see Prov. 11:1). The phrase, "abomination to the LORD," also occurs in Deuteronomy, frequently in reference to sacrifice (see Deut. 7:25), possibly providing a clue to the link between cultic, legal, and wisdom literatures. Interestingly, this form also occurs in ancient Sumerian proverbs where one finds, "X is an abomination to Utu," (the god of justice) These abomination proverbs underscore God's view of right and wrong in the world.

Beatitude

> Blessed is he who is kind to the needy (Prov. 14:21).

A beatitude is a blessing pronounced on an individual by someone in authority (father/teacher/priest/king). In wisdom, it is often used as a motivator to convince the one instructed of the value of the wisdom offered. Wisdom psalms also utilize this form (see Ps. 1:1). One of the ancient functions of the father was to be a blesser of his children (a role sadly lacking in many homes today). Jesus' beatitudes were in the form of a wise king instructing his followers and pronouncing blessings on those embracing the virtues and values of his kingdom. The beatitude form of proverb also appears in Egyptian wisdom literature.

To understand beatitudes, identify the behaviors or character qualities that are being emphasized and any explanation or reward that is mentioned. The focus should be on the value being endorsed rather than on the reward promised. Note also the authority of the person pronouncing the blessing.

Paradoxical Saying

Do not answer a fool according to his folly,
  or you will be like him yourself.

Answer a fool according to his folly,
  or he will be wise in his own eyes (Prov. 26:4–5).

Paradoxical proverbs are sayings in which two descriptive elements of the proverb appear to conflict, resulting in a high level of cognitive dissonance or dilemma. The juxtaposition of Proverbs 26:4 and 26:5 on whether a fool should or should not be answered comprise the best known paradoxical proverbial pair. Recent discussions manifest how effectively these two proverbs call the wise to manage the complex ambivalences of life and to weigh each situation and consequence carefully.[13]

The sages were very aware of the chaotic elements inherent in a fallen world. This is reflected in what has been called their world-upside-down cosmology. As seen in the Book of Job, this perspective shows the other side of wisdom where the wicked receive what they desire and the righteous innocently suffer.

Sumerian proverbial collections also contain this paradoxical form: "From 3,000 oxen there is no dung." Modern versions of paradox are evident when one juxtaposes sayings like: "Haste makes waste" and "He who hesitates is lost." Does "Absence makes the heart grow fonder" or is it "Absence makes the heart to wander" ("Out of sight out of mind")?

Paradoxical proverbs encourage the listener to ponder more complex levels of thought. They force one to go beyond the simple right/wrong mentality of a single proverb and face the diversity of reality. Special care is needed here, for Proverbs warns about

---

13. K. G. Hoglund, "The Fool and the Wise in Dialogue," in *The Listening Heart; Essays in Wisdom and the Psalms in Honor of Roland E. Murphy, O. Carm.* K. Hoglund, et al., eds. JSOT Supplement 58; (Sheffield: Sheffield Academic Press, 1987), 161–80.

the proverb in the mouth of a fool (see Prov. 26:7, 9). Those wishing to be wise cannot merely memorize a proverb and mechanically apply it to a complex situation. This is perhaps the most frequent misuse of the proverbial genre today, but proverbial paradoxes should lead to mental and moral development, not a reductionistic harmonizing.

Acrostic

The acrostic form uses the alphabet as a structuring device. The poem on the virtuous woman in Proverbs 31:10–31 is an example of this alphabetic crafting in which the first word of each successive line begins with the next letter of the alphabet. The Babylonian Theodicy and Psalm 119 also employ this form.

In Proverbs 31, the acrostic is significant on several levels. As an artistic device, the poet adorned the virtuous woman with a poem aesthetically fitted to her character. In addition, the idea of completeness was emphasized as the acrostic listed everything from A to Z and gave the sense that the topic under discussion had been thoroughly and completely discussed. The superlative character of the topic discussed was also highlighted by the acrostic form. This superlative idea fits well both with Proverbs 31 (virtuous woman) and the acrostic in Psalms 119 (wonders of the law). Furthermore, the acrostic may have served as a mnemonic device to aid the memorizing of the text. This pedagogic function works well for Proverbs 31 but seems stretched by application elsewhere (Ps. 119 and Lamentations). These levels of significance for the acrostic aid the understanding of the text regardless of whether one spiritualizes the attributes of the virtuous woman, thinks of her as the ultimate woman of virtue, or sees the poem as a concluding description of Madame Wisdom (cf. Prov. 8–9).

Popular/Folk Saying

As is the man, so is his strength (Judg. 8:21).

A folk saying can be distinguished from the more artistic wisdom sayings because they are apparently passed down by and appeal to common people, and because they are anonymous, brief, paradigmatic, more secular, and nondidactic. Such simple one-line proverbs appear in narrative texts throughout the Old

Testament (see Gen. 10:9; 16:12; Judg. 8:2, 21). There are four types of traditional folk sayings: (1) ones explicitly identified as a *mashal* (proverb), (2) those introduced by the formula "And therefore they say. . . ," (3) sayings that sound like proverbs, and (4) those converted into poetic two-line wisdom sayings.[14]

Pairs

In addition to the proverbial forms recorded by the biblical authors, there were collectors/editors of the proverbial sayings. These editors often employed the proverbial pair to organize their sayings into collections. Proverbs were paired based on catchwords, semantic bonding, syntactic dependence, syntactic repetitions, and thematic cohesion. Almost one-third of the sayings in Proverbs 10–22:17 are found in paired structures and may reflect the work of collectors (Prov. 10:4–5)

Strings are a series of connected sayings in Proverbs 10–22:17 and 25–29. Proverbs 10, for example, is normally considered a disorderly collage of independent proverbs. However, loose cohesive strings may be detected (see Prov. 10:1–5, 6–11, 12–21, 22–30). In discovering strings, the careful reader can better understand what the collectors intended as they put the sayings together. When reading the paired sayings, the reader should keep an eye on how the adjacent proverbs may be connected and impact one another.

Are Biblical Proverbs Always True?

Before turning to a list of specific principles of interpretation, a question confronting the genre of proverbs in Scripture needs to be examined. What authority does a proverb have? Proverbs 10:4 says, "Lazy hands make a man poor, but diligent hands bring wealth." Is this true in every case? Are not some people wealthy even though they are lazy, while others are poor throughout their whole lives even though they are diligent? Among the various attempts to address this problem, three proposed solutions merit discussion.

First, some assume that proverbs are promises and suggest that believers should "name and claim" the positive promises of the

---

14. O. Eissfeldt, *Der Maschal im Alten Testament*. BZAW 24 (Giessen: Alfred Topelmann, 1913), 33.

proverbial writings. Thus, God guarantees the desired consequences if people will just believe. However, such believers equivocate on the meaning of the proverb or skew how they apply the proverb to present situations, sometimes resulting in spiritualized views of proverbs. For example, the "promise" that diligent hands bring wealth means that for poor people who are diligent, God will eventually reward them with fortunes like he did for Job. When that fails to happen, suspicions may be raised about whether the diligent poor person is really as diligent as it appears. Or the meaning of wealth is changed from material to spiritual: The diligent whose poverty persists will nevertheless be rewarded on earth and in heaven with spiritual blessings. But this is surely not the original intent of the proverb and is contrary to the bounds of the genre. The reasoning may seem tight, but the premises are faulty. Equating a proverb with a promise is a frequent and elemental mistake when interpreting proverbs.

Second, some react to the proverb-is-a-promise view and conclude that a proverb is not a promise. A proverb is a generalization about life, and the truth of the statement depends on the circumstances. A proverb does not apply in all situations, and there are no guarantees; it has authority only when other things are equal, that is, when the circumstances are right.

Though this view recognizes that in the proverbial form truth can be presented in generalizations, several complications arise for this approach to proverbial authority. (1) Other things are never really equal, thus the authority of the proverb all but evaporates in this view. What if the circumstances are never right? (2) How far can this methodology be carried? Statements in several psalms, Jesus' Sermon on the Mount, and the Book of James are also formulated as proverbial statements. Are these statements deprived of authority because they are proverbs? (3) When proverbs are cited in biblical narratives or employed in other cultures, they seem to be cited with authority. When, if at all, do proverbs in the Bible have authority? (4) Is empirical verification needed to establish the truth of an inspired statement? Do real-life counter-examples disprove a proverb?

The core flaw of this view is that it tells what a proverb is not but leaves unanswered the basic questions: So what is a proverb?

What is a proverb's relationship to divine truth? If the biblical proverbs are only true sometimes, then what is the difference between an inspired proverb and an uninspired proverb?

A third explanation makes an attempt to reinstate the original authority of the proverb as a genre and part of inspired Scripture. This view suggests that a proverb presents a slice of reality. The biblical proverb is always true, since it is simply specifying only one aspect of reality. Diligence does bring wealth, and laziness brings poverty. Though that is a true statement, life is complex with complex acts and complex consequences, and other factors may convolute the consequences. Thus, a lazy person may have a parent who bails him out so he never receives the poverty consequence which should have come upon him. A diligent son may choose friends who squander the wealth acquired by his diligence (see Prov. 1:10ff.). Nevertheless, the proverb is always true in the slice of reality it describes. It does not pretend to describe all of reality, just one segment of it.

If one is going to approximate the complexities of real life, then all the proverbs must be taken together as a canonical whole. A single proverbial sentence is not meant to be taken as a comprehensive statement of life. Thus, it is critical for the reader of proverbs to understand the collection of proverbs in all its diversity. It is the canonical whole that gives a better description of the actual complexity of life than a single proverb.

Therefore, in order to interpret Proverbs correctly, one must come to terms with each individual proverb's limits. One should look for verifying examples and also counter-examples. Having isolated counter-examples, one must ask what other factors influence the result. How do other proverbs treat these other factors? Thus, each proverb should not be isolated but seen within the context of the whole book, all of Scripture, and life.

How to Interpret Proverbs

If Scripture is to be understood accurately, careful procedures must be followed for each of the genres. The following guidelines will aid readers in discovering the intended meaning of the proverb and the correct application.

Guidelines for Interpretation

1. *Accept a proverb for what it is.* Proverbs focus attention on specific situations and concepts, but they are not intended as complete statements about those situations or concepts. Rather than dealing with theory, they deal with individual situations. However, generalization is common in proverbs. Expect proverbs to look at specific circumstances from one perspective or to make general statements about common situations in life.

2. *Look for verifying examples and counter-examples within the collection of proverbs.* The truth of an individual proverb is limited to the specific slice of reality that it portrays. Various factors may affect the outcome of certain conduct. How do other proverbs treat these factors? Proverbs should not be studied in isolation but within the context of the rest of Scripture.

3. *Recognize the poetic ways that sages expressed their wisdom.* The parallelism between lines and the relationship between paralleled words should be examined carefully. Metaphors and similes abound in the proverbial genre as a means to give life and lasting value to the piece of wisdom. Proverbs were meant to be remembered.

4. *Look for pairs and strings of proverbs.* Some proverbs stand alone without any surrounding context. But for some proverbs, the context is determinative of the meaning. Identifying pairs and strings of proverbs can be important for correct interpretation.

5. *Look for evidence of the setting of the proverb.* Proverbs originated in family life, royal courts, schools, and scribal circles. Think about the meaning of individual proverbs in each of these settings.

6. *Examine the proverb itself.* Study the word order and the meanings of words. If possible, look at the proverb in Hebrew, for a Hebrew proverb translated into English usually loses the aesthetics of the poetry. Analyze the core structure of the proverb in comparison with other proverbs.

7. *Identify the specific value the proverb is communicating.* Restate the proverb in your own words, trying to capture its proverbial punch. Relate the proverb to real-life situations, looking for circumstances in modern life that illustrate the point of the proverb and that may provide exceptions to what the proverb is saying.

The Joy and Grief of Parenting

A wise son brings joy to his father,
  but a foolish son grief to his mother (Prov. 10:1).

Looking at the structure of this sample proverb, each line begins with the word *son* and ends with a reference to a parent. Juxtaposed in the middle of each line are the counter processes "wise makes happy" and "foolish (causes) grief." Thus, the outer words (son/son; father/mother) give a sense of the synonymous while the inner elements present the antitheses between characters (wisdom versus folly) and the results (joy versus grief). The structure of the proverb indicates that character produces a certain consequence. However, the verse provides an interesting twist by suggesting that the child's character causes consequences in the parents.

Restating this proverb in short, pithy, poetically crafted English verse may be helpful in underscoring the point of the proverb:

A wise son, a dad's glad,
  a foolish son, a mom's sad.

The reference to "son" in this proverb links it with the repeated "Listen, my son" of Proverbs 1–9 and with Proverbs 10:5. The collectors may have used this first verse of the sayings as a transition between the instructions and the sayings. Here the connection to the parents is no longer through parental admonition but through a clear look at the consequences of the son's choices. The son is told of the impact that his decisions will have on his parents. But note that the proverb also assumes that the son has some concern for the feelings of his parents. Thus, the proverb calls the young to transcend the egocentric concerns of adolescence to consider and make decisions based on how their character will impact others.

The proverb addresses different issues, however, if we read it from the parents' point of view. While the parents are intimately involved in the instruction and discipline of their children, the child is allowed to choose either wisdom or folly. The proverb shows that good parents are emotionally vulnerable to a child's characterological choices. The parents are not distant but involved, not controlling but supportive of individuation while letting the child know that individuation does not mean isolation. Thus, this proverb warns parents that child-rearing may be a joyful or a painful process. The verse motivates the child to wisdom and informs the child that what he/she does matters.

Wisdom and folly are two words that need to be understood in light of the rest of wisdom literature. Proverbs 1–9 in particular clearly defines what constitutes a wise and a foolish son. A wise son observes moral, social, and theological limits. He is able to master life by implementing the principles of wisdom, crafting it according to the piety of the fear of the LORD. Defining and describing wisdom and folly is an important backdrop to understanding this verse.

Joy and grief are the emotional responses exhibited by the parents. This saying informs the son that he can bring joy to his father. The father is not aloof, distant, or absent. How many sons/daughters have longed to hear a word of praise from the heart of a delighted father? This consequence (i.e., the desire to please) can be a strong motivation. The son is also warned he can hurt his mother, compounding the motivation to pursue being wise. This portion of the proverb may be highlighting the mother's vulnerability to elicit the son's compassion for his mother as a motivation to wisdom and away from folly.

Connecting this verse to other proverbial passages confirms the father and mother's participation in both emotions (see Prov. 15:20; 17:21, 25; 23:24f.; 23:15f.; 27:11; 29:3; cf. 28:7; 19:26). It is interesting that in the Egyptian instructions of Ptah-hotep similar sentiments are voiced.[15]

Illustrations of the truth of this proverb are sprinkled throughout Scripture. On the negative side, examples of a foolish son and a pained parent are David/Absalom, Eli and his sons, Samuel, the prodigal son, and even God with his children, Israel (see Isa. 1:2). Good children causing parents joy are found in the Jacob/Joseph cycles and in Jesus' relationship with his Father who exclaims, "This is my Son, whom I love; with him I am well pleased" (Matt. 3:17). Jesus himself provides the ultimate model of one lovingly bonded to his children both in his grieving over the rebellious children (Matt. 23:37–38) and rejoicing over the wise (see Luke 15).

---

15. *ANET,* 413a.

Modern examples may be seen in the stories of fathers who were really proud of their children and in tales of parental grief over children that have chosen the way of folly. This verse also suggests that parents who embrace and value wisdom may unfortunately have foolish children.

As a counter-example, many absent, distant, or angry parents have little emotional attachment with their children. Because of their egocentric folly, they are unable to bond and feel either joy or sadness over the character of their children. This often leaves the child feeling abandoned, angry, rebellious, or unmotivated in a world where no one really cares. The connectedness and bonding this verse talks about is lost to many. In short, if the parent values or embraces folly, the proverbial presupposition upon which this proverb is based is overturned.

Many modern studies of the causes, consequences, meaning, and processes of grief would be appropriate resources for grieving parents.[16] Studies on the adolescent's impact on the parent would also be relevant.[17] These studies are important resources for those desiring to understand and comfort parents who have been impacted by their children and will aid the deepening of one's understanding of this proverb. The reader should not be afraid to use real life as a tool in interpreting proverbs.

Conclusion

Proverbs are delightful because, in such short space and with striking literary devices, they stimulate thinking about principles for daily living. The metaphorical ways in which they capture life make

---

16. M. Bristor, "The Birth of a Handicapped Child—A Wholistic Model for Grieving," *Family Relations* (Jan. 1984): 25–32. M. Miles and A. Demi, "Toward the Development of a Theory of Bereavement Guilt: Sources of Guilt in Bereaved Parents," *Omega* 14 (1983–84): 299–314. R. Bell and L. Harper, *Child Effects on Adults* (Hillsdale, N.J.: Lawrence Erlabaum, 1977). B. Simos, *A Time To Grieve: Loss as a Universal Human Experience* (New York: Family Service of America, 1979). T. Rando, ed., *Parental Loss of a Child* (Champaign, Ill.: Research, 1986).

17. B. Scott, *Relief for Hurting Parents* (Nashville: Thomas Nelson, 1989). G. Greenfield, *The Wounded Parent: Coping with Parental Discouragement* (Grand Rapids: Baker, 1982). J. White, *Parents in Pain: Overcoming the Hurt and Frustration of Problem Children* (Downers Grove: InterVarsity, 1979).

them timeless. Because proverbs have been subjected to many mistakes of interpretation, readers must beware of several pitfalls: (1) taking the proverbs as promises for success, wealth, and happiness; (2) focusing on the rewards rather than on obedience to the commands that the rewards are trying to motivate; (3) trying to split hairs over the meaning of synonymous terms; (4) trying to read ideas into the proverbs when those ideas are not explicitly stated; and (5) using proverbs to provide simplistic solutions to complex modern problems.

The proverbs in the Bible are kernels of truth that are intended to provide spiritual nourishment for all readers. It is up to us to crack open the kernels by carefully understanding the unique features of the genre of proverbs.

Recommended Reading

Bostrom, L. *The God of the Sages: The Portrayal of God in the Book of Proverbs.* Stockholm: Almqvist & Wiksell, 1990. An excellent treatment of an often ignored topic in Proverbs.

Camp, C. V. *Wisdom and the Feminine in the Book of Proverbs.* Sheffield: Almond Press, 1985. Camp does an excellent job on Madame Wisdom in Proverbs 1–9. She is rightly sensitive to the feminine in wisdom and Israelite culture.

Crenshaw, J. L. *Studies in Ancient Israelite Wisdom.* New York: KTAV, 1976. This classic collects many of the best articles written on wisdom up to 1976.

Fontaine, C. R. *Traditional Sayings in the Old Testament.* Sheffield: Almond Press, 1982. This work focuses on how the sayings function in narrative contexts.

Gammie, J. G. and L. G. Perdue, eds. *The Sage in Israel and the Ancient Near East.* Winona Lake, Ind.: Eisenbrauns, 1990. This is a massive work on the sage and his/her role in ancient wisdom.

Hubbard, D. *Proverbs.* Dallas: Word, 1989. This is the best commentary on Proverbs available. It is practical, easy to read, and yet gives a competent treatment of the text.

Mieder, W. and A. Dundes, eds. *The Wisdom of Many: Essays on the Proverb.* New York: Garland, 1981. This is the single best source on modern paremiology (proverbial) studies to date. Covers many cultures from ancient to modern.

Van Leeuwen, R. C., *Context and Meaning in Proverbs 25–27*. Atlanta: Scholars Press, 1988. Van Leeuwen utilizes the results of paremiology studies to benefit the understanding of the biblical proverbs.

von Rad, G. *Wisdom in Israel*. Nashville: Abingdon, 1972. This is a superb overview of wisdom. He is incredibly insightful and does justice to many wisdom themes.

13

NON-PROVERBIAL WISDOM

Andrew E. Hill

The prophet Ezekiel was mocked as an eccentric and ignored as little more than a "riddler" by a sin-numbed, spiritually bankrupt, and "me-first" generation (see Ezek. 20:49). His parables and allegories were divine signs for a decadent society. Jesus also resorted to ciphers to make eternal truth plain to the seekers of God's kingdom (Matt. 13:34–35). Such non-proverbial wisdom in the Old Testament is both the key and the lock to the great mysteries of divine wisdom, both light of revelation and cloud of judgment. If proverbial wisdom sets truth on the table openly visible and within easy reach of all, then by analogy non-proverbial wisdom ties truth securely in a wrapped package and places it on a high shelf well out of reach and almost out of sight. Non-proverbial wisdom literature invites the inquisitive, the curious, the cerebral, and the risk-taker to probe the mysteries of the way of God's wisdom. Such exploration is not for everyone. Indeed, the sage found but one in a thousand capable of pursuing the wisdom of God that leads to righteousness (see Eccl. 7:28). However, the journey is its own reward and the benefits of attaining such wisdom are priceless (see Job 28)!

What Is Non-Proverbial Wisdom?

The idea of wisdom is basic to human existence. The sheer survival of individuals and societies (ancient or modern), given the vicissitudes of life, necessitates the application of human reason to the problems of coping with reality. This application of reason to the human experience is scientific in the sense that wisdom is based upon careful observations collected, tested, and codified over the years. Basic to this universal wisdom tradition is the notion that the accumulated knowledge and experience garnered by observing and experiencing life can be transmitted to the next generation. It is for this reason that much of the literature collected, preserved, and published by the sages takes the form of instruction intended to steer one safely and successfully through the course of life.

Indeed, one of the several Hebrew terms for wisdom (*hokmāh*) has connections to the technical skill necessary for sea navigation. However, wisdom was far more than acquiring technical skill to secure a serene and prosperous existence. The concept of the fear of the LORD infused Hebrew wisdom tradition with religious and ethical dimensions as well, distinguishing it to some degree from its ancient Near Eastern counterparts (cf. Prov. 3:5–7; 16:6). The teaching of the fear of the LORD connected Hebrew wisdom with knowledge of Yahweh, the one true God and the source of true wisdom (cf. Job 28:23–28; Ps. 111:10; Prov. 9:10). This meant wisdom for the Hebrews extended well beyond the pragmatic pursuits of sheer survival and material success. The Yahweh orientation of Hebrew wisdom had profound implications for moral, emotional, and spiritual well-being of the Hebrew community. Ultimately, Hebrew wisdom was a lifestyle of doing right predicated upon right thought and belief (cf. Prov. 2:6–11).

Like Old Testament proverbial wisdom literature, non-proverbial wisdom is essentially poetic. The poetic tendencies of such didactic literature (e.g., repetition, parallelism, rhythm of idea and sound) serve instructional purposes well. They lend a cryptic quality to the literature which both piques the curiosity of the learner and inherently provides a pedagogical framework for learning by means of mnemonic feature and device.

By way of contrast, the instructional type of proverbial wisdom in the Old Testament tends toward that of practical or declarative wisdom rooted in authority structures (e.g., clan elders, parents, etc.); whereas the instructional type of non-proverbial or alternative wisdom literature is that of reflective or speculative wisdom rooted in the observation of human experience (cf. Eccl. 1:12–14). The predominant literary form of proverbial wisdom is the proverb or saying, instruction based upon comparison or directives, and prohibitions for behavior (cf. Prov. 4:10–27). However, non-proverbial wisdom tends to employ a variety of somewhat exotic and more indirect literary genres and forms (see Job and Ecclesiastes below for Old Testament examples of this mix of literary genres and forms), at times even including the traditional wisdom saying (cf. Eccl. 11:1–4). Thus, proverbial wisdom is characterized by an authoritative quality, a pragmatic worldview, and an ethical purpose (see Prov. 3:1–4); while non-proverbial wisdom adopts a reflective stance toward institutions and authority figures, a speculative—occasionally counter-wisdom—worldview, and a theological and philosophical approach to personal ethics (see Eccl. 3:16–22).

How Non-Proverbial Wisdom Is Stated

Non-proverbial wisdom literature springs from the same three sources underlying the Hebrew proverbial wisdom tradition: tribal or clan wisdom geared toward taming life, royal wisdom designed as a type of leadership training for the elite of Hebrew society, and theological wisdom instilling the entire literary tradition with religious and ethical goals. While the sources of the Hebrew wisdom tradition remain constant, the Old Testament actually dispenses non-proverbial wisdom by means of several peculiar forms.

Riddle

> Out of the eater, something to eat;
> Out of the strong, something sweet (Judg. 14:14).

The riddle is an enigmatic question or an ambiguous saying in the form of a verbal puzzle. It is both *clue* and *snare* because the essential ingredients of a riddle are "[1] cipher language that [2] simultaneously informs and conceals."[1] Riddles have both an entertainment and a pedagogical function; they are valuable in the educational process because they incite curiosity and excite the imagination.

The Old Testament mentions the riddle on several occasions as part of the Hebrew wisdom tradition (e.g., Ps. 49:4; 78:2; Prov. 1:6), but preserves only fragments of this literary form (identified as "disintegrated riddles").[2] Samson's challenge to his attendants at the marriage feast offers one example of this verbal puzzle (see Judg. 14:14). Elsewhere we learn that Moses enjoyed a privileged position because Yahweh spoke with him "clearly, and not in riddles" (Num. 12:8), and that the queen of Sheba tested Solomon's famed wisdom with riddles (see 1 Kings 10:1; 2 Chron. 9:1). The taunt song of Habakkuk 2:6 is indeed a riddle, produced by the combination of the proverb and the mocking byword or taunt.[3]

The riddle is by no means unique to Hebrew wisdom tradition, as similar genres may be found in both the Mesopotamian and Egyptian wisdom literature. These ancient Near Eastern counterparts share both the entertainment and the didactic functions characteristic of the Hebrew literary form. However, the use of the riddle in prophecy for heightening aspects of divine judgment seems peculiar to the Hebrew Bible. Theologically, the riddle is appropriate to wisdom literature because it issues out of the mystery of both the natural and divine order. The riddle addresses topics like theodicy (the problem of evil, Ps. 49:4 ff.), the paradox of God's immanence and transcendence (see Num. 12:8), and even the enigma of teaching mysteries to the next generation (see Ps. 78:2; Prov. 1:6). The genre of riddle reminds us of our finitude,

---

1. J. L. Crenshaw, *Old Testament Wisdom: An Introduction* (Atlanta: John Knox, 1981), 37.

2. J. Crenshaw, *ABD* 5 (1992): 722. Here Crenshaw catalogs Proverbs 5:15–23; 6:23–24; 16:15; 20:27; 23:27, 29–35; 25:2–3; and Cant. 4:12 among his examples of "disintegrated" riddles. This article is a complete survey of the riddle subgenre in the Old Testament and includes ancient Near Eastern parallels.

3. O. P. Robertson, *The Books of Nahum, Habakkuk, and Zephaniah* (Grand Rapids: Eerdmans, 1990), 185.

God's inscrutability, and the magnificent grace associated with divine revelation.[4]

Allegory/Parable

> Son of man, set forth an allegory and tell the house of
> Israel a parable.

> Say to them, "This is what the Sovereign LORD says:
> A great eagle with powerful wings, long feathers, and full
> plumage of varied colors came to Lebanon. Taking hold
> of the top of a cedar, he broke off its topmost shoot and
> carried it away to a land of merchants, where he planted it
> in a city of traders" (Ezek. 17:2–4).

Allegory and parable are subgenres of figurative speech forms. *Māshāl,* the Hebrew term for allegory and parable, is used to describe a wide range of wisdom forms in Old Testament narrative and poetic literature. The essence of the *māshāl* is a comparison. As such, this wisdom feature includes a variety of (sometimes overlapping) literary forms on a continuum from the simple proverb to prophetic discourse (cf. Balaam's oracles in Num. 23:7, 18; 24:3, 15, 20–21, 23), to taunt (cf. Isa. 14:4; Jer. 24:9), to parable, to riddle, to fable, and finally to allegory. Despite a lack of scholarly consensus for the boundaries between allegory and parable, the basic distinction is that allegory employs metaphorical language to make a direct comparison, often in an extended narrative (e.g., Ezekiel's description of Judah as a cooking pot set to boil, 24:3–14), while a parable is a more compact figurative speech form that (usually) draws an indirect comparison with the routine experiences of daily life (e.g., Isaiah likens Yahweh's dealings with Judah to the knowledgeable farmer applying his trade, 28:23–29).

One type of Old Testament allegory is the description of a scene or story comprised of multiple metaphors or representative

---

4. V. Hamp, "*ḥîdâ,*" *TDOT* 4 (1980): 323. This article is a complete discussion of the riddle in the Old Testament. On riddles in ancient Near Eastern literature, see E. I. Gordon, "A New Look at the Wisdom of Sumer and Akkad," *BO* 17 (1960): 122–52; K. A. Kitchen, "Proverbs and Wisdom Books of the Ancient Near East: The Factual History of a Literary Form," *TynBul* 28 (1977): 111–14; and R. J. Williams, "The Sages of Ancient Egypt in the Light of Recent Scholarship," *JAOS* 101 (1981): 2–4.

figures. A good example is Ezekiel 17:2–10, a story of two eagles, a cedar tree, and a vine. A second type of Old Testament allegory develops a scene or story by means of a single metaphor.[5] The description of a man's wife as a cistern or well (see Prov. 5:15–23) is representative of this kind of allegory.

As a speech form in wisdom literature, allegory has primarily a didactic function. According to Psalm 78:2, the allegory characteristic of a parable and riddle is integral to the instruction of the succeeding generation. Here the wisdom forms are connected to the explication of Israel's past history for the purpose of engendering covenant faith and obedience in the generation contemporary with the psalmist. In one sense the *mysterious* (i.e., the allegorical speech form) actually gives clues for solving a *mystery* (in this case, the relationship of the past to the present) by means of a simple comparison of past and present. [6]

Allegory is able to underscore a given truth or heighten the impact of divine revelation. The powerful use of allegory in the "old age" poem of Ecclesiastes 12:1–8 is designed to portray the stark contrast between youth and old age: ". . . in the day when the guards of the house shake, and the strong men hunch over, and the millers cease their grinding because they are few, and the ones looking out the windows are darkened" (12:3, author's translation). Noting how loss of fine motor skills causes the limbs to tremble, that once-straight backs stoop, that teeth are now missing, and that cataracts cloud the eyes prompts young people to cultivate habits of faith in God and obedience to his commands at an early stage in life.

For the purposes of interpretation, it is important to distinguish between *allegory* as a speech form in any given biblical text, and *allegorizing* as an interpretive method. Allegory is a literary feature employing the language of metaphor to say one thing in order to

---

5. On the two types of allegories in the OT, see Scott, *The Way of Wisdom* (New York: Macmillan, 1971), 80–81; note Crenshaw (*Ecclesiastes*, OTL [Philadelphia: Westminster, 1987], 30–31) identifies the lengthy poem in Ecclesiastes 11:7–12:7 as *parable*, with the exception of 12:3–4a, which he marks as true *allegory*.

6. See D. Kidner, *Psalms 73–150* TOTC 14b (Downers Grove: InterVarsity, 1975), 281.

convey another deeper or less obvious meaning. However, the allegorical method understands a given passage as metaphor or allegory whether or not the author intended (and in some cases labeled) it as such.[7]

The *parable* is another form of figurative speech utilizing comparison to make a point or to teach a lesson by analogy from experiences of daily life or imaginative stories. It communicates a pictorial message by means of image and symbol in emblematic language. Figurative speech in the form of parable may be found in both the wisdom and the prophetic literature of the Old Testament.

Since the reader or audience is left to unravel the meaning and application, a knowledge of both the setting and the intended audience of a parable is important to the interpretation of the figurative speech forms. The symbolic language of the parable is especially pertinent to situations of personal or national crisis because the figurative speech both emphasizes the urgency of the moment and the necessity for divine perspective and insight in responding to the trial (cf. Ps. 49:5–7). And most often, the intended audience is not a homogeneous crowd, but consists of a mix of so-called insiders and outsiders. That is, people with a listening ear and obedient heart (the insider, cf. Isa. 32:1–8; 50:4–5) and people with blind eyes, deaf ears, and a rebellious spirit (i.e., the outsider, cf. Isa. 42:18–25; 48:8).

The parable may be akin to the riddle at times, in that the mysterious nature and foolish character of this figurative speech form is both *clue* and *snare* to the audience. Hence, the literary purposes of the parable are often directly related to the directness or obscurity of the symbolic language employed. An examination of didactic and prophetic texts yields four distinct functions for the parable in Old Testament literature: instruction in the way of wisdom (see Prov. 1:6), oracular prediction (see Num. 23:7, 18; 24:3, 15, 20, 21, 23; Ezek. 17:2), enhancement of the message for the audience of insiders (cf. 2 Sam. 12:1–15), and the pronouncement of judgment on the audience of outsiders (see Ezek. 24:3–14; Mic. 2:4–5; Hab. 2:6; cf. Isa. 6:9–13). Though the best example of

---

7. On allegorizing as an interpretive method, see A. C. Thiselton, *New Horizons in Hermeneutics* (Grand Rapids: Zondervan, 1992), 143–78.

parable in the Old Testament is the prophet Nathan's parable to David about the rich man with great flocks and the poor man with one lamb (see 2 Sam. 12:1–4), other texts sometimes labeled parable include 2 Samuel 14:4–17 (the story about a brothers' quarrel ending in murder likened to an affair in David's household), Isaiah 28:23–29 (the story of the simple farmer instructed in the ways of nature by God contrasted with the foolish teaching of the political and religious establishment of Judah, cf. 28:9–10), Isaiah 5:1–7 (the "Song of the Vineyard" that yielded only wild grapes compared to the house of Israel and the people of Judah), Hosea 1 (Hosea's marriage to a wife of whoredom), and Hosea 3 (the life of the prophet and his relationship to the promiscuous Gomer).

Wisdom Poems

> Where then does wisdom come from?
> Where does understanding dwell?

> It is hidden from the eyes of every living thing,
> concealed even from the birds of the air (Job 28:20–21).

The wisdom hymn in the Old Testament is an adaptation of the poetic hymnic form for the purpose of showcasing one or more of the motifs basic to wisdom teaching (e.g., the incomparability and the inaccessibility of wisdom). The Hymn in Praise of Wisdom (Job 28) and the Hymn in Praise of Dame Wisdom (Prov. 8) are often cited as parade examples of the wisdom hymn. In each case the hymn opens with a summons to seek the incomparable wealth of wisdom (cf. Job 28:1–12; Prov. 8:1–5), then proceeds to identify God as both the motive for the quest and the very source of wisdom (cf. Job 28:20–27; Prov. 8:22–31), and closes with a recapitulation to "find wisdom" (cf. Job 28:28; Prov. 8:32–36).[8]

Though the *wisdom poem* is not a distinct genre, it is a deliberately structured and consecutive piece of poetry dealing with wisdom themes, ideas, and stylized features characteristic of the Old

---

8. This three-part outline is typical of psalmic hymns, which include an introduction calling the faithful to worship God, a main section giving the motive for praise (usually introduced by the conjunction *kî*, "for," and a conclusion with the recapitulation echoing the summons to praise God) B. W. Anderson, *Out of the Depths: The Psalms Speak for Us Today* (Philadelphia: Westminster, 1983), 136–37.

Testament sages. Examples of the wisdom poem include Job 9:2–24; 28:1–28, the poems of Proverbs 1–9 (especially the alphabetizing poem of Prov. 2:1–22), and Proverbs 31:10–31 (the alphabetizing poem celebrating the ideal wife). Likewise, those psalms commonly recognized as wisdom psalms include Psalms 32; 34; 37; 49; 73; 111; 112; and 128.

Dialogue and Disputation

> Then Bildad the Shuhite replied:
> "When will you end these speeches?
> Be sensible, and then we can talk" (Job 18:1–2).

Dialogue is simply the exchange of speech in the biblical narrative and usually is not identified as a literary genre. Disputation is more difficult to define because it is an overarching genre found in Old Testament wisdom, legal, and prophetic literature, and often makes use of an array of subgenres. For wisdom literature, the dialogue or disputation is "perhaps the supreme achievement of sapiential rhetoric."[9]

As one of the genres comprising instructional literature in the Hebrew prophets, the purpose of the *disputation* speech form in prophetic literature is theological, leaving "the opponent devoid of further argumentation and resigned to the divine decision."[10] The disputation of wisdom literature does share this didactic function with the prophetic disputation, as well as the literary function of enticing the reader (or listener) to existentially enter the plot of the narrative by skillfully exploiting the human interest factor. Unlike the prophetic disputation, however, the disputation of wisdom literature seeks to foster continued dialogue and reflection on important issues as much as it seeks to bring closure to the dialogue,

---

9. Crenshaw, *Old Testament Wisdom*, 38. On the definition of disputation in the literary analysis of prophetic literature, see A. Graffy, *The Prophet Confronts His People: The Disputation Speech in the Prophets*, AnBib 104 (Rome: Pontifical Biblical Institute, 1984), 23; D. F. Murray, "The Rhetoric of Disputation: Re-Examination of a Prophetic Genre," *JSOT* 38 (1987): 99; and W. E. March, "Prophecy," in *Old Testament Form Criticism*, ed. J. H. Hayes, (San Antonio: Trinity University Press, 1974): 168.
10. R. D. Patterson, "Old Testament Prophecy," in *A Complete Literary Guide to the Bible*, ed. L. Ryken and T. Longman (Grand Rapids: Zondervan, 1993), 303.

since that continued dialogue furthers the didactic purposes of the writer (or speaker).[11] Hence, three cycles of speeches between Job and his friends![12]

The book of Job provides clear examples of three speech types.

1. *Dialogue in the form of discussion.* The first speech of Eliphaz in the first speech cycle of Job and his companions is a sharing of differing viewpoints constructively and amicably (cf. Job 4).

2. *Dialogue in the form of disputation* (containing a thesis, counter-thesis, and dispute pattern of argumentation both confrontational in stance and contentious in tone): Bildad's first speech is a derogatory and condescending rebuttal in that he calls Job a "windbag" (8:2), and belittles Job by suggesting through rhetorical question that Job does not know the "abc's" of the retribution principle foundational to wisdom tradition (8:8–19; note Job's sarcastic response in 12:2 where he quips, "with you [three companions] wisdom will surely die!").

3. *Directed soliloquy:* to the three companions (Job 27), to God (Job 29–31), and even in a form of imagined speech in Job's challenge to God where he deludes himself into thinking his case is so airtight God would be at a loss for a rebuttal (see Job 23:1–7).

---

11. The more open-ended use of disputation in Old Testament wisdom literature is due in part to what Crenshaw (*Old Testament Wisdom,* 123) understands as "the partial nature of all answers to ultimate questions." The didactic quality of wisdom literature lends a certain timelessness to these ultimate questions, whereas the Hebrew prophets employ the disputational speech form in contexts governed by very specific situations and circumstances in the history of Israel.

12. For examples of ancient Near Eastern parallels to disputation and dialogue speech forms in Old Testament wisdom literature, see (Egyptian) "A Dispute Over Suicide," in *ANET,* 405–7, a form of imagined dialogue in that a man disputes with his own soul; and "The Protests of the Eloquent Peasant," in *ANET,* 407–10, including dialogue bordering on disputation between an Egyptian peasant and a governmental official. Also see (Mesopotamian) "A Dialogue about Human Misery," in *ANET,* 438–40; "Dialogue of Pessimism," in *ANET,* 437–38, 600–601; "A Man and His God," in *ANET,* 589–91; "The Babylonian Theodicy," in *ANET,* 601–4; and "The Dispute Between the Tamarisk and the Date Palm," in *ANET,* 592–93; although considered an Akkadian fable, the work utilizes the discussion or disputation speech form.

Wisdom Narrative

> So I reflected on all this and concluded that the righteous and
> the wise and what they do are in God's hands, but no man
> knows whether love or hate awaits him (Eccl. 9:1).

Like dialogue and disputation, the literary category of *didactic narrative* is somewhat broad, giving rise to overlap among wisdom forms and a lack of consensus as to both definition of literary form and identification of Old Testament examples (e.g., at what point is the riddle or parable didactic narrative). One thing is certain: The purpose of didactic narrative is instructional. The expanded treatment of a given topic in didactic narrative (e.g., the folly of sexual sin, Prov. 7:6–23) underscores the gravity of the issue at hand and is intended to make the teaching unforgettable and the insight permanent.

The reflection, the most common form of didactic narrative, consists of a thesis that is tested and evaluated. The reflection is loosely structured and often employs rhetorical questions, example stories, and wisdom sayings. The key elements of the reflection are observation and examination which validate the sage's conclusions. The reflection is especially prominent in the Book of Ecclesiastes, comprising half of the literary pericopes in the composition.

The reflection is common to both the ancient Egyptian and Mesopotamian wisdom traditions. Two widely recognized extra-biblical examples of this reflection genre in wisdom literature are the "Dispute Over Suicide" and the "Dialogue About Human Misery" (see *ANET*, 405–7, 438–40). Both tackle the problem of tragedy in life and the inevitability of death, and both offer instruction based upon carefully considered observation of the human experience. There may even be a connection between the reflection genre of Hebrew wisdom tradition and the prophetic judgment speech characteristic of the preexilic Hebrew prophets, since both are linked to the scrutiny and assessment of human beings and their behavior in the laboratory of life.

A second specialized type of narrative genre was developed by the Hebrew sages for the express purpose of communicating lessons of wisdom. The *autobiographical narrative* is a first-person description of a personal experience, real or imagined (cf. Cant. 3:1–5) or stylized as a literary fiction (i.e., a description of a personal experience created by the biblical writer or editor for literary, and/or theological, and/or didactic reasons; cf. Eccl. 7:23–29). As such, the autobiographical narrative naturally overlaps with both the *reflection* and the *example* story of didactic narrative.[13]

The exact nature of the personal experience reported in the autobiographical narrative is a key issue in the interpretation of this literary form. The memoir may be an actual description of an experience, or it may be a stylized account akin to a type of literary fiction where "poetic, prophetic, and allegorical features often override historical reminiscence in the service of religious interpretation."[14] Thus, the biblical interpreter must first decide whether or not the text in question is a description of a personal experience or a literary fiction. If the latter, it then becomes "difficult to know exactly how much of this [i.e., the autobiographical narrative under investigation] derives from personal experience or how much the literary genre [of literary fiction] demands."[15] Further, the interpreter must examine the larger context of the autobiographical narrative in an attempt to discern the theological agenda of the author or editor shaping the form, structure, content, and placement of the autobiographical account.

The most commonly cited example of autobiographical narrative in Old Testament wisdom literature is Qoheleth's "royal experiment" in Ecclesiastes 1:12–2:16. This first-person description of a personal experience is not only autobiographical narrative, but also an example story since it concretely illustrates the author's point, and a reflection in that the narrative states a thesis which is then

---

13. The genre of autobiographical narrative in the OT has its counterpart in the wisdom literature of the ancient Near East as well. Well-known examples from Mesopotamia include "A Man and His God" in *ANET*, 589–91, and "Ludlul Bel Nemeqi" ("I Will Praise the LORD of Wisdom") in *ANET*, 434–37, 596–601. Though less well developed, the description of personal experience offered as instruction also occurs in ancient Egyptian literature, especially "The Instruction of King Amen-Em-Het" in *ANET*, 418–19, and the opening section of "The Satire on the Trades" in *ANET*, 4332–34. See further Walton, *Ancient Israelite Literature*, 170–75, 199–200.

14. R. N. Soulen, *Handbook of Biblical Criticism*, 2d. ed. (Atlanta: John Knox, 1981), 27.

15. Crenshaw, *Ecclesiastes*, 30.

tested. Whether a real or contrived narrative of personal experience, widespread agreement exists as to the wisdom principle taught here: the futility of finding satisfaction in the human endeavor, or meaning in human life, or in wisdom (apart from God), or wealth, or accomplishment, or pleasure.

Fable

> But Jehoash king of Israel replied to Amaziah king of Judah:
> "A thistle in Lebanon sent a message to a cedar in Lebanon,
> 'Give your daughter to my son in marriage.'
> Then a wild beast in Lebanon came along
> and trampled the thistle underfoot" (2 Kings 14:9).

A fable is "a short story, usually involving animals or plants as characters, that expresses either implicitly or explicitly a moral principle."[16] The Old Testament contains only two fables: Jotham's story of the trees and kingship (see Judg. 9:7–15) and the brief saying about the marriage between the thistle and the cedar tree (see 2 Kings 14:9).

In the first example, Jotham, the sole survivor of the massacre of Gideon's household by his renegade (half-Canaanite) brother Abimelek, pronounces a fable to condemn the murders by the usurper Abimelek, rebukes those who crowned Abimelek king, and warns the Israelites of the dangers inherent in petty kingship. The fable itself tells the story of trees who decided to appoint a king to govern them. In the end, all the trees decide to appoint the bramble bush as king over them since they already have prominent roles in the natural order. By way of correspondence, the trees portray the role of the elders of Shechem in anointing Abimelek (the bramble bush) king. Finally, the mutually destructive relationship of the two parties is prefigured in the symbol of fire. The moral of the fable is pressed home in the summation of Abimelek's kingship (see Judg. 9:56–57). Here we learn that Jotham's fable was a type of curse, illustrating the retribution principle (a common theme in Old Testament wisdom literature) and reminding Israel of a key theological truth—the sovereignty of

---

16. Murphy, *Wisdom Literature*, FOTL 13 (Grand Rapids: Eerdmans, 1981), 176.

God in human history, especially Israel's history as his covenant people.

The second example actually comprises part of a response by the Israelite king Jehoash to a request by King Amaziah of Judah challenging him to a face-to-face meeting. In case King Amaziah missed the point of the fable, King Jehoash warned the Judahite not to become overconfident given his trivial victory over the Edomites (see 2 Kings 14:10). Apparently Amaziah failed to comprehend the meaning of the parable, since he did invade Israel, and he was captured by Jehoash—who subsequently plundered Yahweh's temple in Jerusalem!

Fables circulated in the literature of ancient Mesopotamia, but regrettably only a few examples of the genre exist. The fable of *The Snake and the Eagle* is preserved in an Akkadian anthology of popular sayings, and six examples of Babylonian fables are known (e.g., *The Tamarisk and the Palm* and *The Ox and the Horse*; cf. *ANET*, 410–11, 592–93). These stories represent a literary hybrid of the fable known as "contest literature," a development that has its precursors in Sumerian texts. A stock pattern has been identified in the contest literature, including a mythological introduction which sets the stage for the meeting of the two contestants, the debate between the parties, and concluding with a judgment scene before a deity who settles the dispute. While these stories no doubt had some didactic value, it has been suggested that they were primarily a form of entertainment for the royal court.

Where Non-Proverbial Wisdom Is Found in the Old Testament

Aside from instances of non-proverbial wisdom within other genres (such as riddle within narrative), special consideration needs to be given the mix of genres present in three Old Testament books.

Job

As a blend or mix of several genres and speech forms, the Book of Job almost defies literary description. The rich collage of literary forms in Job includes proverb or wisdom saying (e.g., 8:11; 15:34–35; 28:28), riddle (e.g., God's questions to Job about the created order, 41:1–5), lament (e.g., chaps. 29–30), hymn (e.g., chap. 28), curse (e.g., 3:1 ff.), and theophany (chaps. 38–41); numerous speech forms like disputation (cf. 15:1 ff. and 16:1 ff.), dialogue (e.g., the speeches between Eliphaz and Job in the first speech cycle, chaps. 4–7), lawsuit or trial speech (e.g., chap. 23:1–7), and soliloquy (e.g., chap. 31); and a variety of rhetorical features like irony (5:17), sarcasm (12:2), simile (14:1), metaphor (e.g., 29:15), and rhetorical question (4:17). Given this array of genres and literary features, Job has been defined as epic drama, epic history, lament, disputation, judicial process, comedy, tragedy, and parable, among others. Although there is no consensus to the overall literary genre of Job, nearly all biblical scholars agree that the dominant literary strand of the book is wisdom.

Job does not have a literary parallel in ancient Near Eastern wisdom literature, and a single genre classification cannot adequately describe the literary form of the book. Therefore, it seems best to consider the book of Job a *sui generis*—a unique composition. As a hybrid of several literary genres and forms, Job constitutes one of the great compositions of literary history. "*The Iliad* is great because all life is a battle, the Odyssey because all life is a journey, the Book of Job because all life is a riddle."[17] Like the *Iliad* and the *Odyssey*, Job is a quest—a quest for God. The other Old Testament wisdom book sharing this quality of quest with Job is Ecclesiastes, a quest for meaning in life. But unlike the detached empiricism of the lab notes journaling Qoheleth's experiment in life, Job is a tear-stained diary, drenched with the pathos of the human experience.

However, the Book of Job is regarded a classic for more than its sheer literary artistry and existential qualities. The greatness of Job also rests in its content and themes, especially its shameless probing of questions and issues basic to the human experience. Questions like, "Why worship God?" (cf. 1:9–10), or "Why do righteous people suffer?" (cf. 2:3), "Is God good?" (cf. 10:15–17), or "Is God just?" (cf. 24:2–4), or even "Why pursue righteousness?" (cf. 40:8; 41:11); and issues like life and death (cf. 3:11–19), God's justice (cf. 16:6–17), and God's inscrutability (cf. 23:3; 40:2 ff.).

---

17. Scott, *The Way of Wisdom,* 140–41, quoting G. K. Chesterton.

Thus, while Job is instructional wisdom on select topics (e.g., worship, the sovereignty of God), it is also speculative wisdom on other subjects (e.g., the nature of God, retributive justice, etc.). Like Ecclesiastes, Job represents a type of *counter-wisdom* because it assumes a skeptical posture to the teachings of conventional wisdom literature. So Job challenges the validity of the retribution principle (i.e., human suffering is simply and always a matter of cause [human sin] and effect [divine judgment]), and puts forward the venturesome proposition that some human suffering may indeed be undeserved—but necessarily mysterious because the deep things of God are beyond finding out (11:7). For this reason, Job is *wisdom in revolt* because the composition courageously and confidently poses *ultimate questions* to God.[18] The greatness of the Book of Job resides in its superbly crafted account "of the symbiotic interaction of the beauties of language and the drama of the human encounter with God that lies at the core of the Judeo-Christian heritage".[19]

Ecclesiastes

The Book of Ecclesiastes (or Qoheleth) is a collection of personal reflections composed by a Hebrew sage after musing upon the meaning of life, the finality of death, and the utter transcendence of God. This book constitutes the main biblical example of the genre known as speculative, pessimistic, or discussion wisdom (cf. the Sayings of Agur in Prov. 30, especially vv. 1–6). This type of wisdom literature is *counter-wisdom* or *anti-wisdom wisdom,* in that it challenges both the teachings of conventional wisdom literature and the very notion that wisdom alone could ensure one a successful life or lead one to the knowledge of God. The Book of Ecclesiastes is a blend of wisdom forms composed primarily of non-proverbial wisdom features, especially didactic narrative (notably the reflection and soliloquy). Other types of wisdom forms identified in Ecclesiastes include proverb (10:8), precept (5:2; 7:21–22), parable (11:7–12:7), comparison (i.e., ma sha7ll7-5), rhetorical questions (5:6, 16), example story (9:13–16), and autobiographical narrative (1:12–2:16).

18. Scott, *The Way of Wisdom,* 141.
19. Gladson, "Job," in *A Complete Literary Guide to the Bible,* 243.

Although Ecclesiastes consists of a kaleidoscope of wisdom literary forms and counter-wisdom themes (e.g., the vanity of life, the apparent finality of death, the inscrutability of God, the obscurity of the future, the inequities of life, etc.), polarity constitutes the unifying structure of the book. This polarity (or tension created by the juxtaposition of two basic ideas or elements to one another, like life and death or wisdom and foolishness) is the most important characteristic of the book.[20] The use of tension is the real genius of speculative or discussion wisdom. The polarization that characterizes Qoheleth's treatise prevents the biblical wisdom tradition from fossilizing, from degenerating into a smug and self-sufficient system of canned theology for life's problems. For this reason, the Book of Ecclesiastes is one of the most important possessions of the Christian church, since it compels us to continually evaluate and correct our understanding of God and our teaching about God in the light of the whole of biblical revelation.

The purpose of counter-wisdom like that found in Ecclesiastes is to force the reader (or listener) to be brutally honest with both self and God. "By making us look straight at the darkness of our ignorance and the unknown beyond, Qohelet compels us to take a stand, to say what we believe, and why."[21] Perhaps more important, the reflections of the sage in Ecclesiastes unmask the myth of human autonomy and self-sufficiency and drive us in all our frailty and inability to find meaning in a crooked world in the Creator-creature relationship—the ultimate polarity (cf. Eccl. 3:14–15; 5:18–20; 11:5; 12:1).

Commenting on the cryptic nature of the speculative wisdom in this most unusual of Old Testament books, Ellul summarizes: "Qohelet does not write this way because he enjoys communicating in code, but because he is dealing with truth, and there is no other way to express it . . . Indirect communication is the only possibility, because it is the only accessible, bearable communication."[22] The New Testament corroborates this need for indirect

---

20. J. A. Loader, *Ecclesiastes: A Practical Commentary*, trans. J. Vriend (Grand Rapids: Eerdmans, 1987), 11; see further his *Polar Structures in the Book of Qohelet*, BZAW 157 (Berlin: de Gruyter, 1979).

21. Scott, *The Way of Wisdom*, 188–89.

22. J. Ellul, *Reason for Being—A Meditation on Ecclesiastes*, trans. J. M. Hanks (Grand Rapids: Eerdmans, 1990), 118.

communication when the evangelist records that Jesus spoke to the people in parables because they were seeing but not perceiving, hearing but not listening (see Matt. 13:13). In this sense, most of the non-proverbial wisdom forms are both a *clue* and a *snare* because they reveal and conceal spiritual truth; they invite penitent seekers into the divine mystery and confirm arrogant rebels in their godless foolishness.

Song of Solomon

The Book of the Song of Solomon (or Canticles) was numbered among the seven works broadly considered wisdom literature by early church tradition (Job, Psalms, Proverbs, Ecclesiastes, Canticles, and the apocryphal Sirach and Wisdom of Solomon). While traditionally regarded poetic literature by Jewish and Christian interpreters, Canticles is also a type of wisdom literature; it has the same distinct interests featured in the Old Testament literature cast in wisdom forms.

This shared interest is primarily the humanism basic to the nature of wisdom tradition, coping with life in all its facets. One essential facet of that coping involves human sexuality and its implications for personal behavior and interpersonal relationships. Canticles addresses issues fundamental to the human experience, romantic love and fidelity in the heterosexual marriage relationship. The book's love songs celebrate the God-ordained goodness of the physical nature of human beings created male and female in his image, extol the virtue of sexual love between a man and a woman united in marriage before God, and exhort marriage partners to a life of faithfulness and fidelity. Thus, Canticles is wisdom literature in the sense it seeks to inform behavior, encourage (biblical) morality, and steer the reader (or hearer) down the good path of righteousness, justice, and equity (see Prov. 2:9).

By way of genre, Canticles is usually understood as lyric love poetry. As such it contains no specific wisdom forms, save what may be disintegrated riddles (e.g., 4:12; 8:6).

How to Interpret
Non-Proverbial Wisdom

Unlike Old Testament historical narrative, which tends to focus on the election of Israel, Israel's covenant relationship with Yahweh, God's sovereignty and providence in dealing with Israel and the nations, and the formal religious life of Israel, wisdom literature emphasizes creation, the realm of nature, personal piety, familial relationships, and personal ethics. Whereas narrative is expositional, wisdom is instructional. Wisdom is rooted in the practical and the concrete.

Most of the Old Testament wisdom literature is poetic. This means the interpreter must possess a working knowledge of the literary nature, structure, and form of Hebrew poetry, as well as a basic understanding of Hebrew wisdom traditions. A sound interpretive approach to the Bible reads the Old Testament as both revelation and literature.

Macro-Principles of Interpretation

Given the relationship of non-proverbial subgenres and speech forms to wisdom literature in general, the following macro-principles foundational to the interpretation of the wisdom genre in the Old Testament also provide a baseline for understanding the diverse form of wisdom:

1. *Identify the specific subgenre(s) and/or speech forms contained in the portion of wisdom under investigation.* Wisdom literature appeals to human emotion and imagination and interpreters need to interact with the text reflectively at this level.

2. *Note the distinction between proverb and law.* Wisdom presents itself as normative truisms—not absolute claims.

3. *Always interpret a specific wisdom teaching in light of the whole of Old Testament wisdom tradition.* Keep in mind the basic theological themes of wisdom literature including creation, human experience, moral action, skepticism, personification, and immortality. Likewise, read the whole of Old Testament wisdom tradition in the context of the entire Old Testament. For example, the sage's death wish (see Eccl. 4:2; 7:1–2) must be informed by the psalmist's passion for life (cf. Ps. 119:176).

4. *Recognize that non-proverbial wisdom tends to be contradictory (i.e., given to polarity) or reflective in nature and prefers more indirect communication* (e.g., Eccl. 7:3, "sorrow is better than laughter," or Eccl. 4:12, "a cord of three is not quickly broken"). Proverbial wisdom, on the other hand, tends to be repetitive and direct in its instruction, inviting topical or thematic study.

5. *Expect figurative language since wisdom literature attempts to capture universal truth through the assessment of particular experiences.* Be alert to the arresting strangeness of wisdom, since the literary forms are designed to overcome the cliché effect of ordinary discourse and make the teaching or insight permanent.

6. *Heed the admonition of the sage who aptly reminds that understanding wisdom is practicing wisdom.* In other words, the teachings of instructional literature must be applied to daily living (see Prov. 2:8–9).

Guidelines for Interpretation

In addition to the principles for interpretation, students of the Bible need a process to direct this examination of non-proverbial wisdom.

1. *The interpreter must determine the poetic quality of the literature.* This is done once the wisdom subgenres and speech forms have been identified in a given text. Poetic parallelism may be present in the wisdom sample under investigation; that is, the meaning of the wisdom text in question may depend in part on the type of poetic parallelism employed.

2. *The interpreter must mine the wisdom sample for rhetorical features and devices.* The Bible is both a literary text (creative and imaginative writing given to story and experience) and a non-literary text (explanatory or expositional). Literary texts in the Old Testament use rhetorical features to capitalize on the human factor of shared experience in life, and to heighten the impact of the message being conveyed. Hence, recognition and identification of these rhetorical features in literary texts enhances the reader's appreciation and enjoyment of the literary artistry of biblical literature, contributes to the overall understanding of authors' meaning in context, and facilitates the application of this meaning to the contemporary setting. The majority of rhetorical

features in Old Testament wisdom literature have already been identified.[23]

3. *The interpreter must identify figurative speech.* The primary concern in interpreting the subgenres and speech forms is understanding the figurative language often characteristic of wisdom literature. Proper biblical interpretation depends upon distinguishing literal speech from figurative language, since the former can be read at face value and the latter requires decipherment. Figurative language normally operates according to one of two literary devices: comparison (i.e., simile and metaphor) or substitution (i.e., synecdoche and metonymy). Two guidelines help discern figurative speech in wisdom literature: first, "figures of speech arise when concrete words are employed in ways other than their primary meaning"; and second, "when an attempt to understand words in their most concrete sense yields nonsense or some meaning inappropriate in context, then the words are being used figuratively."[24]

4. *The interpreter must identify extended figures of speech.* The following paragraphs present rules for interpreting the most prominent examples of extended figures of speech in the Old Testament.

- Allegory. Identify explicitly the original audience of the allegory, determine the occasion of the allegory if possible, note the details and features of the allegory, search out the points of comparison in the allegory, look for explicit internal identification of the features or symbols of the allegory, and list the points of comparison and the items they represent, noting if a likely meaning for any of the features of the allegory surfaces in another biblical text.

- Parable. Analyze the literal story (noting the attitude, spiritual condition, and response of the audience, and the occasion prompting the parabolic speech), interpret the symbolic details (i.e., identify those elements of the parable that may be allegorical), and determine the theme(s) or major emphasis of the parable. Note also the immediate context of the parable and, if possible, the larger context of the speaker's

---

23. L. Ryken and T. Longman III, eds., *A Complete Literary Guide to the Bible* (Grand Rapids: Zondervan, 1993), 230–95.

24. W. E. Mouser, *Walking in Wisdom* (Downers Grove: InterVarsity, 1983), 83.

message and teaching, as well as the presence of hortatory sayings that may serve as clues to the main point of the parable.

• Fable. Recognize the contemporary situation prompting the speaker to resort to a fable, take note if the fable is simple (stressing one point) or complex (stressing several points), and observe the response of the audience to the fable.

Nathan's Parable of the Stolen Sheep

The numerous subgenres of non-proverbial wisdom literature in the Old Testament complicate the analysis of any single pericope as an exemplar of this literary category. Here the parable told by the prophet Nathan to King David after he had committed adultery with Bathsheba will demonstrate how the interpretive principles for non-proverbial wisdom literature may be applied to a sample text (see 2 Sam. 12:1–4).

This parable was directed primarily to King David, although other members of the royal court or personal attendants may have been in the audience as well. Other literal details of the story include the foil of the two chief characters, the selfish rich man, and his poor but loving and faithful counterpart. The occasion prompting the parabolic speech was David's sin of adultery with Bathsheba (and the subsequent murder of her husband Uriah, 2 Sam. 11:2–5, 14–15). The spiritual condition of King David at this point in time is difficult to assess. He may have been plagued by guilt. Yet the purpose of figurative speech is self-discovery on the part of the audience or reader. Since the prophet had to interpret the story for the king, it seems David had forgotten or dismissed the incident entirely and was thoroughly consumed by royal duties and responsibilities (see 2 Sam. 12:7–10). David's initial response is one of juridical rage, supporting the thesis that the king is engrossed in his official fealty (the story especially animates the king, given his role as Israel's last court of appeals). Once David grasped the truth of the parable, he confesses his sin (see 2 Sam. 12:13), and elsewhere we learn that David's response was one of genuine repentance (cf. Ps. 51).

The symbolic details of Nathan's story may be distilled in three basic points: the respective status of the rich man (possessor of multiple wives, including the harem of former King Saul; cf. 2 Sam. 12:8) and the poor man (whose sole treasure is his wife), the action of the rich man against the poor man, and the possession of the ewe lamb. The larger context of Nathan's parable and the prophet's own commentary indicate the rich man of the story is equated with David and the poor man with Uriah. The lone ewe lamb of the poor man is a figure for Uriah's wife Bathsheba (see 2 Sam. 12:9–10). Nathan explicitly connects the rich man's taking of the ewe lamb with David's murder of Uriah (see 2 Sam. 12:9).

Nathan's declaration, "You are the man!" is the hortatory signal identifying the theme or emphasis of the parable. The parable is not so much about adultery with Bathsheba or the murder of Uriah as it about the person and character of King David, the LORD's anointed. Not only has David violated the law of God by lusting and killing, but by these actions he has also eschewed the very grace of God that elevated him to the position of king in Israel. The response of the prophet to David's confession (see 2 Sam. 12:13–14) and David's prayer of repentance (see Ps. 51:1–4) confirm that the gist of the parable is David's relationship with Yahweh, the covenant maker.

The parable suggests many personal applications. However, in keeping with the basic interpretive rules for parables, application consists in transferring the meaning of the symbolic speech for the original audience to the contemporary situation. The reversal dramatically emphasized by the parable provides the necessary clue for ascertaining the meaning of Nathan's story for David. The king decreed the rich man must die (see 2 Sam. 12:5), but the prophet counters that David will not die (see 2 Sam. 12:13). No doubt as David reflected on his role in the story as the rich man he was overcome by the grace of a merciful God in sparing him and his dynasty. Little wonder God's steadfast love is the preeminent theme in the Davidic psalms (e.g., Ps. 18:50; 21:7). How much more should the New Testament Christian praise God for the gift of grace in Christ Jesus that "brings life for all who believe" (see Rom. 5:15–19).

Conclusion

Whereas proverbial wisdom in the Old Testament tends to be direct and practical, non-proverbial wisdom is an alternative form that is usually reflective or speculative, sometimes even a *counter-wisdom* view. Since wisdom literature in general is highly poetical, the interpreter must come to wisdom texts with a basic understanding of how poetry in the Old Testament works. For non-proverbial wisdom forms, interpretive steps such as looking for polarity within the same book, or examining a broader context of wisdom literature when encountering a topic, are critical.

The aphorisms of the intertestamental sage, Jesus ben Sirach, framed in a numerical saying, offer a fitting way to conclude this essay and pay tribute to one at ease with the obscurities of parables and whose scholarship penetrates the intricacies of riddles to the glory of God and the benefit of the church of Jesus Christ (cf. Sir. 39:2–3).

> Three saws distill Old Testament wisdom tradition,
> even four fix the craft of the Hebrew sage:
> all wisdom derives from Yahweh;
> wisdom imitates her name, invisible to most;
> happy indeed, those who muse over ciphers;
> and the sum of wisdom is reverence for Yahweh
> (Sir. 1:8; 6:22; 14:20–21; 19:20).

Recommended Reading

Bullock, C. H. *An Introduction to the Old Testament Poetic Books*. Chicago: Moody, 1979. See especially "Wisdom in the Old Testament" 20–37, and "Theology in the Wisdom Books," 49–62.

Crenshaw, J. L. *Old Testament Wisdom: An Introduction*. Atlanta: John Knox, 1981. Innovative and balanced treatment of the literature and teaching of the Old Testament wisdom tradition. The best of the introductions to Old Testament wisdom, although not always evangelical in its conclusions.

Gammie, J. G. and L. G. Perdue, eds. *The Sage in Israel and the Ancient Near East*. Winona Lake, Ind.: Eisenbrauns, 1990. Exhaustive treatment of the religious and sociological significance of the sage in the ancient world.

Garrett, D. A. *Proverbs, Ecclesiastes, Song of Songs*. NAC 14. Nashville: Broadman Press, 1993. Includes useful introductions to and examples of various forms of wisdom literature.

Hill, A. E. "A Jonadab Connection in the Absalom Conspiracy?" *JETS* 30 (1987): 387–90. Explores the role of the sage and wisdom tradition in the Absalom coup.

————. and J. H. Walton. *A Survey of the Old Testament*. Grand Rapids: Zondervan, 1991. See "Introduction to Hebrew Poetic and Wisdom Literature," 247–62, on the form, practice, person, and content of the Old Testament wisdom tradition.

Hoglund, K. G. et al., eds., *The Listening Heart: Essays in Wisdom and the Psalms in Honor of Roland E. Murphy*. Sheffield: JSOT Press, 1987. Wide ranging collection of essays treating the literary form, content, and extra-biblical parallels of the Psalms, and biblical and post-biblical wisdom literature.

Kitchen, K. A. "Proverbs and Wisdom Books of the Ancient Near East: The Factual History of a Literary Form." *TynBul* 28 (1977): 69–114. Includes a comprehensive listing of all the extant wisdom literature from the ancient Near East.

Lambert, W. G. *Babylonian Wisdom Literature*. Oxford: Clarendon Press, 1960. Standard resource on Mesopotamian wisdom literature, includes Akkadian texts, transliterations, and English translations of several wisdom subgenres.

Morgan, D. F. *Wisdom in the Old Testament Traditions*. Atlanta: John Knox, 1981. A tradition history approach tracing the influence of Hebrew wisdom on the literature of the Old Testament.

Mouser, W. E. *Walking in Wisdom: Studying the Proverbs of Solomon*. Downers Grove: InterVarsity, 1983. Basic "how-to" study guide for Proverbs. The interpretive principles outlined for proverbial wisdom apply to non-proverbial wisdom as well.

Murphy, R. E. *Wisdom Literature: Job, Proverbs, Ruth, Canticles, Ecclesiastes, and Esther*. FOTL 13. Grand Rapids: Eerdmans, 1981. Systematic genre classification of every pericope in the corpus of Old Testament wisdom books.

————. *Wisdom Literature and Psalms*. IBT. Nashville: Abingdon, 1983. Interpretive guide to Old Testament wisdom literature, with helpful examples employing a wide range of wisdom texts and literary forms.

————. "Wisdom in the Old Testament." *ABD* (1992), 6:920–31. Currently the best "state of biblical wisdom address" available. Readable for the non-specialist and helpful for the scholar, especially the extensive bibliography.

Scott, R. B. Y. *The Way of Wisdom*. New York: Macmillan, 1971. Especially good on the contemporary relevance of Old Testament wisdom literature.

Williams, J. G. *Those Who Ponder Proverbs: Aphoristic Thinking in Biblical Literature*. Sheffield: Almond Press, 1981. On "counter-wisdom" and "polarity," see chapter 3: "Aphoristic Wisdom of Counter Order," 47–64.

14

LITERARY FORMS IN THE HANDS OF PREACHERS AND TEACHERS
Walter B. Russell, III

In bringing this book on the literary forms of the Old Testament to conclusion, we need to revisit the issue of why paying attention to genres is important. Specifically in this chapter, the goal is to answer two questions: *Why* should preachers and teachers apply the genres of the Old Testament in their ministry? and, if they should, *How* should preachers and teachers apply the genres of the Old Testament in their ministry?

Why Should Preachers and Teachers Apply the Genres of the Old Testament?

After listening to hundreds of sermons and Bible lessons over the years, you may be struck that few of those from the Old Testament even mentioned the issue of genres, let alone seriously interpreted or taught in light of them. This may lead to the conclusion that genres, in fact, do not matter and are peripheral, negotiable aspects of the Bible. The following four misconceptions are expressions of this faulty conclusion that need to be corrected.

Misconceptions of Old Testament Genres

Misconception #1: The genres of the Old Testament can be ignored because they are archaic and irrelevant. It is ironic that this kind of thinking is widespread among Bible-believing people. Its main problem is that it espouses a very radical and skeptical view of meaning. Those who advocate the irrelevance of literary forms in the Bible are the same people who ask questions like, "What does this verse mean to you?" This locates meaning in the hands of the reader, not in the author's intentions as expressed in the biblical text. This is a very dangerous form of literary theory that is generally called reader-response criticism.[1] Many well-meaning Christians have undiscerningly backed into this way of interpreting the Bible. Additionally, many preachers preach as if the life context of the congregation is the only relevant context that matters in interpretation. If this is so, then of course things like literary forms or genres from the biblical context do not matter. However, if the authors of the biblical text should be considered in the process of interpreting the Bible, then the literary forms they chose must also be considered.

Additionally, ignoring the literary setting of biblical passages is also a form of ethnocentrism. "Ethnocentrism" is simply viewing life only through the lens of your own people, or *ethnos*. While this is not bad in and of itself, it is generally accompanied with the uncritical attitude that "one's way of life is to be preferred to all others."[2] Therefore, we wrongly assume that since our way of life is the best way of life, it must be the way of life that is reflected in the Bible. We then feel free to interpret the Bible only within our cultural and literary contexts because we assume that it is the same as the Bible's. Of course, nothing could be further from the truth. The *most recent* Old Testament book is at least 2,300 years old! It

---

1. For a description, see "Reader-Response Criticism" in M. H. Abrams, *A Glossary of Literary Terms*, 4th ed. (New York: Holt, Rinehart and Winston, 1981), 149–52. For an evangelical critique, see Grant R. Osborne, *The Hermeneutical Spiral: A Comprehensive Introduction to Biblical Interpretation* (Downers Grove: InterVarsity, 1991), 377–380.

2. David Bidney, "CULTURE: Cultural Relativism," in *International Encyclopedia of the Social Sciences*, ed. David L. Sills (New York: Macmillan, 1968), 3:546.

and the other books of the Old Testament all reflect ancient Near Eastern culture in ancient Near Eastern languages. It is the height of modern arrogance to ignore or erase these differences since God has chosen these languages and cultural contexts as the setting within which to reveal himself to us. The distinctives from these cultures, including literary forms, simply must be applied to the study of the Bible.

One last impetus is for preachers and teachers to ignore the literary forms of the Old Testament. This comes from the loss of a sense of history, and is very evident even among conservative, orthodox Christians who have a high regard for the Bible. It is evident in how many now assume that God speaks *directly* to them in the Bible. While this is true in one sense, it is not true in another. God does speak *to us* in the Bible, but he speaks to us *through* the original context of another group of people. This is a very crucial distinction. If Christians have lost their sense of God speaking and acting in history, they may make the mistake of collapsing history to a search for personal meaning. In other words, rather than the Bible being about God working out *his* plan in human history as he reveals himself *through* various peoples and contexts, believers read the Bible as if it is about *their* plan for personal fulfillment and happiness. This is what Thomas Oden has called our modern era's "narcissistic hedonism."[3] Christians worship the God who has revealed himself in history through many different genres. These are the genres of people of another time and place, yet God has spoken to us *through* them. Significant distortion occurs when the words "through them" are left out.

Misconception #2: The various genres of the Old Testament should be flattened out because common folks cannot understand them. The Bible itself speaks against such an interpretive strategy. For example, the author of Hebrews 1:1–2a describes God's revelation during the Old Covenant era like this: "God, after He spoke long ago to the fathers in the prophets *in many portions and in many ways*, in these last days has spoken to us in his Son" (NASB,

---

3. See Thomas C. Oden, *After Modernity . . . What?: Agenda for Theology* (Grand Rapids: Zondervan, 1990), 43–57; and idem, *Two Worlds: Notes on the Death of Modernity in America and Russia* (Downers Grove: InterVarsity, 1992), 31–47.

emphasis mine). The point the author is making is that God's revelation during the Old Testament era was incredibly rich in its diversity. To ignore, deny, or negate this diversity is to dilute the intellectual dignity with which God deals with us. The point is not that the genre diversity makes faith in God hard to understand, because history affirms just the opposite. Rather, the diversity in genres reveals how diversely God expects us to think about him and our relationship with him. In other words, he primarily wants us to know the narrative or story of his working in history (hence, more than fifty percent narrative in both the Old and New Testaments). But he also wants us to know about the history of his people and his laws, oracles, warnings, and apocalypses. However, he has also revealed himself in the laments, praises, proverbs, and non-proverbial literature of his people. Our God is rich in the variety of the revelation of himself and his choice to do it this way underscores the richness of our dignity as human recipients of this revelation. How tragic that preachers and teachers would devalue the common folks intellectually under the guise of making the Bible more understandable.

Additionally, flattening out the various genres of the Old Testament in order to make them more accessible to common folks can actually be very harmful. A sad illustration of this is the teaching by well-meaning preachers that Proverbs 22:6 is a promise about child-rearing that is to be clung to in earnest faith by Christian parents. Couples have been doggedly clinging to this "promise" for years with wayward children. Think of the decades of false hope from which such couples could be saved with better attention to the genre of the Bible, since "Train up a child in the way he should go, even when he is old he will not depart from it" (NASB), is a wise saying and not to be equated with a guarantee. Additionally, think of the unnecessary anger and perhaps disillusionment from which countless parents could be saved regarding this one proverb alone if their preachers and teachers would rightly attend to genres when they teach the Bible. The stakes are far too high to mislead God's people by flattening out the Bible's genres.

One last point needs to be stated against the common practice of preachers and teachers of leveling the genres of the Old Testament. This is probably the most ironic of the points and also the most important. There is an underlying premise to the view that says attending to the Bible's genres is too difficult for common folks to understand. The premise is that if a preacher or teacher deals with the biblical genres, he or she will take the Bible out of the average person's hands and place it only in the hands of those who are biblically or theologically educated. To do this would be undemocratic! Therefore, this reasoning goes, wise preachers and teachers will ignore or flatten the biblical genres to keep the Bible more accessible and approachable to the average person.

This appears to be a convincing argument. However, the current actually flows in the opposite direction. This is true because of the very nature of genres themselves. God and humans communicate in literary genres not because this makes communication more difficult, but because this makes communication possible. In other words, the very nature of a genre is that it is *a public, sharable form of communication*.[4] We immediately determine a certain type of meaning when we grasp the genre of the communication. For example, when we pick up the newspaper, we encounter numerous genres or subgenres as we go from news stories to advertisements to editorials to comics to classified ads. Knowing these genres within the newspaper does not hinder meaning, but enables it. Think of how confusing a newspaper would be if we did not know what genre we were reading. We could make the near fatal mistake of interpreting an advertisement as a promise! The role of genres is just as central and indispensable in the Bible. To ignore or level the distinctions between the biblical genres supposedly in order to help explain the Bible actually removes one of the most vital vehicles for understanding it.

Also, this reflects a very dangerous view of the Bible that goes back in interpretive history to Philo, Origen, and the Alexandrian school of interpretation. Their view of Scripture, which lives today in many who would ignore biblical genres, is that the purpose of the Bible was to announce the connection that exists between

---

4. For one of the most lucid and persuasive discussions of the nature of genres and genre ideas, see E. D. Hirsch, Jr., *Validity in Interpretation* (New Haven and London: Yale University Press, 1967), 24–126. See also the helpful discussion in chapter two of this book.

spiritual events.[5] In other words, those who view the Bible in this manner do not attend to genres themselves or even to the historical events of the Bible as meaningful in and of themselves. Rather, they are looking for the *spiritual* truths that are the deeper meaning of the Bible. They implicitly assert that it is these spiritual events or truths *hidden* in Scripture that are really what the Bible is all about. Because they preach and teach this way, they can ignore or level the specific forms in which God has revealed himself in history. They seek as their desired end something mystical that the Word of God allegedly contains. Ironically, preaching or teaching this meaning of Scripture by ignoring or leveling biblical genres takes the Bible out of everyone else's hands because it *privatizes* and *individualizes* interpretation. This occurs because the common ground for understanding and interpreting the Bible is its genres which are public, sharable, and community-oriented. It is these very public and sharable aspects that are eliminated. Therefore, the tragedy is that rather than making the Bible more accessible to all people by flattening the biblical genres, these preachers and teachers actually remove it to an inaccessible, private sphere with no common ground for understanding! This strongly discourages both widespread Bible reading and meaningful interpretation because the typical hearer's response to these types of sermons or Bible lessons is "*I* could never get out of the Bible what Pastor X is getting." By rightly appealing to the biblical genre, preachers and teachers should be encouraging this far more desirable response: "Now I understand what this part of the Bible means and I am encouraged to study it more because of its clarity and relevance."

Misconception #3: Because every word of the Bible is inspired by God, the individual words of Scripture should be our main emphasis, not the larger units of the text such as genre. Although this assertion sounds unusual, it is widely held by conservative Christians. Much contemporary preaching and teaching can be traced to preachers or teachers reading a passage of Scripture and being stirred by a word, phrase, or verse which then becomes the

---

5. Origen, *De Principiis* 4.2.9. Note the brief but helpful discussion in Robert M. Grant with David Tracy, *A Short History of the Interpretation of the Bible*, 2d ed. rev. and enl. (Philadelphia: Fortress, 1984), 52–62.

focal point of their sermons or lessons. Increasingly in recent years, these sermons and lessons are topical in nature. It is as if the word, phrase, or verse is a key that unlocks the topic or idea that hovers above and beyond and sometimes in the passage of Scripture. Such a view of language and meaning is rooted in the very atomistic approach to interpretation begun by the Jewish rabbis in the centuries before Jesus and passed on to the Church through the Alexandrian school of interpretation.[6] They asserted that every word and symbol was filled with meaning. This view sees words like components in a stereo system. We build a stereo from the ground up by combining components and we can allegedly build the meaning of the Bible from the smallest component upward. Therefore, the way to understand the meaning of the Bible is to start with understanding the smallest components, namely words. According to this perspective, meaning comes from the bottom up. One begins by focusing on these smallest components and eventually combines these components to build the system— the meaning. Passages like Matthew 5:18 and 2 Timothy 3:16–17 are misused to validate this emphasis on individual words.

The reader may recall the discussion of the three levels of context at the beginning of Chapter 1: *immediate* (word and sentence), *distant* (whole Bible), and *middle level* (genre of the unit and the biblical book). It was argued that the middle level of context (genre) is the most important consideration in the interpretive process. This is absolutely correct for a simple, but very crucial reason: Meaning does not come from the bottom up, but from the top down. What is the difference? Meaning is not componential like a stereo system, but structural like the ingredients mixed together to make a cake. Each element of the cake (flour, sugar, egg, etc.) has meaning in light of the role it fulfills in the organic structure of a cake. Texts are organic like cakes in that the individual words, sentences, and paragraphs fulfill structural roles in the meaning of the whole text. Therefore, the meaning is shaped most significantly at the genre level where one decides to use an egg to create a cake, and not, for instance, an omelet. The meaning of

6. For helpful discussions, see Frederic W. Farrar, *History of Interpretation* (London: Macmillan, 1886), 47–107, and David S. Dockery, *Biblical Interpretation Then and Now* (Grand Rapids: Baker), 27–34.

texts is most significantly shaped at the level of genre when the author decides to create proverbs, not narrative, or to write laws, not laments (though just as with the egg and the cake or omelet, some of the same words could be found in both genres). Texts are multitiered things and the decisions made at the top level of the text influence all of the lower levels of the text as to their meaning.[7] In other words, to discover if something is a cake or an omelet, you do not start by doing an in-depth study of the egg which each contains. Rather, you see how the egg fits into the organic structure of the whole. The meaning of the egg in our illustration is in the role that it plays in the organic structure of the cake or omelet, not in its independent "eggness."

All of this discussion about meaning coming from the top down and not from the bottom up is very instructive for how we should study, interpret, and teach texts of the Bible. More emphasis should be placed on understanding the genre and the whole meaning of the text (for instance, the biblical book) than we have historically done. Additionally, more time and energy should be invested at the level of discovering the structure of the biblical book according to its genre and its genre idea.[8] Last, more emphasis must be placed on the idea contained in the paragraph. This is really the smallest unit of text that should be closely studied in most of the genres (with some exceptions like proverbs). Unfortunately, this emphasis on the shaping of texts from the top down is directly contrary to several generations of biblical language teaching in evangelical schools. Greek, Hebrew, and Aramaic have been taught for many years following the premise that close analysis of the smallest units of the text (words and parts of words) is the most fruitful path to understanding the meaning of the text. Unfortunately, this "tag and flag" approach to identifying and labeling every Greek or Hebrew word also has drastically affected

---

7. This is the kind of insight that comes from literary critics like E. D. Hirsch, Jr. (*Validity in Interpretation*) and those who use discourse analysis or discourse criticism. For an introduction to discourse criticism, see Robert D. Bergen, "Text as a Guide to Authorial Intention: An Introduction to Discourse Criticism," *JETS* 30 (1987): 327–36.

8. This genre idea of the whole text is called "the generic conception" or "intrinsic genre" in the very important discussion by Hirsch in *Validity in Interpretation*, 68–126.

preaching and teaching. It has led to an atomistic emphasis on the wrong level of texts. It has taken many years to listen to what linguists have been saying for some time: Because language is organized from the top down, start by focusing on the higher structures of the text and work downward.

Misconception #4: The genres of the Old Testament are too hard and too esoteric and thereby the playground of scholars only. We have already addressed parts of this misconception by arguing that the nature of genres is, in fact, just the opposite. Genres make the Bible more accessible to the peoples of the world. This is true largely because most of the genres of the Old and New Testaments are widely known. For example, every culture in the world can relate in some degree to the fifty percent or so of the Bible that is narrative. The same could be said for the vast number of cultures that would instinctively recognize the genres of history, law, lament, praise, and wisdom literature. God in his grace and mercy has chosen to reveal himself in many of the universal and most common literary forms that exist. There is really nothing esoteric about these genres, even in so-called primitive, non-literate cultures. One could recount the narratives and proverbs of the Bible and be basically understood at the level of genre.

However, there is some validity to the accusation that some genres of the Bible are harder to understand and demand clarification and additional input to comprehend them fully. This would be particularly true of the apocalyptic genre and the non-proverbial wisdom genre.[9] This need for additional teaching in interpreting parts of the Bible helps to surface what is a faulty assumption on the part of many in the West. The assumption is that the Bible has been written so that all of it could be understood by every (adult) individual only with the aid of the Holy Spirit as they sit alone and read it. However, this assumption is faulty at two levels. First, the majority of people throughout the history of the Church have had the Bible read to them or have only read the Bible themselves within the assembled community of the Church. Most have not had their own copies of the biblical texts in earlier centuries and many could not read anyway. For example, literacy could

---

9. See chapters 9 and 13, respectively.

have been as low as ten percent in the Roman Empire at the time of Jesus.[10] The point is that having the luxury of your own copy of the Bible and having the ability to read it by yourself is a fairly recent phenomenon. It may well be that God's intention for the majority of his people was that their reading and discussing of the Bible were to occur when his people assembled. This seems to be what Paul instructed Timothy to do as a part of the assembly (see 1 Tim. 4:13).

However, a second faulty aspect of the above assumption is that believers should be totally adequate in their individual state to read and interpret the Bible unaided. Of course, this is negated because God has given teachers and pastor-teachers to the church to aid God's people in this area (see 1 Cor. 12:28; Eph. 4:11). Why would God have given such gifted individuals to the Body of Christ if they were not genuinely needed? Perhaps we have carried our rampant individualism too far in the West and tried to function in a manner that actually works against Christ's design for the church. The difficulty in understanding certain parts of God's Word should be no barrier in light of the design of the body of Christ. The solution is to let the church function as it was designed and let the teachers teach and the people learn. Such functioning does not make the Bible the domain of scholars, but rather the domain of the functioning gifts of the Holy Spirit. In such a domain, Spirit-gifted teachers and pastor-teachers explaining difficult genres should be an exciting learning process.

The answer to the question, "*Why* should preachers and teachers apply the genres of the Old Testament in their ministry?" is derived from at least four perspectives. These genres are absolutely central and essential to understanding the Bible, rather than peripheral and negotiable. God's revelation is in the form of marvelously diverse genres because, rather than hindering clear communication, these genres actually facilitate it. To ignore, level, circumvent, or withhold such information from God's people is to hinder, not help, their understanding of God and his Word. This is *why* preachers and teachers must attend to these genres. Now

---

10. See William V. Harris, *Ancient Literacy* (Cambridge: Harvard University Press, 1989), 3–24.

the issue becomes "*How* should preachers and teachers apply the genres of the Old Testament in their ministry?"

How Should Preachers and Teachers Apply the Genres of the Old Testament?

Given the breadth of hermeneutical principles in the genre chapters (chaps. 4–13), the principles now need to be summarized for preaching and teaching. After doing this, these principles will be applied to a much-preached passage to see how genre-sensitivity should impact sermons and Bible lessons.

Principles of Application

1. *The genre characteristics of the biblical passage should impact the form of the sermon.* The forms of sermons must not violate the genre qualities of the passages under consideration. If they do, they may either detract from the biblical passages or distort the meaning of the passages by distorting the forms of the passages beyond their recognized genre shape. However, this may sound more restrictive than it actually is because this principle is really only a restating of what is intuitively obvious to many preachers and teachers. For example, if the text is a passage in Proverbs, then it is probably best to preach from this genre as Proverbs generally does: topically. In other words, preach or teach from various proverbs that are tied together topically around such crucial issues as God and man, wisdom, the fool, the sluggard, the friend, words, the family, and life and death.[11]

Or if the text is from Psalms, the preacher or teacher who is genre-sensitive will not just pluck some verses out of the middle of these ancient songs. Rather, the wise interpreter will speak about the thrust of the whole psalm and perhaps emphasize climactic points in the lyrics. This is no different from how we would approach the lyrics of a contemporary song that we wanted to use as an illustration. Also, if a passage of narrative is the focus, a preacher or teacher who is genre-wise will not try to preach a

---

11. This is the list of helpful topical studies included in Derek Kidner's brilliant commentary on Proverbs, TOTC (Downers Grove: InterVarsity, 1964), 31–56.

three-point doctrinal sermon. This is because the intention of Old Testament narratives is usually not to teach a theological doctrine in a direct manner.[12] Rather, the preacher or teacher may want to adopt more of a narrative style sermon or lesson that retells the biblical story and punctuates it at appropriate points with additional insights or a final application.

In sum, if preachers and teachers will make these kinds of sermon alignments in light of genre alignments, then they will underscore the centrality of the Word of God in our lives and help encourage vibrant reading and healthy interpretation of it in a more genre-sensitive manner.

2. *Preachers and teachers must establish the meaning of the passage in its original literary and historical setting before moving to its significance to contemporary hearers.* If there is one hermeneutical principle that is repeated in all of the various genre chapters of this book, it is the principle of placing a passage within its broader genre context. Ironically, if there is one principle that is regularly violated by preachers and teachers, it is this principle. Why is this so? One reason may be the rush to demonstrate that the biblical passage and message is relevant to the hearers' needs. Or, as some prefer to describe it, this is the tyranny of the hearers' felt-needs that many preachers and teachers feel. While it is a necessary and worthy goal to address the needs of listeners, this step must be held in abeyance until the meaning of the passage has been established within its original context, apart from its relevance to contemporary hearers.

An effective concept that helps in doing this is the distinction by E. D. Hirsch, Jr. between meaning (what the author meant by the use of a particular sign sequence) and significance (a relationship between that meaning and any other thing).[13] In the face of tremendous pressure and impatience to establish the significance of a passage, preachers and teachers frequently gloss over the meaning of the passage. This, in fact, reverses good hermeneutical process by using a sense of a passage's significance as the means of

---

12. See chapter 4. Also, see Gordon D. Fee and Douglas Stuart, *How to Read the Bible for All Its Worth,* 2nd ed. (Grand Rapids: Zondervan, 1993), 83–84.
13. Hirsch, *Validity in Interpretation,* 8.

interpreting the passage's meaning. That is, they develop a premature sense of the passage's significance to contemporary hearers and use this as the lens for interpreting the passage's meaning to its original hearers. This is, of course, absolutely backwards! It is far better when the preacher or teacher establishes the passage's meaning by studying it in a genre-sensitive manner that adequately emphasizes the appropriate generic context. Such context is one of the three primary safeguards to accurate interpretation of the Scriptures.[14]

3. *The common hermeneutical saying "One interpretation and unlimited applications" should be replaced by "One interpretation that establishes a limited range of applications."* In opposing such a widely held hermeneutical dictum, we step on sacred ground that seems unassailable. However, some reflection about this issue should help clarify how to draw good applications from the various genres of the Old Testament. All that needs to be asked about a given passage is, "Are there any applications that are not legitimate applications?" Of course, the answer is "Yes." For example, Exodus 20:13 is the commandment, "You shall not murder." An application from this law that says that I can murder my friend is obviously an illegitimate application. Exodus 2:15–22 is the narrative where the Hebrew midwives both disobeyed and lied to Pharaoh instead of killing the Hebrew newborn males, and yet God was good to them and established households for them. An application from this passage that asserts that God will bless us if we disobey and lie to any governmental authority is obviously an application that is not legitimate.

The question is, "What establishes the boundaries between legitimate and illegitimate applications?" There can be only one answer. The author's intention as expressed through the chosen genre in the specific idea of the passage is what establishes the boundary for legitimate applications. As a part of the authors' intentions expressed within the particular genres they used, they in-

---

14. In addition to context, the other two safeguards to accurate interpretation are the reliance upon the Holy Spirit to help us interpret and the confirmation of our interpretations by present and former Spirit-gifted teachers in the church (perhaps via conversations, books, or journal articles).

tended that certain specific applications be made in response to what they wrote. God intended that the hearers or readers of Exodus 20:13 make the specific application of not murdering anyone. Moses probably intended that the recipients of Exodus 2:15–22 make the application that God would bless all those who chose to build up and not tear down the nation of Israel (cf. Gen. 12:3 and God's promise to Abraham regarding those who blessed him). Any other applications are secondary at best, or illegitimate at worst.

This discussion about proper applications is very closely tied to the issue of the genres of the Old Testament. Preachers and teachers must have a meaningful understanding of the genre of a passage before they can discern proper applications from the passage—applications are genre-specific! For example, if something is of the genre of law, then the proper application is probably a very specific response in obedience to that law. If something is of the genre of proverb, then the proper application is probably *not* treating this as a promise, but rather choosing to make this wise choice in light of the kind of reality and authority that the proverb represents.[15] Therefore, one of the primary losses that preachers and teachers who do not apply the genres of Bible will experience is the penalty of errant applications that are outside the boundaries that both the genres and the specific passages intend. This is a rather large price to pay for such negligence.

Potiphar's Wife and the Temptation of Joseph

The twenty-three verses of Genesis 39 comprise one of the best known and most widely preached narrative passages in the whole Bible. It vividly portrays Joseph's blessing as a slave in Potiphar's house (vv. 1–6), his refusal of the sexual offer by Potiphar's wife (vv. 7–18), and his imprisonment by the angry Potiphar after his wife framed the innocent Joseph (vv. 19–23). The typical approach to preaching or teaching this chapter is to view Joseph as a model believer and to pull principles from the narrative about how to deal with temptation in general, and sexual temptation in particular. Such an interpretive perspective seems so obvious and so

---

15. See chapter 12 on "Proverbs."

powerful to Western preachers and teachers. But does it do harm to the narrative genre?

Preaching and teaching Genesis 39 in this manner *does*, in fact, distort the primary meaning of this narrative. The distortion occurs by ignoring some of the main characteristics of the narrative genre and by violating some of the basic interpretive principles for interpreting narratives.[16] In particular, in interpreting narratives, smaller sections of the narrative like Genesis 39 must be understood in light of the whole narrative. In the case of this passage, the broader narrative is the section that focuses on Joseph (Gen. 37–50) and ultimately the narrative of Genesis-Exodus (and perhaps Numbers). It is sufficient, however, to focus on the Book of Genesis and especially chapters 37–50 to establish the broader narrative context.

After reading Genesis 1–36, the thoughtful reader will realize that God has a specific purpose for blessing the children of Israel and it is not because of the inherent qualities of their patriarchs. Rather, it is because God is merciful and gracious and desires to preserve this people as a blessing to all peoples (see Gen. 12:1–3). Therefore, by the time we encounter Joseph in Genesis 37 we should realize that this is *another* in the line of unlikely fathers of the nation whom God will use *in spite of* his qualities. Attention to the genre characteristics of the narrative also helps establish the basic interpretive framework that the broader narrative should give us: *God*, not Joseph, is the real hero of the narrative.[17] Additionally, Western interpreters should have been impressed by the corporate or group perspective that the narrative displays by the time they get to Genesis 37. This means that the focus of the narrative is not on Joseph or the patriarchs as individuals, per se, but rather it focuses on them as representatives of the chosen seed of blessing, the people of God. Therefore, their actions must be interpreted in light of how they respect the chosen seed and advance God's purposes for his elect people.

This brief attention to some of the main characteristics of the narrative of Genesis shows that the typical focus on Joseph as an

---

16. See chapter 4 for the full set of these hermeneutical principles.

17. See Fee and Stuart, *How to Read the Bible for All Its Worth*, 84–86 for the same interpretive conclusions.

individual model believer is contrary to the basic thrust of the narrative. Therefore, any insights that center around Joseph's actions as a model believer are probably of secondary value. They may reflect some of the implications of the narrative but are certainly not the main point.

What is the main point of Genesis 39 and Joseph's temptation and subsequent imprisonment? Looking at the flow of the narrative in the immediate context helps to answer this crucial interpretive question. In Genesis 37 the arrogant, insensitive, and favored young Joseph is introduced. He is certainly no hero! However, Genesis 37 also introduces the key contrast within the broader narrative. While Joseph's disrespect for his family is expressed in his youthful arrogance, Joseph's brothers have a more seasoned disrespect for the chosen seed and their family honor. This is obvious when they would sell their own brother Joseph into slavery out of petty family jealousy and then lie to their father about Joseph's death. However, such disdain for the chosen seed in Genesis 37 is heightened in Genesis 38 when the author interrupts the Joseph narrative with the tragic story of Judah and Tamar. The main point of this narrative is that there is even more widespread disobedience in the land regarding disrespect for the chosen seed and family honor. This is important as an immediate contrast to Joseph and also because of Judah's blessing later in the narrative (Gen. 49:8–12).

Therefore, by the time we get to Joseph in Genesis 39 the question should be how God (the hero of the narrative) is going to preserve his chosen people in spite of their actions toward one another. God does preserve them through the obedient choices of the young Joseph in Genesis 39, who shows obedience outside of the land by respecting the seed and family honor by refusing to compromise them with a married Egyptian woman. While such obedience to God and respect for the seed proves initially costly to Joseph, God is with him (see Gen. 39:21, 23) and God uses Joseph to bring blessing, honor, and deliverance to the seed in Genesis 40–50. This is why Joseph can say at the end of the Genesis narrative to his fearful brothers: "Do not be afraid, for am I in God's place? And as for you, you meant evil against me, but God meant it for good in order to bring about this present result, to preserve many people alive" (50:19–20, NASB).

Therefore, what is the primary point of the narrative in Genesis 39? Preachers and teachers will reflect sensitivity to the narrative genre of Genesis 39 if they emphasize that God was (and is) at work to preserve his people so that they can be a blessing to the peoples of the world. This is the basic meaning of Joseph's temptation narrative. The application of the main point of this narrative to us is that God may choose to use us like he did Joseph when we make hard choices in life out of respect for the chosen seed (this is the church under the new covenant) and out of concern for the outworking of God's purposes in the world (to bless all the peoples of the world, under the new covenant through faith in Jesus Christ). As believers, our individual choices should not be viewed primarily in individualistic terms, but rather representatively as to how they affect the people of God of whom we are a part and whom we represent. Therefore, to emphasize Joseph's response to temptation as the choice of an individual in isolation is to miss the basic thrust of the Genesis 39 narrative. The narrative actually points us in a far different direction. Greater sensitivity to the characteristics of narratives and to the interpretive principles of the narrative genre will help to avoid such misreading.

Conclusion

Several responses, both logical and practical, can be made to the question, "Why should preachers and teachers apply the genres of the Old Testament in their ministry?" Far from being irrelevant or out of reach for everyday use, genres are the very fabric out of which God has woven revelation. Since literature works from the top down, primary attention belongs on the middle level of context, that of the literary form and biblical book. The answer to "How should preachers and teachers apply the genres of the Old Testament?" is straightforward: learn the main characteristics of each genre and absorb each genre's basic interpretive principles. Both the structures and the applications of our sermons and Bible lessons should be significantly informed by these characteristics and principles. However, doing this obviously entails some time and hard work. But this should not be troubling to us because

Christ gave gifted pastors and teachers to his Church for this very purpose!

It has been said that what gives meaning to life is a long commitment in the same direction. Commitment involves time, and commitment involves hard work. May Christian preachers and teachers, revelling in the diversity of forms in which God has given his Word, commit the time and work needed to understand literary forms. This is not an option and not a luxury, since literary forms are so much a part of the goal of understanding the Word of God and helping God's people understand it—a goal that is indeed worthy of our time and effort.

GLOSSARY*

Allegorize - An approach to scriptural interpretation that looks for meaning beyond the literal sense of the passage, including a deeper and mystical sense not intended by the author. It was practiced by the Jews of Alexandria in pre-Christian times and adopted by some of the early Church Fathers.

Allegory - A type of literature in which the author uses obvious symbolism to suggest deeper meaning. Allegories use metaphorical language to make a direct comparison, often in an extended narrative; in contrast to a parable that is a more compact figurative speech form, usually drawing an indirect comparison with the routine experiences of daily life.

Anthology - A collection of selected literary pieces or passages.

Antithetical parallelism - A common Hebrew poetical pattern where the second line states the opposite of the first (e.g., Prov. 10:1).

Aphorism - A short, pithy statement of a truth or principle common to proverbs; an adage.

Apokalypsis - A Greek word that means "an uncovering, a laying bare." It functions as the title for the Book of Revelation.

---

* This glossary was compiled by Jeff Crabtree, a former student of Richard Patterson.

Apocalyptic genre - A form of prophetic literature character-ized by a focus on the final, total eradication of evil by God him-self, and on the complete victory of his people who will reign forever. This is portrayed through messages in graphic images, vi-sions, and symbols.

Apostrophe - A literary device where the writer addresses a person usually not present, or a thing usually personified for rhe-torical reasons, i.e., as if the personification could respond to the address (e.g., Deut. 32:1).

Chiasm - Named after the Greek letter *chi* that looks and func-tions like the English letter *x*. A chiasm is a literary device where related elements in parallel constructions are inverted or crossed.

Covenant - A means of expressing or establishing and defining a relationship which has stipulations and obligations for the parties involved.

Convention - A literary convention is any literary habit or rule in common usage. Each genre has its own conventions or ways of doing things.

Emblematic poetry - A common Hebrew poetical pattern that explains a point or truth by using a figurative illustration as one of the parallel units (e.g., Prov. 25:25).

Epic - A long narrative in prose or poetry (usually the latter) written in an elevated style that recounts the deeds of a legendary or historical hero whose destiny determines the future of a nation or of the world.

Foil - A literary device in which one character serves as a con-trast to another.

Form Criticism (German, *Formgeschichte*, for "form history") - A procedure for identifying and analyzing oral forms before they were assimilated into literature.

Genre - A kind or type of literary composition.

Genre criticism - The process of identifying in a text the range of literary-rhetorical features that make the text one type of writing and not another.

Hermeneutics - The study of the methodology and interpretive principles of biblical interpretation.

History - A literary genre that records a series of accounts with cause-effect sequences given more weight than the plot.

Hyperbole - A figure of speech where a writer exaggerates to make a point (e.g., "If I speak with the tongues of men and of angels" [1 Cor. 13:1]).

Inclusion - A literary device where words or clauses are repeated to bracket off or envelope the marked-off material.

Imprecatory psalms - A psalm that includes a prayer for God to punish the enemies of the psalmist.

Lament - A form of poetry expressing grief, sorrow, fear, anger, contempt, shame, guilt or other dark emotions.

Literary criticism - The study that engages in the analysis or artistic evaluation of literature.

Metaphor - A figure of speech which compares two objects or actions showing their similarities and by stating one item or action is another (e.g., "You are the salt of the earth [Matt. 5:13]).

Metonymy - A figure of speech where the name of one object is used for something else with which it is associated (e.g., "In the mouth [i.e., the testimony] of two or three witnesses" [Matt. 18:16, KJV]).

Narrative - A literary form which is a story or a record of a series of events.

Paremiology - The study of proverbs.

Parenesis - A composition for the purpose of exhortation.

Pericope - A section of a book.

Prolegomenon - An introduction.

Prose - A form of writing distinguished from poetry that uses ordinary speech patterns.

Proverb - A short, paradigmatic, poetically-crafted saying; an aphorism, an adage.

Pseudonymous - A literary work bearing a false name, that is, not the name of the actual author.

Qoheleth - The Hebrew title of Ecclesiastes which probably means "the preacher, the speaker in assemblies."

Redactor - Editor.

Sapient - Wise.

Simile - A figure of speech which compares two objects or actions showing their similarities. Similes use the words *like* or *as* (e.g., "In the end she is bitter as gall" [Prov. 5:4]).

Sitz im Leben - German for "setting in life." The social setting in which an oral composition originated and was preserved.

Synecdoche - A figure of speech where the part is put for the whole (e.g., "And my heart despised reproof" [Prov. 5:12, NRSV]).

Synonymous parallelism - A common Hebrew poetical pattern where two or more lines using different words say the same thing; the sense of the first line is repeated in the second (e.g., Ps. 19:1; Matt. 7:7).

Synthetic parallelism - A common Hebrew poetical pattern where the second line extends or finishes the sense of the first line without repeating anything from the first line (e.g., Ps. 103:13).

Scripture Index*

Genesis

*   These indices were compiled by David Barnett.

Proverbs

Ecclesiastes

Names Index

SUBJECT INDEX